D1487304

TRIMARK PICTURES OFFLINE ENTERTAINMENT GROUP & SLAM PICTURES PRESENT
A MARC LEVIN FILM "SLAM" STARRING SAUL WILLIAMS SONJA SOHN
BONZ MALONE BEAU SIA LAWRENCE WILSON EDITED BY EMIR LEWIS
MUSIC BY DJ SPOOKY MUSIC SUPERVISORS HAPPY WALTERS JULIANNE KELLEY
DIRECTOR OF PHOTOGRAPHY MARK BENJAMIN STORY BY MARC LEVIN RICHARD STRATTON
WRITTEN BY MARC LEVIN BONZ MALONE SONJA SOHN RICHARD STRATTON SAUL WILLIAMS
EXECUTIVE PRODUCERS DAVID PEIPERS HENRI M. KESSLER
PRODUCED BY HENRI M. KESSLER MARC LEVIN RICHARD STRATTON DIRECTED BY MARC LEVIN

www.slamthis.com

SLAM

SLAM

Edited by
Richard Stratton
and
Kim Wozencraft

Grove Press
New York

Copyright © 1998 by Offline Entertainment Group

All rights reserved. No part of this book may be reproduced in any form or by any electronic or mechanical means, including information storage and retrieval systems, without permission in writing from the publisher, except by a reviewer, who may quote brief passages in a review. Any members of educational institutions wishing to photocopy part or all of the work for classroom use, or publishers who would like to obtain permission to include the work in an anthology, should send their inquiries to Grove/Atlantic, Inc., 841 Broadway, New York, NY 10003.

"Subterranean Night-Colored Magus" previously published in *4,000 Shades of Blue* by DJ Renegade, Karibu Books; and in *HyperAge* magazine (Spring 1995); and in *The Asheville Poetry Review* (Spring/Summer 1996).

"Paid in Full" written by Eric Barrier and William Griffin. Copyright © 1987 Songs of Polygram International, Inc., and Robert Hill Music. International copyright secured. All rights reserved. Used by permission.

"What's Your Name" written by Claude Johnson. Copyright © It's a Hit Music. International copyright secured. All rights reserved. Used by permission.

Published simultaneously in Canada
Printed in the United States of America

FIRST EDITION

Library of Congress Cataloging-in-Publication Data
Stratton, Richard (Richard H.)
    Slam : the book / Richard Stratton, Kim Wozencraft.
       p.   cm.
     ISBN 0-8021-3575-7
     1. Slam (Motion picture)   I. Wozencraft, Kim.   II. Title.
   PN1997.S5455S76   1998
   791.43'72—dc21   98-21873

Grove Press
841 Broadway
New York, NY 10003

98 99 00 01 10 9 8 7 6 5 4 3 2 1

In loving memory of

Hannah A. Levin

Take me to a place where we can fly.
Take me to a place where she will never die.

Contents

Foreword

This is not just a movie book that prints a screenplay along with a few glam mugshots of actors. This book teaches you how to steal your own movie.

Slam—the book and the movie—flips the pyramid, inverts the hierarchy. What you get here are multiple POVs, from captain to deckswab, from producer to gofer. Collectively, a model emerges on how to make a film *Slam*-style, guerrilla-style, what the filmmakers call *drama vérité*.

To make *Slam,* the filmmakers went right to the ground of their beseeching—got real poets to play poets, cons to play cons, went to prison for their prison "set." *Slam* made real prisoners forget for a few days that they were locked in cages, as their reality was incorporated right into the film during the shooting. They got the actors to develop their own parts, and gave those actors screenwriting credit.

All films are political. If there is zero political consciousness in a film— that's its politics. Luis Buñuel made films about the bourgeoisie—but when his self-absorbed characters totally ignored the terrorist bombs going off in the background—that *was* his political statement. *Slam*-style may not be for everyone, but if you feel passionately about a real story, *Slam* shows you how to go out and get it.

This book is not just the narcissistic wet dream of an auteur, it is an archeological expedition, made by cast and crew, digging for the bones of a lost art—a story that doesn't just entertain, but electrifies.

Annie Nocenti
Editor
Scenario magazine

The Producers: Richard Stratton, Marc Levin and Henri M. Kessler.

INTRODUCTION

SLAMMED in Dodge City

by Richard Stratton

> "This ain't no metaphor. This is my life."
> *Ray Joshua*

On July 30th, 1990, I was released from federal prison after serving eight years for smuggling marijuana. I have now been back in the world for as long as I was locked up, yet the years of freedom seem to have gone by in a rush, like a blurred landscape seen through the window of a speeding train. The prison years sit inside me whole, still undigested, a hard lump of experience pressing against my heart.

I think of prison every day. I often dream I am back behind the walls, or in some abstract prison of the mind. There has been a foul-up in the paperwork; I am still in custody with no definite release date. The prison experience is so profound, so disturbing, I think that no matter how much I write about it, no matter how many films I make about prison, the essence of what it means to be deprived of freedom will always elude me.

It was eerie going back inside to make *Slam*, transforming the setting of my recurring nightmare into a movie set. At one point I was assisting the director, Marc Levin, we were in the lower depths of the jail shooting the Ray/Bay scene as it has come to be known, the compelling moment when gangsta rap meets poetry behind bars. I had to run up and down the tiers to the guard's control bubble to have him open or close cell doors. I thought, "How weird is this? Strange and twisted flashback. Me with a walkie-talkie telling cops to open and close cells just like I was a cop myself."

Imprisonment is harsh punishment. Only physical torture—often part of the experience—or death is more severe than taking away someone's freedom, locking them up in a cage and separating them from family, loved ones, the rest of society. Needless to say, I believe this punishment should be reserved for the worst of us—violent predators who cannot live among us without harming others.

So I keep going back to prison, now as a writer and a filmmaker, trying to understand and illuminate the experience. I am most comfortable when I am with people who have spent time in the joint, shared the experience, like old war buddies. I married an ex-convict. For a couple of years we published a magazine, *Prison Life*, which we called "The Voice of the Convict." Imagine how that went over with the police state propagandists who would have us believe that the answer to all society's ills is to build more prisons, lock up more and more men and women for longer and longer periods of time.

I believe the opposite is true. My own experience and the research I've done have convinced me that this imprisonment binge we're on, if allowed to continue unchecked, will ultimately destroy our society, our country, America, home of the free. We are creating a whole class of angry, frustrated people who have been steeped in violence and have no understanding of or stake in a free, civilized culture.

The United States now has the highest incarceration rate in the world, four times that of any other western industrialized nation. As we near the end of the twentieth century, we have almost two million men and women locked up in a vast American gulag, a prison-industrial complex comprised of brutal human warehouses and driven by profit. I have been there and I can tell you the country club prison is a myth. Even the lower security joints are overcrowded, degrading, staffed by hostile, sadistic cops who are encouraged to treat prisoners as an inferior life form. In prison, you have no privacy. You are never alone; you are always surrounded by strangers and at the same time you are always lonely. Being in even the best of prisons is like living in a public toilet.

Since I have been out, the powers that be have done away with the one redeeming aspect of prison life: educational programs that offered prisoners an opportunity to make positive changes in their lives and become better people. America is in a vengeful mood. Longer sentences, no parole, the "no frills" prison, the death penalty: All are part of a trend away from compassion and healing and back to an Old Testament philosophy of violent retribution. Gang warfare. You hurt or kill one of ours, we kill you. Violence begets violence.

I was the exception to the rule of who usually goes to prison in America. White man from a solid middle-class background, well educated, I had no excuse for my behavior, as both federal judges who sentenced me were wont to remind me. (I had two trials, one in the District of Maine, the other in the Southern District of New York, Manhattan, for essentially the same twenty-year crime spree.) They hammered me. I got fifteen years in Maine for importing pot. Then, in New York, when I refused to cooperate with the *federales*—which, as the public defender explains to Ray Joshua in *Slam*, means, rat, snitch, tell on your friends or enemies (in my case they wanted me to implicate Norman Mailer, a close friend)—they hit me with another charge. I was convicted of conducting a "continuing criminal enterprise," also known as the kingpin statute, and they gave me another ten years running wild with the fifteen for a total of twenty-five with no parole.

Because I was educated, because I could read and write with some facility, I was able to study the law while in prison and eventually discover the elusive loophole the lawyers had missed and get myself sprung. Otherwise, I would still be there, still doing time, of the world but not in it, longing for the simple joys and pleasures of life, like being able to walk to the corner and buy a newspaper, or being able to hold the one you love in your arms.

Worse yet, had I been sentenced under the federal sentencing guidelines that were enacted while I was locked up, I would have received a mandatory sentence of life without parole. For marijuana. Large loads, yes, but nevertheless for importing a plant that is used regularly by millions of Americans, now grown in all fifty states, our biggest cash crop. Today, handle large amounts of weed, son, and you could be locked up for the rest of your natural—or unnatural—life. That is some serious shit.

More than half of the nearly two million souls we have relegated to human warehouses here in the land of the free are black. Although African-Americans account for less than 15 percent of the free-world population, we lock up blacks at a rate nearly eight times greater than we do whites. There is no valid evidence that blacks commit more crime than whites; they simply get caught, prosecuted and sent to prison more often. Chances are, if you were born black, born in the ghetto, if you have no money for a lawyer, no money for bail, and you get busted even for some petty-ass shit like a quarter pound of weed, you are fucked. You are going to prison.

After I got sentenced in Maine, when I was on my way to the penitentiary in Terre Haute, Indiana—known as one of the tougher joints in the federal system—the deputy U.S. marshals who were transporting me tried to put the fear in me by saying that Terre Haute was "full of D.C. niggers" and

I had better be ready to get it on or some big black buck would make me his punk. I laughed at them. I was cocky, maybe trying to hide my fear, but I said that I was more worried about the white boys in Washington who had already fucked me than I was about some black guys who were in the same sorry predicament.

Turned out, I was right. The infamous "D.C. niggers," as they are known throughout the federal system, never did me any harm, never even threatened me; in fact, some became close friends. I learned a lot from the black men I lived with in prison. I learned that if you want to see where and how racism lives on in full blown horror in this country, you need only look at the criminal justice system. I learned that, the worse you treat someone, the harder and meaner they get, just like junkyard dogs. I also learned that, beneath the surface, even the toughest hard-ass from the meanest streets and cellblocks wants basically the same things everyone else wants: love, respect and understanding, and an opportunity to live a decent life. All the rest is just posturing, or survival tactics, often honed in prison.

In the words of another ex-convict, a man I admire greatly, former Black Panther and criminal justice system reform activist Eddie Ellis—who served twenty-seven years in New York state prisons for a murder he didn't commit—the black man's journey in America has taken him "from the plantations to the projects to the penitentiary." Nowhere is this more apparent than in our nation's capital.

Washington, D.C., with its gleaming white monuments to liberty and justice for all, has an incarceration rate four times that of the rest of the nation, making the District the undisputed incarceration capital of the world. The rate of black to white prisoners in D.C. is greater than ten to one. On any given day in the District, one in two black men between the ages of eighteen and thirty-five are in jail, on probation or parole, or wanted on warrants. In the shadows of Capitol Hill, the D.C. City Jail festers with trashed lives, men and increasing numbers of women who have been thrown away, condemned to the living hell of prison for the crime of being poor, uneducated, born in the ghetto.

Well over half of these prisoners are serving disproportionately long sentences for nonviolent drug and property offenses. The drug war has become the new Vietnam, another vicious quagmire and political smoke screen, this time waged in our own backyards, in the streets of our cities, against our own citizens. It is the driving force behind the imprisonment boom and the law and order orgy that has robbed Americans of many precious civil liberties and turned this country into a land of informants where children are urged to rat on their parents, a land of paranoia where many citizens hate the government and fear the all-powerful police.

In writing *Slam*, Marc and I wanted to tell a story that would dramatize issues we were faced with in our personal and professional lives, Marc as a documentary filmmaker, I as a writer and editor of *Prison Life*. As much as we hoped to make a film that would be entertaining, fresh and moving, we wanted it to be about something, to have a theme with resonance and meaning beyond the usual commercial crap polluting our artistic lifeblood. The first film we worked on together was a documentary for HBO, *Prisoners of the War on Drugs,* about the impact of the drug war on our prison system. One of Marc's best friends died while in jail on drug charges. My years as a POW still haunt me. The subject is as close to us as our skin.

One of the initial creative questions we faced was whether to make Ray Joshua's crime marijuana or crack. Though my own bust had been for marijuana, and although I believed a pot dealer would be a more sympathetic character, I was concerned we would be criticized for being politically naive when it is the violence of the crack wars that has given rise to the latest rash of drug war hysteria.

Marc and Henri Kessler, the third producer, favored making it a pot bust that propels young Ray on his mythic journey. I spent a day in D.C. Superior Court watching arraignments, observing the procedure so I could write the courtroom scene, and I saw that at least 70 percent of the cases called were for simple possession, or possession with intent to distribute (PWID, as the D.C. convicts call it) small amounts of drugs, mostly marijuana. With a prior conviction, under the new federal sentencing guidelines, Ray would be facing enough time to up the stakes. Raymond Joshua, universal Buffalo Soldier from the projects, then became the local herb merchant and poet, mystic dispenser of truth.

Slam may well be the first movie ever made about a sympathetic drug dealer. A favorite scene of mine is the dope deal in the first ten minutes of the movie when Ray sells a bag of herb to his dreadlocked, browbeaten brother. No guns. No fear. No stereotypical heavies draped in gold chains lurking in the shadows. It's more like a spiritual transaction. When we were working on this book, there were those who urged me to edit out all references to marijuana. "C'mon," I said, "this is a book about the making of *Slam*. And, finally, no matter how you slice it, this movie is the story of a marijuana dealer." A low-level, subsistence pot dealer to be sure ("I'm just out there surviving," Ray tells his court-appointed lawyer), but a dealer nevertheless.

The journey of our main character, Raymond Joshua, a talented young rapper and poet from the 'hood, would, we decided, be the simple and commonplace story of a street kid surviving by his wits, hustling a little contraband on the side. He gets caught up in the gang warfare raging in our inner cities as young men fight their way up the food chain with automatic weapons. Busted for a quarter pound of weed, caught fleeing the scene of a shooting, Ray winds up in the D.C. City Jail. That could very well have been the end of Ray's story. Another casualty of the drug war, another young black man whose life will be wasted because as a society we ignore the underdog until he bites us on the ass, then we lock him up in a cage and turn him into a killer. If we want these young men to stop behaving like animals, we had better stop treating them like animals.

But Ray is a poet, he uses the Word as his weapon. There was a lot of discussion about the climactic scene, the moment in the yard when Ray defuses the escalating violence between the warring crews, Thug Life and Union, and saves his own skin by unleashing a barrage of verbal blows to the psyches of gang members poised to do battle. People told me the scene would never work, it was too unrealistic, too contrived. And it might not have worked if we hadn't found the extraordinarily talented Saul Williams to play the part of Ray. But I had seen it happen, I had seen men quash potential violence with words, either with basso profundo bombast or wit or humor, in bullpens, cellblocks, and on prison yards. I used language, the language of the law, to get myself out of prison. And rap music, the latest mutation of poetry, holds a generation in thrall, white and black alike.

"Democracy needs her poets, in all their diversity, precisely because our hope for survival is in recognizing the reality of one another's lives," Bill Moyers writes in the introduction to his book about a festival of poets, *The Language of Life*. When Ray bellows to China, charismatic boss of Thug Life crew, "Stealing us was the smartest thing they ever did," China glowers with recognition. Zen Gangster Hopha, played by the multigifted Bonz Malone, tells Ray he is a great man because, quoting Sun Tzu in *The Art of War*, he won the war without using violence. And Lauren Bell, teacher of a self-expression class about to become extinct in the latest round of get-tough-on-tough-guys cutbacks, recognizes Ray's gift as her students' hope for salvation. Sonja Sohn, in developing the character of Lauren, volunteered to teach a poetry class at Rikers Island. The actors all created their own characters from discussions with Marc and me, from experience and research. Among other books, Saul read *Convicted in the Womb* by Carl Upchurch, who tells of re-creating himself with a volume of Shakespeare's sonnets he found in a solitary confinement cell. In *Prison Life* he read the story of Jimmie Santiago Baca, another convict who saved his life with poetry.

The actor/poets wrote their poems and composed much of their own dialogue ad lib in workshops and while the camera was rolling. Early on, we decided to do away with the notion of a conventional screenplay. I told Marc from the beginning there was no way we could write dialogue better than what our actors would come up with. We worked with them on the story and they helped us develop the scene outline that would be our road map through the projects in Anacostia, on the cellblocks and in the yard of the infamous D.C. City Jail, to the base of the great white man's totem pole, the Washington Monument, where the available imagery provided us with a padlocked gate.

The people we drafted to be actors along the way—prisoners, prison guards, ex-cons and ex-con mayors we snatched from the available talent pool—also made up some of their own dialogue based on Marc's direction. Marc would tell the actors how to get into the scene, where to take it, and how to get out. But God is in the details. The amazing side trips the actors took came from the inspiration they got telling a story they knew was vital to their own lives. Working with the prisoners was a kind of vindication for me and for them. Here men who have been demonized were laying bare their souls. When Jerome Goldman stood up during the classroom scene in the jail and recited his poem "Why?" which begins, *I shot three motherfuckers/and I don't know why*, he asked the fundamental question the film proposes: Why perpetuate a cycle of violence, crime and imprisonment that has failed miserably?

The story of *Slam* begged to be told. Marc's vision of Ray's tale was so clear he had no trouble recognizing it, coaxing it from those who are living it and, with Mark Benjamin's magical-realism style of cinematography, capturing it on film. But it couldn't have happened if it hadn't been for a cosmic conspiracy of events that resulted in what Marc called "a seam in time" that made it possible for us to slip into the capital and make a guerrilla-style revolutionary film right under their noses.

Writer Robert Leaver, who worked as a production assistant and driver, tells the off-camera story of the making of this film in a wry *Slam* diary entry entitled *Wheel Man*. Washington was in flux. The cops were looking the other way. The production itself was a kind of caper—a covert operation. Using Marc's concept of the stealth bomber media mission worked. We came in under the radar, superimposed a dramatic narrative on the shocking reality we had discovered while making documentaries, then got out of Dodge City before the *federales* figured out what we were doing.

The mayor of Washington, Marion Barry, is another drug war casualty who knows firsthand how the criminal justice system works. "Some people call it the criminal *injustice* system," I heard him tell an audience of ex-cons and family members of prisoners while I was following him around doing research for an article for *George* magazine. At the time of my last interview with the mayor, we were prepping to shoot in D.C. Casting on the fly, I knew we needed a judge for the courtroom scene, so when the interview ended I asked Mayor Barry if he would play the role.

He studied me with a slight smile and twinkling of the eye. "What's the movie about?" he asked.

I pitched him like I would have pitched an enlightened studio executive.

"You know the story," I said.

Many white Washingtonians and middle-class blacks who have fled the District are quick to blame Mayor Barry for all Washington's woes. That's about as accurate as giving Giuliani credit for what's happening in New York. Truth is, like everything else in America, it's all about money. The white boys on Capitol Hill who control the purse strings loathe Barry because he refuses to kiss ass and because he has consistently spoken out for the angry, dispossessed blacks who live in the other Washington, D.C. While shooting the courtroom scene, I savored the irony of playing a prosecutor to Mayor Barry's judge. What we saw happening in Washington while we were making *Slam* was the glaring reflection of an open sore on the face of the nation.

The District's Department of Corrections, which corrects exactly nothing and makes everything worse, has been given over to the feds and to private industry. The same folks who brought us Kentucky Fried Chicken have opened a private prison in Youngstown, Ohio, to house some of the more than 14,000 D.C. prisoners. It will be interesting to see how they deal with the "D.C. niggers." Most of these men have grown up in prison or on the mean streets of the war zones. They have nothing to lose. As Americans, we have everything to lose if we continue to think of the least fortunate of us as somehow *other*. What we do to the least of us, we do to all of us.

Now that President Clinton has been caught with his pants down, maybe he will come to see that the hypocrisy and viciousness, the police state law enforcement tactics and strategies promulgated during the drug war, with his eager participation—wiring people up and getting them to implicate themselves and others on tape, coercing people to go before grand juries and rat out their friends, threatening citizens and using the brutal punishment of imprisonment to condemn what should be private behavior—have turned around like a whole junkyard full of rabid dogs to bite him on his ass.

We committed a Hollywood sin and left the ending of the movie ambiguous. During a Q&A after a screening of *Slam* at the Sundance Film Festival, someone in the audience asked Marc why he had chosen to leave Ray's fate dangling on the locked gate at the foot of the Monument.

Marc answered, "Because finally, it seemed to me, what matters is not what Ray does. What matters is what we do, how we as a society respond to the many Ray Joshuas out there who have been locked up and locked out."

Film is our most collaborative art form. I was honored to work on this film with so many gifted people and I am honored to help tell this story. I hope the book mirrors the extraordinary mix of vision and talent that converged to make *Slam*. Heartfelt thanks to my wife and partner, coeditor Kim Wozencraft, and to Pam Widener and Fionn Reilly, whose help in making this book about *Slam* was invaluable.

Film has become our most popular medium for telling the stories of one another's lives. Democracy needs her brave and committed filmmakers. My big hope for *Slam* is that it helps to exorcise some of my own and society's demons.

The
Slam
Diaries

MARC LEVIN

DISPATCHES FROM THE FRONT
A DIRECTOR'S JOURNAL

John Kirby

July 22, 1997

On the road to D.C. with Robbie driving, Daphne and John relaxing in the back of the minivan. Beautiful sunset over oil refineries on Jersey Turnpike. Postmodern pollution landscape. That's why the Garden State has one of the nation's highest cancer rates. My mom and dad have been hit.

I close my eyes and try to forget the crisis of the moment and remember how this *Slam* journey started.

FLASHBACK TO:

April 1996

On a warm spring evening my wife, Ellin, and I are walking the streets of the East Village when who do we run into but Bonz Malone—street legend, raconteur, journalist, writer of the Tuph Street column in *Vibe* magazine. Bonz is an old friend; I haven't seen him in six or seven months. We met over a decade ago when Bonz was seventeen and I was making a documentary for CBS on troubled youth called *What's Going On*. While shooting the film, I got to know this young black writer who was working for a teenage newspaper called *The New Youth Connection*.

At that time, Bonz was known as Kevin Haslem, and he was already a legendary graffiti artist whose tag had traveled on subways from Coney Island to Yankee Stadium. He had been kicked out of a number of high schools in Brooklyn. (As he said, "I grew up on tough street. School and I didn't get along.") He'd been busted for graffiti and thrown in Rikers Island. Luckily, someone recognized that Bonz was a good kid with talent, and they hooked him up in a special program where he could work on a newspaper and graduate from high school. He was the first writer I met who used a hip hop slang style artfully as a journalist and commentator. Since then, he's become a nationally known magazine writer and personality.

"Where you been, buddy?" I ask, reconnecting with my old friend and partner in crime.

"Rehab," he answers with a straight face.

I'm in shock. Bonz Malone in rehab. America has really become *One nation under rehabilitation*.

Bonz assures me that no rehab could neutralize his head. He tells Ellin and me that we have to go with him to check out the action at the Nuyorican's annual Grand Slam. "There's some phat talent," he says and smiles mischievously.

The Nuyorican Poets Café is one of the great mixes in the New York scene. People of all kinds have made it a true safehouse for creative work and play. I've been going to the café slams since they started in the early '90s. Bob Holman, New York's poetry slam impresario, is an old friend.

Bonz, Ellin and I step into the club just as this handsome, dreadlocked poet takes the stage—Saul Williams. I get a comfortable spot at the bar, order a beer. I've seen most of the talent that has passed through the café, some great spoken-word artists, but Saul Williams is spitting out dense multi-dimensional word bombs that explode in a mix of street culture and classical mythology, a unique mix of rap, word play and poetry that takes you straight from the street corner to the twilight zone. His movement and presentation have a princely stature and dignity, almost Shakespearean. As he gains momentum, he seems to be reinventing his words, each loaded with mega-tons of meaning, one blast after another.

Wow, the man is hot. Possessed. A true brother from another planet, and definitely a ten—the Grand Slam winner!

May 1996
A few days after Saul wins the Grand Slam, the Offline team (me, Henri Kessler and Richard Stratton) is off to Cannes. We are working on a feature film project called *Acid Test* about the secret testing of LSD by the CIA back in the '50s. Yes, it was LSD that originally brought us together.

I met Richard in the early '90s, right around the time Oliver Stone's *JFK* came out. I was working on a documentary, *Beyond JFK*, with Danny Schecter and Barbara Kopple, and we all went to Town Hall in Manhattan one evening for a symposium called "Fact and Fiction: The Artist's Responsibility."

Afterwards, at a bar across the street, Danny Schecter introduced me to Richard and his wife, Kim Wozencraft, both writers. We got to talking about drugs and politics, two of our favorite subjects, when Richard said to me, "Kim and I just saw the ultimate movie about drugs and politics."

"Oh, really?" I replied, eager to hear more.

"You wouldn't have seen it," he said. "We were the only two people in the theater. It was called *Blowback*."

"I made that film," I told them.

"You're that Marc Levin?" said Richard. "Amazing. I told Kim when we left the theater that I had to meet the man who made that movie."

Blowback is a crazy underground black comedy I made around the time of the Iran/Contra debacle. The intelligence community uses the term blowback to describe the fallout when a covert operation backfires and comes back to haunt the Agency—like when they trained Afghan freedom fighters to kill the Russians only to have them blow back later as terrorists trying to blow up the World Trade Center.

Kim's first novel, *Rush*, was a fictionalized story of her experience as an undercover narcotics cop in Texas. She got strung out on drugs and was eventually busted by the FBI and sent to prison. So Kim had her own story to tell about drugs, politics and blowback. Richard had been an international marijuana and hashish smuggler, bringing in boatloads of pot from Colombia and freighters of hash from Lebanon. He was busted on a drug kingpin charge, convicted and sentenced to twenty-five years in a federal penitentiary. He became a jailhouse lawyer, successfully appealed his sentence and got out after serving eight years. While in prison, he wrote a novel called *Smack Goddess*. Richard and Kim met at a PEN Prison Writing Awards ceremony shortly after Richard's release from prison in 1990. Two ex-con writers—one a former narc, the other a former smuggler—they went on to publish and edit the award-winning magazine *Prison Life*.

I told Richard about a story that had always intrigued me, the CIA's early LSD experiments and how they boomeranged (blew back), helping to catalyze the '60s counterculture. It was a historic irony that fascinated both of us. We decided to try and make a movie about it—*Acid Test*. And that's how we met Henri.

Henri is the man who took our idea and raised the money to develop it as a screenplay. Henri is an original, one of the first New York club kidz who ended up running his own nightclub, The Grollier. The turning point in his life came at age thirteen, when he was bar mitzvahed. He grew up in Brooklyn, worked after school as a groundskeeper at a small tennis club run by Phil Rubell, the father of Steve Rubell, who had just opened Studio 54. Phil Rubell came to Henri's bar mitzvah and asked him what he wanted. "A new tennis racquet?"

Henri told Rubell, "I want to go to Studio 54."

Rubell did him one better. He gave Henri a gold VIP card and said, "Just tell my son to treat you right."

The next night, Henri snuck out and went to Studio 54. He ended up in the VIP room with Andy Warhol and Calvin Klein, Mick and Bianca Jagger and the whole clubland scene. He never went home.

Ten years later, he opened The Grollier. One of his investors was David Peipers, a bright, adventurous venture capitalist. Henri brought Richard and me to meet David, we all hit it off and David put up the money to develop *Acid Test*.

So here we are in Cannes, trying to get foreign financing to make *Acid Test*. After partying late, Henri and Richard somehow find the energy to get up and motorbike into town for the 8:30 a.m. screening of *Trainspotting*.

I'm still comatose. They wake me with a call at about 10:30, and they are over-the-top, flipping out.

"We just saw a great film, man, *Trainspotting*, about a bunch of Scottish dopers. Can you imagine some executive in Hollywood green-lighting a project about Scottish junkies? Never happen. These guys just went out and did it, made their own goddamn movie. That's what we've got to do. Fuck Hollywood. Fuck stars. Fuck packaging and all the rest of that crap. We need to come up with a project only we can do, our way, and then go out and do it."

I stagger up and out, walk the half mile along the Mediterranean to town. It's a beautiful day, I'm thinking about Henri and Richard's enthusiasm, their frustration with the system and their faith in me. I think about all the kids we'd met in prison on bullshit drug charges while Richard and I were working on a documentary for HBO called *Prisoners of the War on Drugs*.

The drug war is the engine driving the explosion in the nation's prison population, creating an all new prison-industrial complex and warehousing people for years on petty drug charges. We had met so many talented people who were wasting away behind bars, from teenage crack dealers to grandmothers busted for pot. The whole drug war is total madness. If Richard had been busted today, with the current sentencing guidelines, he would be looking at mandatory life without parole; he certainly wouldn't be waiting to have brunch with me on the French Riviera.

Then I think about Bonz. If someone hadn't given him a break, he might well be serving time instead of expressing himself as a writer. Finally, I recall the Grand Slam Bonz had led me into a few days earlier, and the amazing performance of Saul Williams.

Suddenly, it hits me—*Slam*. What an irony that it comes to me as I'm strolling along the beach on the luxurious French coast. But there's also myth, magic and history in the Mediterranean, and that's how I see it: A talented young guy gets busted on a small drug charge; we follow him into the black hole of the criminal justice system, where somehow he discovers his voice and emerges as an artist on stage at a poetry slam, just like I'd seen two days ago at the café. *Slam* is a film I can make my way, my style, using incredible talent.

I sit down for cappuccino with Henri and Richard and tell them, "It's the story of the poet from the 'hood—*Slam*."

They are instantly intrigued, nodding their heads, smiling. "Yeah. Yeah. *Slam*."

June 1996

A few weeks after my return, Saul Williams comes over to my loft on 26th Street and we have our first discussion about *Slam*. I've sketched in a little more of the idea and explain to Saul how the key dramatic question for the movie's main character is whether to "cop or cooperate." Is he going to cop a plea and go away to prison for a few years, or will he cooperate with the police, snitch and go free? Our character has a week to decide, most of it to be spent in the D.C. City Jail. As he struggles to survive in the dog-eat-dog world of prison, he discovers his voice, his mission as a man and as an artist, and he becomes free.

Saul likes the high concept. I like Saul a lot and am impressed to learn that he is also a student in the prestigious New York University graduate drama program.

We start a dialogue. I show him my work, he shows me his. Richard,

Henri and I see him in a play by Athol Fugard, *A Lesson from Aloes*. Saul goes on to take third place at the National Slam Championship in Seattle. He is obviously a major talent, and, just as important, a beautiful, gentle soul. I guess our only real question is, can he be hard enough to pull off the street realism?

September 1996

We start to look for our female lead. Mouth Almighty Records is doing a spoken-word happening at S.O.B.'s. Daphne Pinkerson, my partner in documentary film production, takes her Hi-8 camera down to tape the talent. Bonz and Bob Holman are the MCs and there are about eight poets, including Saul.

Two-thirds of the way into this really hot night, a blazing beauty takes the mic and blows everyone away. Boom. Sonja Sohn. Afro-Asian mocha explosion.

We go back to the studio to check the video and make sure we haven't had a communal hallucination. When the Dutch Angle Close-Up of Sonja doing her poem "run free or die" comes on, the party grows silent. There she is, just like we saw her in the movie before the movie was even shot. Slowly, everyone is drawn closer and closer to the TV screen. The whole room is mesmerized. Her performance is so powerful, and the words, it's as if they were written for *Slam*: "My back is against a brick wall and I got a Mack truck two inches from my face...I got two mothafuckin minutes, y'all, before I smash my face into the grill of a Mack truck, before I get ten thousand bricks shoved up my ass, before I run free or die!"

I keep repeating those words, "run free or die." We are all in love with Sonja. A few days later, she comes over and we lay out our game plan.

Sonja is down with the *Slam* posse. We hook her up with Saul and start workshopping. The chemistry between Saul and Sonja is great right from the beginning. They have known of each other but have never worked together before.

The first improv we do is in my living room on a fall afternoon. I go through the basic scene setup, then the actors take over. We start with them meeting in a writing workshop in jail. Then we do the climactic fight scene that will come at the end of the film. Daphne tapes the workshop and we see it is charged, we know we have some heat.

One of the key lines in that scene emerges from the first session. As Sonja is pushing Saul's character to face up to his responsibility and make a decision, Saul leaps off the couch and yells, "This ain't no metaphor! This is my life!"

We are pretty confident Saul is our lead, but I still want to talk it over with Bonz, so we schedule a sit-down with the early *Slam* team. Bonz works on his own schedule, so when he doesn't show up on time, we don't think much of it. A while later, I get a call from him.

"Hey, Marc, I'm sorry, I can't make it down," Bonz tells me.

"What's the problem?"

"Oh, man, you won't believe it. I'm back in Rikers."

Oh, shit. Here we are trying to do a story about a talented guy who gets thrown in jail, and once again Bonz is racing ahead of us, living out the real story. It seems he had been in a fight, he put a few pool balls in a sock and went after some guy. Bonz had expected the judge to give him a suspended sentence, but His Honor was in a bad mood and told Bonz he was going to jail for four months.

November 1996

I take the subway out to Queensborough station and wait in the cold with a large group for a public bus out to Rikers. I am the only white person on the bus packed full of moms, kid brothers, sisters and girlfriends.

I wait for hours in a small room with lots of frustrated, anxious folks who have been herded from one place to another. An officer finally calls my name. I am led into a large cafeteria-style visiting area. About five minutes later, Bonz appears in a blue jumpsuit for our sit-down.

"I'm cool," he assures me. Not many people bother him, he says, since he's always reading *The Art of War* and *How to be an Executive Leader*. "They don't know what to make of me. I haven't told anyone here who I am."

I update him on *Slam*. Bonz has started writing some scene ideas for us and I encourage him to use this experience to develop material for the film. Bonz and I have been talking about doing a down-and-dirty guerrilla film production for years. We have acted out hundreds of scene ideas and character monologues since we first met. In fact, Bonz's closing monologue in *What's Going On* was such a classic that the morning after it aired *The Cosby Show* called CBS to ask about "that incredible talent."

Bonz was a hard-core renegade with little interest in network TV sitcoms. But over the years, we have discussed Bonz's performing talent.

At one time we talked about him as a possible lead in *Slam*, so I'm a little apprehensive about how to handle our enthusiasm for Saul. I remind Bonz that he turned me onto Saul and tell him about how exciting some of the improvs between Saul and Sonja are.

"Saul would be great as the lead," he says. I smile in relief. "Bonz, you're beautiful."

"Hey, I still want a major role in this film," he says.

"Brother, you got it. Who do you want to be?"

"I want to play the Zen Gangster. I call him Hopha, and his crew is the Union. It's time to get organized, Cuz."

Winter 1996–97
We continue to workshop with Saul and Sonja while producing two major documentary projects: an HBO show on Texas Death Row; and a three-hour miniseries for the Discovery network, *CIA: America's Secret Warriors*. We are also doing follow-up on a documentary we did with Bill Moyers and Dateline NBC, *Oklahoma City: One Year Later*. So *Slam* is percolating in a stew with a lot of other interesting projects.

One afternoon, I am on the phone with CIA headquarters in Langley, Virginia. Another line rings and it's the godfather of the Christian Identity movement and head of the Elohim City commune in the hills of eastern Oklahoma. (Timothy McVeigh allegedly spent some time there before the Oklahoma City bombing.) Daphne gets on the phone with him, trying to set up a possible shoot. Then a third line rings; it's a collect call from a federal penitentiary, a major organized crime figure on the line. One of our production assistants has to deal with it. Here we are at our loft on 26th Street with the CIA, the Christian militia movement and the Mafia on our phone lines simultaneously.

For a moment, I get paranoid, wondering, "Doesn't the Agency have some supercomputer that can cross-reference these calls and set off a flashing red warning light, pinpointing us on West 26th Street in Manhattan?"

Early March 1997
Since 1975, my loft on 26th Street was known to an underground global cadre as "the situation loft" or "loftland." For almost a decade it was an international crash pad and party central; for over twenty years it has been my office and production studio. My father, Al, was my original partner, and then Daphne Pinkerson came aboard. By the late '80s, Daphne had brought some order to the chaos, but we were still a home-grown, family film–and–TV production company. Now, with all of our films coming together at the same time, and on the precipice of *Slam*, it is becoming clear that we've outgrown our crib. It's time to make a move.

For years, driving down the West Side Highway to 26th Street, I have marveled at the great beast of a building on the corner of 26th and the Hudson River: the Starrett-Lehigh building, a huge, art deco, ocean liner–like structure that takes up an entire city block, with glass windows looking out at the city and the river from all sides. A New York landmark.

With Henri on the case, we soon find ourselves looking at an enormous, gutted space on the northwest corner of the 17th floor of the Starrett-Lehigh building. The space was once an industrial print shop, and there is grease and grime all over. We climb through the debris to filthy windows looking west to the Hudson, north to the George Washington Bridge and east to the midtown power skyline. We make our way around the tapered mushroom columns, through the garbage to the northwest corner. There is something about the rounded corner and the curved bay windows that stops us. We're on point, almost like on a ship's bridge, looking out for whatever is coming next. It's the big sky, the big vista, the big picture. We know immediately: This is the spot.

Late March 1997

The light in the new space is amazing, especially the sunsets and the city skyline at night. Our grand opening party is one of those nights you remember for a lifetime; hundreds of people flowing in and out and joining in the excitement. The *Slam* team is there in force: Bonz, Saul, Sonja, Liza, Beau Sia, Bob Holman. My parents and sisters are there. My youngest sister, Jules, informs me that she is pregnant with her third child. The evening has that feeling; we're all about to give birth to something new and exciting.

At about 1:30 a.m. Richard has the DJ play our new anthem, the George Clinton song "Dope Dog." The place goes wild, dancing to the beat of the drug war from the point of view of a crazed dope-sniffing canine. There is a meltdown and I become a whirling dervish, spinning over to the northwest corner, the magic spot, the lookout point. A full moon is rising like a large yellow tennis ball spinning between the Chrysler building and the Empire State building. I slowly turn my head and pan the full arc from the midtown Manhattan skyline to the Javits Center in front of me, to the twinkling jeweled necklace connecting New York and New Jersey. A lone boat heads up the river, across to New Jersey. I can see the ridge where my folks still live. I literally see my whole life in front of me. I was born in New York and was a baby over on East 36th Street, playing in the park by the Queens Midtown Tunnel. Then my folks, deep in the labor movement, moved to an Italian working-class neighborhood in Elizabeth, New Jersey. I was a kid growing up on 45 Orchard Street. All my crazy friends would go on a daily rampage on their release from Catholic school, even terrorizing my sisters. So as I was about to become a teenager my parents decided their union organizing days were over and they began to pursue professional careers. I think they were also worried that I was about to become a juvenile delinquent on the mean streets of Elizabeth. My folks moved to a vintage middle-class suburb, Maplewood, and bought a house on the top of a hill. That's where I came of age during the '60s, with my blond WASP friends and their country club parents lost in an alcoholic daze like Mr. and Mrs. Robinson in the movie *The Graduate*. And that's where I made my first tapes and movies—those teenage days, live.

Suddenly I realize what is so special about this place. Dancing on point, surrounded by the *Slam* crew, by family, friends and colleagues, looking out at the shimmering light and water, I know I have found the spot. I can review my whole life in one long panorama.

April 1997

The CIA series premieres and now I'm dealing with the critical response—and the fallout. Discovery is in a state of shock. They know how to deal with snakes, sharks and sabertooths, but not controversy. Someone in their PR department actually sent a preview copy of the series to the CIA. The Agency freaked, claiming they were misled.

"We were told this was an historical documentary, not an investigative report," they squawk. The CIA crying foul? Ha! The Agency complaining they've been lied to! Now they want the last show, the segment called *Blowback*—which includes a look at the CIA's cocaine connection—canceled.

The executives at Discovery have no idea how to deal with the situation. After all, the military and the intelligence communities are primary sources for all their boy-toy shows. That's where they get all that footage of airplanes, rockets, tanks, aircraft carriers and spy satellites.

Thank God the critics heap praise on the series; it offers Discovery some defense. But they are still very nervous. For me, there are three phone calls that make it all worthwhile. First, Norman Mailer calls. We had dined together more than two years earlier, me, my father, Richard, and Norman, talking spooks, conspiracies and counterintelligence in a grand brainstorming powwow.

"The CIA is a living organism," Norman tells me now over the phone from his home in Provincetown. "You captured that. You did it! You may have laid them to rest forever."

Then Oliver Stone calls, raving, "How the hell did you ever get Richard Helms to say that shit? Did you drug him?"

Finally, Dick Gregory checks in. "That was the most amazing television experience of my life. This could change America."

I hang up the phone, touched by this troika of heavyweights; their praise inoculates me against the crisis raging at Discovery and the Central Intelligence Agency.

The phone rings again. It's my mother. "How's everything going?" I ask.

"Not too well," she responds. My first flash is that something bad has happened to my father. He has been dealing with a low-grade bladder cancer and I immediately assume that it has spread and is serious.

"What's wrong? Is Dad all right?" I ask, waiting for bad news.

"He's fine. It's me. I have a brain tumor. It looks very bad."

I am stunned, numb, silent. Then she breaks down.

Frightened and disoriented, I just mutter, "What!?"

My mom dying? It can't be. She is indestructible. It must be a mistake. Then my dad takes the phone and says, "It looks serious."

I can tell he's struggling to keep it together. "But you know your mama," he says. "If anyone can pull out a miracle, she can."

My mom is an incredible force, capable of the impossible. She and my father have devoted their lives to trying to make the world a better place and they have accomplished amazing things, built up quite a reservoir of good karma.

For many years, I have given thanks and praise for being part of such a blessed family, full of so much love, joy and goodness. There is a lifetime of magic that has touched my grandparents, my parents, my sisters and me, and now all our children. My two kids, twins, were born six weeks premature, and my son was in critical condition because his lungs were not fully developed. He pulled all the tubes and wires out, driving the nurses and doctors crazy. But he pulled through and kept the string of Levin luck going.

We are a family that has survived and thrived through every crisis, protected by the grace and power of my parents' love, and their commitment to making a difference. I had always wondered how long the magic could last. Someday, I knew, our lucky streak would have to come to an end.

As my father fights to stay composed, he sums it up: "We have nothing to complain about. We've had one incredible run."

The doctors give my mom three to six months to live. Her entire left side is partially paralyzed by a seizure from the tumor. They call it glioblastoma, the most aggressive and deadly brain cancer. It is incurable.

I want to make the most of my remaining time with my mom. I also have to help my father and three sisters deal with the day-to-day care—the oncologists, the brain surgeons, the nurses, the CAT scans, the radiation, the antiseizure drugs, the steroids—and investigate all the alternative treatments that might offer hope to prolong her life and minimize her suffering.

At the same time, I throw myself into all of our film projects, becoming a total workaholic. It is my way of coping, my escape.

May 1997

We start making plans to shoot *Slam* in NYC. After all, it is our home, and it would be cheaper and easier. Henri and I start meeting with people from the mayor's motion picture office. It quickly becomes clear that as long as Giuliani is running the show, any media access to Rikers Island and the criminal justice system will be impossible. If Dinkins were still mayor, maybe we would have a chance, but with ex-prosecutor Rudy Giuliani clamping down, we can't even get permission to take a Hi-8 camera out to a poetry workshop that Sonja is doing in the jail.

Meanwhile, we're shooting another HBO doc, *Thug Life,* on the jailing of black youth in Washington, D.C. The nation's capital is a real tale of two cities. Behind the façade of the monuments and federal buildings is another Washington, where one out of every two young African-American men is caught up in the criminal justice system. It is American apartheid in the capital of the free world. As the Gingrich Congress does away with welfare and affirmative action, the District spirals down the drain. Across the Anacostia River in Southeast, it's like being in another country. The only growth industry seems to be the criminal justice system. And now they're talking about closing that down and shipping D.C.'s prisoners to private and federal prisons around the country, far from family and friends, in a new diaspora.

It is almost as if the federal government is punishing the District for re-electing Marion Barry, a convicted drug abuser. "Just say no" seems not only to be their lame antidrug mantra, but also the feds' attitude toward helping the District.

Daphne sets up a meeting with the director of the D.C. Department of Corrections, Margaret Moore, sometimes referred to as "Iron Panties" because she can break down hard-assed male wardens and leave them in tears. We enter her spacious office with trepidation. I explain who we are, the work we do and what we are hoping to do in D.C.

Ms. Moore is extremely responsive, especially when I talk about exploring what is happening to all the young black men moving through her system. We are surprised. We give her tapes of some of our other films, *Gang War: Bangin' in Little Rock* and *Prisoners of the War on Drugs,* and make plans for another meeting so she can introduce us to the wardens of the various prisons in the Lorton Correctional Complex.

A few weeks later, we are crammed around a long table at the D.C. Department of Corrections headquarters. Daphne and I are the only white people in the room. At least Daphne is from D.C. I am just another middle-aged, white Jewish producer from New York City.

But this has become our beat. Usually, Daphne and I are suspected of being undercover FBI or DEA agents. This crowd is a lot more hospitable than the Crips and Bloods were when we first started *Gang War*.

Ms. Moore asks me to lay out my vision for the film. I give a short pre-

On location at D.C. City Jail.

sentation. Instead of the usual cautious bureacratic double-talk, the wardens make moving, passionate pleas for someone out there in media land to wake up and tell it like it is.

By the end it is almost like a revival meeting. "Hallelujah, someone wants to tell our story, someone wants to tell the truth. Who cares if it's two white producers from New York? We've been waiting a while. You came to the right place at the right time."

Daphne and I are completely surprised. It's hard to believe we're listening to wardens and corrections officials. They speak with such candor, compassion and conviction about the tragedy of what is happening in our nation's capital. Many of the key movers in the system are strong, articulate black women. They are running a system that is locking up so many of their men—husbands, brothers and sons—it hurts them and they want to do something about it.

One of the most powerful voices at that first meeting is that of Pat

Jackson, the acting warden of the D.C. Jail. She challenges us and says that if we are going to do any film on the young black men in the system, it has to start and end in the D.C. Jail.

We take Pat Jackson up on her proposal, and within a few weeks we're filming in the D.C. Jail. We start with the juveniles, the teenagers under eighteen, who are facing adult charges, mostly homicide. We start talking to them. We find out that almost all of them have seen *Gang War: Bangin' in Little Rock.* Our film has become a cult classic in jails and prisons, one of the most watched HBO documentaries in history. *Gang War* is our passport into the lives of these young prisoners.

In many ways, that summer of 1992 was the birth of the *Slam* style. Our initiation came the afternoon we got caught in the middle of—and captured on film—a drive-by shooting. Our guide, Steve Nawojczyk, Little Rock's crusading coroner and peacemaker, had brought some pizzas for the gang. We were saying good-bye to Lafeil Jackson and his brother Dewitt, the Crip OGs. As our car was about to pull away, a red car pulled up beside us. I was in the driver's seat watching the scene through the windshield. Daphne had the Hi-8 camera and was saying good-bye to the guys on the porch of the Crip house. All of a sudden an arm reached out of the Bloodmobile and started firing a Tech 9. The guys on the porch bolted in all directions.

"Keep rolling," I barked, diving under the dashboard for cover. Crouching behind the open car door, Daphne courageously continued, pointing her camera at everybody running for cover and screaming for retaliation. Is this for real? I thought. Caught in the middle of the Bloods and the Crips during a drive-by in the president's hometown? How the fuck did I ever end up here!

Amazingly, no one was hurt.

A twelve-year-old Crip came up to me afterwards.

"Are you ever going to make a real movie?" he asked.

"Real movie?" I laughed nervously. "I can't think of anything more real than what we just saw."

"That's for HBO," he reminded me. "Not a movie with actors playing in the mall theater."

"I hope I make a movie like that someday," I confessed to him. "Why do you ask?"

He surveyed the scene, still buzzing from the drive-by. "Well, y'all spent a summer down here with us and seen what it's really like. I want to know what kind of story you'd tell."

May 1997

What about *Slam* in D.C.? The more Richard and I talk about it, the more intriguing the idea becomes. Maybe we have found a jail where we can actually bring in actors and shoot our own feature film.

Before going too far, we decide to bring Saul down as a production assistant on the documentary crew. Saul is a middle-class kid from New York state, he has never been in jail, so regardless of what happens it is good research for his Ray Joshua character.

We go back to D.C. for another shoot. Saul is part of the crew but he has time to talk to a lot of the young guys in the jail. A number of times, officers and other inmates mistake him for a prisoner. He is fascinated, constantly taking notes, sketching ideas and images we will work with later.

On the third day of the shoot, we wind up in the concrete courtyard that serves as the jail recreation yard, with about fifteen of the hard-core juvenile offenders. Bay and Face rap for us and Saul is totally into it. He has relaxed over the past few days and I can see he is ready. When Bay and Face finish, I tell them that our dreadlocked production assistant can also rap.

The prisoners want to hear some New York style so they implore Saul to kick a few rhymes. As he begins, Mark Benjamin, our cameraman, starts rolling, slowly panning the faces of these D.C. teens while they listen to Saul.

At first, they're thrilled to be sharing the same language with a brother. Then, as Saul's poetry lifts off and becomes more metaphysical, their faces begin to show confusion and apprehension. Is he dissing us? Where's he headed? What the fuck's he talking about?

As he lands back on earth and wraps it up, they leap to their feet, yelling, "South Side! South Side!" and claiming him as their own.

The moment becomes a touchstone. When we get back to New York and look at the footage, we realize it really can work. You can have a poet of Saul's caliber freestyling with hard-core bangers from the street; it isn't just a filmmaker's conceit. We study the ever-changing expressions on the prisoners' faces—the recognition, confusion and solidarity. It becomes our topography of truth.

Late May 1997

It's a cold, gray spring day in D.C. and we're shooting at a housing project called Simple City. It's a hot spot because there's been a recent kidnapping and shooting of a twelve-year-old. We're talking to some of the kids and a group of the ex-offenders who are working with them when this big guy in shades steps forward and introduces himself as Lawrence or Big Mike. I ask him which name he prefers.

"Whichever you want, man," he says. "I have many names."

It's obvious Big Mike is well known on the streets of Southeast. He tells us his story: One day he was sitting in a car when someone came up, put a pistol to his temple and pulled the trigger. BAM! The bullet bounced around inside his skull, then shattered into five pieces. He could smell the powder burn his flesh, but he couldn't see anything. He was still conscious as the emergency team loaded him into an ambulance and took him to the hospital.

The doctors saved Big Mike's life but he was blinded. Everybody thought he had died, so when he returned to the 'hood it was like the resurrection of Lazarus. People thought they were seeing a ghost. Since then he's been trying to broker a peace between the warring cliques. A warm, magnetic bear of a guy, he's rocking like Stevie Wonder when he says, "I see more now than I ever did then."

Richard's main D.C. contact, the man who brought us into the 'hood, is Rhozier "Roach" Brown. Roach greets Richard with a "Merry Christmas," and, when introduced to me, "Happy Chanukah, Marc."

Roach is a real piece of work, always coming up with off-the-wall expressions— "Roachisms," we call them. "You have about as much chance of winning your case as throwing a snowball into an elephant's mouth at a hundred feet" is a typical example. Roach runs the mayor's Office of Ex-offenders Affairs. As he puts it, "Most cities have some kind of office of veterans affairs. Well, in D.C. we have the only office for ex-offenders. We're trying to reintegrate."

Roach is an ex-offender, as is the mayor. Richard hooked up with them while working on a piece about Marion Barry for *George* magazine. Richard has also been trying to organize a national conference for ex-offenders and community activists. He's convinced that the best hope for reform of the criminal justice system is to try to mobilize the ever-expanding ex-con population. It's an idea both Roach and the mayor share with him.

Roach was a convicted murderer who became a writer and actor in a theater group he organized at one of the Lorton prisons. Somehow he got a pardon from President Ford in 1976 for his prison troupe's community work. Unfortunately, after a stint as a television producer in the '80s, he got caught up again in the drug scene. He and the mayor both got lost in a haze of cocaine, women and power politics. Roach was busted again and sent back to prison.

Of course, Mayor Barry was also busted in the famous FBI sting when one of his old girlfriends set him up and had him videotaped smoking crack in a hotel room. As Roach tells it, the mayor just wanted to get laid, but the woman kept insisting they hit the pipe first. When the FBI team busted in, the mayor let go his memorable line, "The bitch set me up."

So Roach and the mayor know both the inside and the outside. In fact, the mayor caught a lot of flak for putting Roach on the city payroll. Richard, having been an international drug smuggler and ex-con with eight years in the pen, quickly bonded with Roach and Mayor Barry. We are aware that many people in D.C. feel the mayor is a disgrace and Roach is just one of his crooked cronies. But from our perspective, however slippery Roach's reputation, he's an effective coordinator and ebullient collaborator. After all, we're working with characters in the D.C. Jail and on the streets of the ghetto. Roach's effervescent personality and his life history make him an ideal *Slam* ambassador to the 'hood.

We are considering Simple City for the opening scenes in the film. Roach arranges a sit-down with some of the local young guys and the ex-offenders, The Alliance of Concerned Men, who are working with the warring crews to bring peace to the neighborhood. Richard, Henri and I meet with them in a local community center and try to explain what we want to do.

The men are polite but suspicious. Roach vouches for us but, as one of the older men explains it, they have been burnt by the media too many times.

"All you know how to do is exploit us and stir up a lot of negative publicity. It's nothing personal but it's hard to for us to trust any film or TV people," he says, and that seems to be the end of it.

Then Richard stands up and says, "Look, I did eight years in the penitentiary on a drug conviction. I met and became friends with a lot of men in the joint just like you." The room goes silent. "This is the first feature film I've produced and I want to do it with people who know the real story, who've been through what we've been through. I want it to be real."

Once again, Richard makes the connection. The mood changes. The suspicion evaporates and soon it's all about how can we work on this project together.

June 1997
Washington is definitely gaining momentum as the place to shoot *Slam*. Here we have the Gingrich Congress, with Clinton's acquiescence, condemning all the social outreach programs—health care for children and poor people, public education and the whole idea of home rule for the District—and nobody seems to give a shit. Only blocks away from democracy's show-

place are crime- and drug-infested neighborhoods whose citizens have been condemned. Set against the white marble façades is an endless parade of young black faces being imprisoned for bullshit petty drug charges, as the official drug warriors keep mouthing the same "get tough on crime" nonsense. Where else could two white Jews and our token WASP walk into the municipal jail and ask in all seriousness, "Can we shoot a movie here?"

To get official permission to shoot *Slam* in the D.C. Jail, and to use real prisoners and corrections officers in supporting roles and as extras, we need to convince Margaret Moore, director of the District's Department of Corrections. She has been fair and supportive so far, she's given us access to shoot our documentary, but the legal and bureacratic problems of shooting a feature film inside could make it impossible. There are insurance and release nightmares, not to mention the public relations problems, security concerns and personnel demands. The risks are endless. The job of a corrections executive is to minimize risk, not maximize it. If anything goes wrong while we're in the jail filming, Margaret Moore will catch the heat. Her career is on the line.

This is going to be a tough sell. Not only am I asking to use the jail in a feature film, but I'm doing it without a script. All I have given her so far is a one-page synopsis of *Slam*.

Walter Woodward, the public information officer, leads me into Ms. Moore's large office. She hangs up the phone, sits on the couch and turns on the local news. She has just come from testifying on the Hill. Congress is taking over the District's operations, including corrections. I start cautiously.

Soon I understand that Ms. Moore doesn't want to talk about all the potential problems and headaches; she wants to escape her reality and talk about the story and the characters. I act out the story line and explain our style, how we will involve the staff and prisoners, give an opportunity to those who want to participate. I tell her I hope we can reach an oral agreement without lawyers and middlemen because we are financing the movie ourselves and it is a leap of faith for all of us. I promise her that if we succeed we will give something back to the jail by creating a book and videotape library (the jail has no library) so prisoners who want to educate themselves will have an opportunity.

As we get into it, I realize Margaret is going back through her own personal experiences, using them as a source for story and character suggestions, especially those concerning the female lead, Lauren. Lauren is a beautiful young volunteer who runs a writing workshop in the jail where she meets the main character, Ray. I describe how we will have different prisoners perform poems for the class. Afterwards, when everyone else leaves, Lauren and Ray will have a moment alone.

"They talk and then there is an awkward moment of silence where they both feel an attraction," I tell her. "Then Ray moves toward her to steal a kiss."

Ms. Moore stops me. "No, Marc, it wouldn't happen like that. It is certainly possible that a teacher, or volunteer, could have personal feelings for an inmate. And it's even possible that they could have a private moment together where she encourages him to develop his talent. But if an inmate crosses that line, and puts her career in jeopardy by trying to take advantage of her openness, she would be very upset."

I listen intently. "Not even a little kiss?" I ask.

"No way. I would be so upset and so disappointed if he tried that on me. I'd be furious. You want to make it real, right?"

It dawns on me that she is getting personally involved; maybe something like this happened to her. The whole negotiation is coming down to my willingness to consider her creative input in this crucial scene.

I tell her I am open to her suggestions. It does add a note of tension and drama to our characters' budding romance. Maybe she's right, that's the way to play the scene.

"You've convinced me," I admit.

She smiles and says, "Good, I think it's going to be a great movie."

Walter sits up and smiles. Ms. Moore is green-lighting the project.

Late June 1997

There is still the overriding question of how we're going to finance this movie. Even if it is no-budget, we need cash just to get the cast and crew down to D.C. and start shooting.

Our first flash is to try to hook up with an executive producer who will godfather the project. Henri and I talk to Ted Field of Interscope Records. He has just finished shooting *Gridlock* with Tupac and says he's more interested in our *Acid Test* project.

"The CIA and LSD are two of my favorite subjects," he says. "Unfortunately, I'm doing a CIA story with Arnold Schwarzenegger and an LSD movie, the Tim Leary story, with Nic Cage."

We move on to try Sheila Nevins at HBO. Sheila is undoubtedly the most talented television executive I've worked with. She has her name on more quality documentaries than anyone I know. She has also found a way to appease the ratings monster while keeping the artist and social critic alive.

"Lose the message, gain the heat" has always been Sheila's decree. She works from the gut. Find the heat and the beat first, then worry about meaning and message. In many ways, Sheila helped me develop my style in the five *America Undercover* documentaries we've done. Now that I'm working on the D.C. doc for her, she seems like a natural to executive produce *Slam*.

The problem is that Sheila and Richard have been working on HBO's dramatic prison series, *Oz*, with Tom Fontana, and both of them have been frustrated by the experience. Fontana is an auteur and he really doesn't need Richard or Sheila.

Richard and I go to HBO to meet with Sheila and her vice president, Nancy Abraham. Richard advises Sheila, "Forget about *Oz*. Let's do our own prison movie." We put on a *Slam* promo tape of Saul performing and some of the D.C. Jail footage.

When it's over, we ask Sheila if she wants to join us.

"What do you need actors for?" she asks. "I'm sick of drama. Just give me the real thing."

She seems disillusioned by her recent experience with *Oz* and she can't even consider trying anything else in the dramatic genre. We strike out again.

Who else is there? One hot June day Bonz calls me. "Come to Times Square," he says. "Be here in forty-five minutes."

"What's up, Bonz, a secret mission?"

"We're going to talk to Chris," he says cryptically.

"Chris? You mean Chris Blackwell?"

"You got it, brother."

For years Bonz has been telling me about Blackwell. One of Bonz's first jobs was at Island Records and Chris had taken a liking to him. So now we're going to have a sit-down with the man who did *The Harder They Come* and brought Bob Marley to the world.

Bonz and I meet on the sweltering pavement in front of the Virgin megastore. He's dressed in Bermuda shorts, shades and one of his trademark straw bowler hats. We walk over to the Polygram building and take the elevator up to Island Records.

No one knows where Chris is. His movements are mysterious, known only to a few. We wait. After an hour I am ready to split. Just then, we're ushered into a small meeting room. We sit at a beautiful wooden table and Chris comes in. He's charming and relaxed. Bonz is at one end of the table, Chris at the other.

Bonz quickly gets down to business. "Chris, I know you are a man of vision. That's why I've come here with my people. You always told me that when I had it together, I should come to you first. Well, here I am."

Chris laughs and tells us how he is sick of the entertainment business. "The global corporations have sucked the fun and excitement out of this business," he says. "I'm starting something new—a truly no-budget studio using the new digital technology. I need someone like you, Bonz, to help me start up the operation. You interested in being a no-budget studio exec?"

It's quite an offer. Bonz's reply is classic.

"I know you're a generous man and I appreciate that," he tells Blackwell. "You're talking about the future and I know you're a man who can see the future. But I'm thinking about right now. Today. We're here and we're ready to shoot a film in Washington, D.C. You down with us, or not?"

Chris smiles, shakes his head. "I know you'll do it. And I can't wait to see your movie."

July 1997

It's time to make our move and there's still no money. I've got major deadlines coming up in the fall. *The Execution Machine: Texas Death Row* is due to premiere on HBO at the end of September. I'm also working on a new series for Bill Moyers, someone I admire greatly and have worked with on and off for more than twenty years. Moyers is doing a five-hour series on addiction and recovery for PBS. Daphne and I are doing the last hour, *The Politics of Addiction*. This is a topic Bill and I have been discussing for years. He and his wife, Judith, have struggled with their own son's drug and alcohol addiction and they are calling the series *Close to Home*.

When we first talked about the project, Bill cautioned me, "Marc, this isn't about the war on drugs. This is about addiction and recovery."

I got the message. "I'm there, Bill. I think this is a new way to approach the whole issue."

It's nine months later and he is now considering wrapping up the series by saying, "The war on drugs is the Vietnam of our time. A big lie."

Much has transpired and a lot is at stake on that production, which also has to be done by the end of September.

Meanwhile, my mother is continuing her incredible struggle to stay alive. Her first major decision after being diagnosed with brain cancer was to go to the Grand Canyon in her wheelchair with my father, my sister, Nicole, and her son, Benji. She went to the edge of the Canyon and looked out to contemplate the beauty and mystery of the abyss.

The woman is awesome. She taught us how to live and now she is teaching us how to die. Despite the doctors' grim prognosis I know there is no way she's checking out until my younger sister gives birth to her baby, due in November. Mom's willpower is stronger than any cancer.

My mother and I make plans to go to my sister's place in Amagansett, Long Island, for the Fourth of July weekend. It's my dream to walk in the sea with my mom, and, amazingly enough, it's a dream that comes true.

We have an incredible holiday. My wife and I; my sister Danielle and her husband, Dave; their two daughters, Julia and Sophia; and my mother and father. My mom is so alive and full of humor, passionate opinions and forceful advice. She is inspiring all of us with her strength and courage. Every morning we go out to the bay, where they have a special beach wheelchair for the handicapped. We lift my mother out of the car and into the dune buggy, then wheel her down to the beach. My sisters and I get her ready, wheel her right down to the water, lift her from the chair and slowly float her out until the water is almost up to her shoulders. Then she can walk.

We walk back and forth, back and forth, talking about life and death, family and love and how important it is to appreciate every moment we have together.

My mom rests in the afternoon, and then, at the end of the day I wheel her down to the peninsula at Louse Point to watch the sunset. As the sky turns into a brilliant pink orange purple glow, I tell her, "That's my vision of eternity right there. Every time I see that, I'll think of you and how much of you lives in me and always will."

She looks at me, her face bathed in a deep rich gold glow, free of the pain and fear, radiating peace and beauty.

"You changed my life," she says. "I was a wild woman. Then I had you and I became a mother. You were such a playful, joyous baby. We decided to have another child immediately. I've learned so much from you children. I've been so lucky to have your father and you and your three sisters. Your love is what keeps me alive. But the day will come when the sea takes me back and then it's your turn, Marc. It's your family now."

July 6, 1997
Coming back from the holiday weekend, I'm overwhelmed, beginning to think it's too much.

"I have two shows due in September, my executives are breathing down my back, and my mom is dying," I tell Henri. "Let's wait. We'll shoot *Slam* in October."

This is not what he wants to hear. Saul is thinking about moving to San Francisco in the fall. And at the end of the summer, Sonja is going to London to record an album. Now I'm talking about pushing *Slam* back. Henri sees his plans all slipping away and he flips out. Bonz and I tell him to chill but he's panicked.

"I'm at a turning point in my life," Henri pleads with me. "I don't care what it takes. I have to do this. It's time for me to put up or shut up. I'll do whatever it takes." He throws his credit card on the table. "I'm ready to run up a hundred thousand dollars to get us started. Let them come looking for me. I've got nothing to take. I'll leverage everything I've got. Just give me the last ten days in July."

Henri is serious. Someone has to light the fuse and risk it all to make it happen. I did it once ten years ago with *Blowback* when I mortgaged my loft and my future to make a movie. Now it's Henri's turn and he's ready to take the leap.

I squint my eyes, look at Bonz, his bald black crown glinting as he puffs on his cigarette like some wise man.

"I'm down if you're down," I say.

Bonz grins and nods yes. I nod back and turn to Henri.

"Let's do it."

We all shake hands and embrace.

"Guess you got us, bro."

Just then, the sun explodes in the sky, a brilliant sunset outside our West Side office windows. God is our gaffer. We see a glowing future.

July 18, 1997

Now it's all about organizing a small gonzo squad to slip into a timeless zone and steal the moment. Henri organizes the production while I screen cuts for Bill Moyers and Sheila Nevins. Then we run. I know I have at least five days before they will start looking for me.

Henri and Richard have put together quite a crew. As we load in to caravan south, I am amazed by the cast of characters. The *Slam* circus is coming to the capital. We're traveling into a dreamworld together, covert operatives on some counterintelligence mission. Our lives are in sync, somehow all at a turning point, charging to the edge, hoping for a harmonic convergence.

"It's all in the timing," I say. "Seize the moment and slip through a seam in time."

We are part of a vast unseen underground movement for change. Players and provocateurs plotting a free-form creative conspiracy of consciousness to push the culture one step ahead of the reactionary forces of fear and greed. Our mission: Tell stories that reveal the truth of our time. It isn't about movies, it's about life. It's about being part of a posse that breaks on through to the other side and rides the next wave together. Surf's up!

We're cruisin' south. "What's the plan?" someone asks.

My partners have christened my style *drama vérité*. I guess I've always been wandering in the no-man's-land between fiction and nonfiction, asking, "What is real?" Following the trail of many others. The Italian neorealists after World War II, films like *Open City* and *Bicycle Thief*. Buñuel's films in Mexico like *Los Olvidados*. The French new wave, Godard's *Breathless*. Haskell Wexler's *Medium Cool*, Pontecorvo's *Battle of Algiers*, right up to Larry Clark's *Kids* a few years ago.

For me, it all started with my first job as an editing apprentice for the Maysles brothers on the classic rockumentary, *Gimme Shelter*. Right from the beginning it was sex, drugs, rock and roll, politics and murder. A black guy stabbed and killed by Hell's Angels at Altamont during the Stones concert. All captured on film. The line between the performance and the people was smashed. That's where my film education began. Since then it's been simple. Find the spot where the real is radiating, throw talent in, mix and start shooting. The chaos theory of production. Capture the rapture.

My mom goes to Dr. Doom tomorrow. She's struggling for every minute. In many ways, I feel her fight for life has somehow inspired *Slam*.

She's been a freedom fighter from the start. As a young radical, they called her "Hannah the Red." She, my father and their comrade, Norman, all headed off to rebuild Europe after the war in 1948. When my father's parents found out that he and my mom were living together in Paris out of wedlock, they flipped. My dad had to return home to prevent his parents from committing kosher hari-kari.

My mom went on to an international youth festival with Norman and they ended up at this huge socialist rally in Milan, Italy. The organizers wanted one of the Americans to say something. Norman and my mom flipped a coin. My mom won and took the podium, ranting the party line to more than a half million enthusiastic students, workers and activists gathered in the huge Piazza del Duomo. She blew them away. I've always imagined she was like Janis at Monterey.

Standing in the wings was a handsome Israeli Mossad agent, smitten by her ferocious passion. He immediately made a move to recruit her for Israel's war of independence. But waiting back in New York was her soul mate, Al Levin. With the cheers and chants of hundreds of thousands of screaming Italians ringing in her head, she had to make a fateful decision. Which way? Which man? Which life? She chose the kid from Argyle Road in Brooklyn and a life committed to the fight for peace and justice here in the United States.

Heading to D.C. now, I fee like I am at a turning point in my life. My first trip to D.C was in the summer of 1963, the March on Washington. My sisters and I were just kids, but our parents wanted us to witness history and Martin Luther King's famous "I have a dream" speech. When King was assassinated five years later, my mom was once again on the front lines, working with black activists during the Newark Riots. By then she had become a Ph.D. in psychology. She went on to teach and organize, setting up community health programs in the South Bronx during the '70s.

In the '80s and '90s my mother moved on to the juvenile justice system in New Jersey, trying to give troubled, disadvantaged kids a second chance. She has devoted her life to helping people and challenging the system. There was a fire in her, and now I feel it burning in me. A rage to live. A rage to make the world right.

I asked my mother about this rage. She laughed. "That's from me," she said; "that rage is a gift."

My mother had fought the good fight and now she was passing on the torch.

I know that it is my mother's rage—her intense passion and her clear focus—that is driving me now to make this movie. Her spirit has touched *Slam*. It is our magic, our guide, our protection. This is the story she has always wanted me to tell. I know, Mama, this one's for you!

I open my eyes. It's dark as we approach D.C. Tomorrow it all begins. This is it, a true under-the-radar stealth production. Savor every moment, team, because it may never be this good again.

Donny Brice

SAUL WILLIAMS

Saul Stacey Williams first electrified the spoken-word circuit in 1995. In 1996 he became the Nuyorican Poets Café's Grand Slam Champion, following in the esteemed footsteps of Reg E Gaines, Paul Beatty, Maggie Estep and Tish Benson. He has since represented the Nuyorican Poets Café at poetry festivals throughout the country.

Sharing the stage with such renowned artists as The Last Poets, Allen Ginsberg, Amiri Baraka, Sonia Sanchez, The Fugees, The Jungle Brothers, the Roots, and Eryckah Badu, Saul has been a featured performer at Rock Against Racism, C.B.G.B.'s, Boston's Museum of Fine Arts, The American Craft Museum, the Knitting Factory, S.O.B.'s, New Music Café and at numerous colleges and universities.

Saul's poetry has been featured in *The New York Times, Bomb, Red Clay, New Word, African Voices* and the anthologies *In Defense of Mumia* (Riverside Press) and *Catch the Fire* (Putnam). His own book of poetry, *The Seventh Octave,* is now in publication at Moore Black Press. He has also collaborated with several musicians and is featured on numerous albums.

Saul has an M.F.A. in Drama from New York University and a B.A. in Drama and Philosophy from Morehouse College.

prisons be like magnets
attracting delinquent habits
maybe that's why niggas ste (al)...
...el wheels spinning to counter the attraction
spray my name on steel horses
to loosen the reins
cry the eyes of a thousand storms
galloping o'er the clouds

chariots of the morn
foot soldiers of the wind
hand maidens of the dawn

the archers are aimed at the unnamed
the rain bows and arrows
truth is blood stained

yet, Brutus is an honorable man
although he has Caesar's blood on his hands
and claims that his palms are bleeding
but no doves grace the sky
of his eyes
and the Sun
still must set
in the West

By no means the darkest Ray of the Sun
a shaman of shadows
cast your net in my lungs
and reap the dreams of my breath
of these hymns seldom sung

Black's the gift
to be young...
to be young...

dreams deferred
so Ray sinned in the Sun

i sold clouds
in a rainless season
nickel bags
dimes
of rhymes and reason

as if clouds were treason:
the warden storms
through wintered cells
avalanched rhetoric
me and reason rebel
my mind's consciousness in snow suit
my third eye strapped in ski boots
they crucified their lord on snowboards
the iceman cometh
plug the sun in
one hundred Miles' trumpets
and running
with the music
loop the drumbeat
tambourine gone
shake the shackles
i'm handcuffed to the sample machine
shoot the sheriff
and throw me the key

bulls eye
blood shot
matadors of the wind
i'm charged
with possession of illegal substance
yet, my substance makes eagles of the ill

July 21, 1997

This is the third day of the *Slam* shoot and the first day of this journal... As we approached the prison, i felt as if i wasn't going to feel... i couldn't feel that i was about to enter another world, although my mind knew it. it was such a gray day. there was much less drama entering the prison. let's not forget that Bonz wore a bathrobe. so we met a group of prisoners whom we had seen on the videotape of Marc's meeting the previous day. That's when i met China. China is the draft pick to be the leader of the Thug Life clique. it's amazing he sounds like Tupac. i want to remember the way he said, "hol uh gyuhn im dat nigger mow ain boom blow of his heee" (hold a gun in that nigga's mouth and, boom, blow off his head). So China, like them all, clearly understood what we were there to do. It amazes me how clearly they understand the picture. it amazes me how seemingly impossible it is for me to not think less of these brothers simply 'cause they're locked up. when actually their conditions surely must heighten their senses and their intuitive shit. they could probably smell the money in our pockets and the rug from the hotel lingering from the bottom of our shoes. they were prepared to add all the missing links, which i must say is probably what they would do best having been chained as they have. i must confess: i am so confused by the story that i could hardly tell them what was going to happen with any certainty. but if i use that properly that will keep me fresh as we enter new scenes and approach the obstacles of communication and poetry. interestingly, they paid attention to all of the details that lead to what and how we can successfully get from A to B without seeming fake and so, of course, the question arose, "well, what kind of poetry is it that's gonna make a group of people that's about to jump a nigga stop in their tracks?" and so i finally recited Amethyst Rocks for them. they froze, they felt it. they understood. this is a mission. now back to China. i can see how he's the perfect rival and will be the perfect partner. he wants to say so much to let me know that he understands. and he's come up with this wonderful concept of his character being an emcee and feeling my talent—in fact they all came up with the thought of them deciding not to touch Ray because they see that he is an asset to our community. because he's talented and because he's on a mission. they see how they should begin to simply wish him a safe journey. and China envisioned a third scene between us where he expresses his desire to express and we squash the beef and begin to communicate. i kinda—never mind. i love the idea. we gotta make it work. also i want to...

did you put on your best attire for this occasion?
sky blue jump suit
when gravity's got you grounded
and bending your knee
but will you Spring?

...decide how i'm going to amend Amethyst for the courtyard scene. how much should i make it an actual commentary on what's going on? Amethyst Rocks is and was my coming out and if anything it should help me map out what Ray should sound like.

but before i go...

so after the rap session and brainstorm dialogue we went up to the juvenile block where i saw all of the old gang.

> "yo, man you brought me a note?"
> what?
> "you got a note for me?"
> what?
> "you can't kick a little rhyme for me?
> just a little, man.
> i need to hear some lyrics.
> i'll make a beat for you."

...and he starts banging the bars. i couldn't believe how hungry these kids are for lyrics. it's beautiful. met a new kid who's serving 75-to-life. what the fuck is that? i wish i had had more rhymes for them. maybe i should trust myself and kick some poetry to them. i hope to feed them every day while i'm there. damn, it's like prison ministry. going cell to cell reciting lyrics to prisoners.

after we left the juvenile ward we went down to the bullpen where a guard preached statistics to us that let you know that we were not merely in any jail. that we were in the founding fathers' nest of genocidal vultures. i successfully held back my tears until we got in the van. i want to take full advantage of this situation. i want to cast a spell.

> these gray walls
> clouds of the sky
> of our pain
> another Sun to be slain
> but this Ray has a name
>
> shackled
>
> another link
> in a chain letter to God
> self-addressed

alright, alright
i'm God
i confess
guilty
and yet you plot my pain
without realizing the ellipse of your own orbit

you can't extinguish the Sun
there's not enough water in your wisdom
your puddled logic
is damned

i remember the awkwardness of walking through the projects of southeast D.C. feeling uncomfortable because i was walking with white people who were holding cameras.

i remember our initial trip to D.C. Jail in February '97 and everyone joking about the fact that if i were to stray away from the rest of the film crew i would definitely be mistaken for a prisoner.

i remember realizing that they were right.

i remember the warden being very concerned about whatever it was that i was writing in my little journal as if she knew the power of word.

i remember being introduced to the kids in the juvenile ward and being told that they were all there for a Murder One charge.

i remember how after being prodded to talk about how it felt to be locked up they eventually all looked at each other, started banging a beat on the table and speaking in rhymes.

i remember the endless rhyming ciphers that we had around the lunch table when i was in high school.

i remember the looks on their faces when i entered the cipher and how they started screaming, "South Side!" when i was done as if they took my rhymes to be the anthem of where they were from.

i remember two or three of them reciting my three or four minutes of material back to me as they returned to their cells. verbatim.

i remember that that day was my twenty-fifth birthday.

i remember hearing statistics that most Black men are either dead, in jail, or have at least been to jail by the age of twenty-five, and here i was visiting this prison on my birthday looking at all of these brothers standing like candles in a cake waiting to be blown out.

i remember thinking that performing my poetry in prison would be

like performing an exorcism.
i remember how months later, when we were shooting the scene of me
being led into the prison a storm cloud opened up in the sky.
i remember how depressed i became when we had been shooting inside of
the prison for three days and i had not recited any poetry yet.
i remember deciding that Joshua should be the last name of the character
because of the effects of Joshua's trumpet on Jericho.
i remember introducing myself to residents of Woodland Terrace and prisoners as Raymond Joshua since i never knew when the camera might be on.
i remember many people thanking us as if we were doing community service.
i remember shooting the bullpen scene and one inmate asking me if we had
signed any paperwork that would forbid us from suing if we got hurt in the
prison and after telling him that i hadn't he proceeded to say that if i were to
let him stab me, i could sue and that he wouldn't charge much for his services.
i remember, as we were shooting the booking scene, someone screaming,
"how many mothafuckas did that nigga have to snitch on to get that job?" as
if i were a real convict who had agreed to be on the news.

the silver waist chains
the keloid outline of a face
the early presidents names
the burning toilet paper wicks
the juvenile division
the judge's dooms day decision
the kufis
the shackles
the brand new sneakers

i remember hearing on the news something about a white bull that was
born in Wyoming, Minnesota, or someplace. a white bull... they said that
native Americans were traveling from all over the country to see it because
their people had predicted years ago that it would be the sign of a new
day.... a second coming, or some shit.

ain't no white bulls in this bull pen
...none at all...
and when i close my eyes
i'm on a ship in the Atlantic
when i close my eyes

there's talk of a new world
and little sunlight

when i close my eyes
even my eyelids seem shackled shut

ain't no white bulls in this pen
no signs of a new day
or life hereafter
...none at all...

THE WIND'S SONG

the square root of kiss is a hum
i hum under my breath when i contemplate the drum
of your heartbeat
and my heart beats for your breath
i revel in the wind for mere glimpses

i'm tornado over you
would you look into the eye of my storm
i whirlwind through your life like breeze
and fill your lungs
as we achieve the second power of a hum

i love...

as instruments come to life
through breath
the wind sends my high notes to indigo communions
with Coltrane's Favorite Things

...this is my body which is given for you,
this is my blood which is given for you...

my love like the wind, uncaged
blows time into timeless whirlpools

transfiguring fear and all of its subordinates
(possession, jealousy, fear)
into crumbling dried leaves

my love
is the wind's slave
and, thus, is free

my love
is the wind that is shaped
as it passes through the lips of earthly vessels
becoming words of wisdom
songs of freedom
or simply hot air

my love
is the wind's song:
if it is up to me, i'll never die.
if it is up to me, i'll die tomorrow
one thousand times in an hour and live seven minutes later.
if it is up to me, the sun will never cease to shine
and the moon will never cease to glow
and i'll dance a million tomorrows
in the sun rays of the moon waves
and bathe in the yesterdays of days to come
ignoring all of my afterthoughts
and preconceived notions
if it is up to me, it is up to me.
and thus is my love:
untainted
eternal

***

the wind is the moon's imagination wandering:
it seeps through cracks
explores the unknown
and ripples the grass

my love is my soul's imagination
how do i love thee?
imagine

SHA CLACK CLACK

i know you are but what am i?
infinity

if i could find the spot where truth echoes
i would stand there and whisper memories of my children's future
i would let their future dwell in the past
so that i might live a brighter now

now is essence of my domain
but it contains all that was and will be
and i am as i was and will be
because i am and always will be
that nigga

i am that nigga

i am that timeless nigga
that swings on pendulums like vines
though mines of booby-trapped minds
that are enslaved by time
I am the life that supersedes lifetimes
i am

it was me with serpentine hair
that with a timeless stare
turned mortal fear into stone time capsules
they still exist as the walking dead
as i do: the original suffer-head
symbol of life
and matriachy's severed head
Medusa, i am

it was me the ecclesiastical one
that pointed out that nothing was new under the sun
and through times of laughter and times of fear
saw that no time was real time
'cause all times were fear
the wise seer
Solomon, i am

it was me with tattered clothes
that made you scatter
as you shuffled past me on the street
yes, you shuffled past me on the street
as i stood there conversing with wind-blown spirits
and i fear it's your loss
that you didn't stop and talk to me
i could have told you your past
as i explained your present
but instead i'm the homeless schizophrenic
that you resent for being aimless
the intuned nameless, i am

i am that nigga
i am that nigga
i am that nigga

i am a negro
negro from necro, meaning death
i overcame it
so they named me after it
and i be spittin' at death from behind
and putting "kick me" signs on its back

because

i am not the son of sha clack clack
i am before that
i am before

i am before before

before death is eternity
after death is eternity
there is no death there is only eternity
and i be riding on the wings of eternity
like: yah! yah! sha clack clack

i exist like spit-fire
which you call the sun
and try to map out your future with sun-dials
but tic-toc-technology can no tic toc me

i exist somewhere between tic and toc
dodging it like double-dutch
got me living double time
i was here before your time
my heart is made up of the quartz crystals
that you be makin' clocks out of
and i be resurrectin' every third
like: tic-tic-tic

sha clack clack

no i won't work a nine to five
because i am setting suns and orange moons
and my existence is this:
still yet ever moving
and i am moving beyond time
because it binds me it can set me free
and i'll fly when the clock strikes me
like: yah! yah! sha clack clack

but my flight does not go undisturbed
because time makes dreams defer
and all of my time fears
are turning my days into day-mares
reliving nightmares
that once haunted my past
sha clack clack
time is beating my ass

and i be havin' dreams of chocolate covered watermelons filled with fried chicken like piñatas. with little pickaninny sons and daughters, standing up under them with big sticks and aluminum foil, hittin' them, trying to catch pieces of fallen fried chicken wings. and aunt jemima and uncle ben are standing in the corners with rifles pointed at all the heads of the little children. "don't shoot the children," i shout. "don't shoot the children." but it's too late. they've already been infected by time. but this shit is before my time...(i need more time! i need less time!) but it's too late. they start shooting at the children and killing them:

one by one
two by two
three by three
four by four
five by five
six by six

but my spirit is growing seven by seven
faster than the speed of light
'cause light only penetrates the darkness
that's already there
and i am already there
i'm here at the end of the road
which is the beginning of the road beyond time
but where my niggas at?
oh no
don't tell me my niggas are lost in time
my niggas are lost in time
my niggas are dying before their time
my niggas are dying because of time

AMETHYST ROCKS

"What i got
come and get some
(get on up)
hustler of culture"

i stand on the corner of the block slingin' amethyst
rocks
drinkin' 40s of Mother Earth's private nectar stock
dodgin' cops
'cause five-0 are the 666
and i need a fix of that purple rain
the type of shit that drives membranes insane
oh yes, i'm in the fast lane
snorting...candy yams
that free my body and soul
and send me like Shazam!

"never question
who I am
God knows"

and i know God personally
in fact, he lets me call him me

i be one with rain and stars and things
with dancing feet and watermelon wings
i bring the sunshine and the moon
and the wind blows my tune

...meanwhile
i spoon powdered drum beats into plastic bags
sellin' kilos of kente scag
takin' drags off of collards and cornbread
free-basing through saxophones and flutes like mad

the high notes make me space float
i be exhalin' in rings that circle Saturn

leavin' stains in my veins in astrological patterns

yeah, i'm sirius B
Dogon niggas plottin shit. lovely
but the Feds are also plottin' me
they're tryin' to imprison my astrology
to put my stars behind bars
my stars in stripes
using blood splattered banners
as nationalist kites

but i control the wind

that's why they call it the hawk
i am horus
son of isis
son of osiris
worshipped as jesus
resurrected like lazarus

but you can call me lazzie

lazy

yeah, i'm lazy
'cause i'd rather sit and build
than work and plow a field
worshipping a daily yield of cash green crops

your evolution stopped
with the evolution of your technology
a society of automatic tellers and money machines
nigga what?

my culture is lima beans
and tambourines
dreams manifest
dreams real
not consistent with rational

i dance for no reason
for reason you can't dance
caught in the inactiveness
of intellectualized circumstance
you can't learn my steps until you unlearn my thoughts
spirit soul can't be store bought
fuck thought
it leads to naught
simply stated it leads to you
tryin' to figure me out
your intellect is disfiguring soul
your beings not whole
check your flag pole:
stars and stripes
your astrology is imprisoned
by your concept of white
of self
what's your plan for spiritual health?
calling reality unreal
your line of thought is tangled
the star spangled got your soul mangled
your beings angled
forbidding you to be real and feel
you can't find truth with an ax or a drill
in a white house on a hill
or in factories or plants made of steel

stealing me is the smartest thing you ever did
too bad you don't teach the truth to your kids

my influence on you is the reflection you see
when you look into your minstrel mirror
and talk about your culture
your existence is that of a schizophrenic vulture
who thinks he has enough life in him
to prey on the dead
not knowing that the dead ain't dead
and that he ain't got enough spirituality
to know how to pray

yeah, there's no repentance
you're bound to live an infinite
consecutive executive life sentence
so while you're busy serving your time
i'll be in sync with the moon
while you run from the sun
life of the womb
reflected by guns
worshipper of moons
i am the sun
and i am public enemy number one
one one one
one one one
that's seven
and i'll be out on the block
hustlin' culture
slingin' amethyst rocks

John Kirby

SONJA SOHN

Sonja has been unleashing her brand of raw performance poetry on unsuspecting audiences since 1992. She has toured England and performed extensively in New York at places such as the Public Theater, Nuyorican Poets Café, Woodstock '94, Lollapalooza, S.O.B.'s, Supper Club and Fez.

In 1993, Sonja began acting, studying briefly at Lee Strasberg in New York, then privately with Susan Batson. She has appeared as Natasha in the Actors Studio production of *At the Bottom* (an adaptation of Gorky's *Lower Depths*) and in other theatrical productions in New York, as well as in an independent feature entitled *Work*.

Sonja hosts and performs her own work at small performance spaces in New York, in her performance-art variety show, *Sonja Sohn's Finger in the Socket Salon*. She recently recorded an album for Arthrob, a London-based Warner label.

A STORY OF SYNCHRONICITY, DIVINITY AND MAGIC

The night I met Marc Levin, Richard Stratton and Henri Kessler I had just arrived home from a two-week trip to South Korea. I had taken my mother back to search for family she had not seen in more than thirty years. Traveling with her, my two daughters and my husband (from whom I was in the midst of separating) had been less than a picnic. Tears. Tantrums. Family secrets. Death. And screaming children. All on videotape. Scary. But that's another movie. Anyway, here I was straight off a seventeen-hour flight, jet-lagged and cranky as hell, muttering, "Damn, I do not feel like going to this fucking reading tonight." But something was telling me I had to—that there would be somebody there I had to meet.

Following those little crumbs of intuition has never led me astray. In the past, they have prevented me from getting hurt, busted or killed. They've given me a daughter who saved my life. And they led to the dreams I now live.

I had come a long way toward recapturing myself and defining my purpose. I had come a long way from being the eight-year-old who lost all her dreams because what was in her heart was so far from the reality she was living in the projects of Newport News, Virginia. I had come to realize that my whole life had been spent trying to patch up a broken heart and battered dreams, patch up my life with anything I could get my hands on, as long as it dulled the pain. And everything I did to try to patch it up was destructive. Everything I touched I destroyed. Everything I did to keep up the façade destroyed me a little more and continued the vicious cycle. Until the day the cycle revealed itself to me.

Finally, I learned that everybody on this earth has a purpose, a reason for living, and oftentimes, it is first revealed as a dream.

So I spent the next several years uncovering—stripping myself of every patch and false front I wore. Unraveling until I saw my mummified self for what I really was. And then I had the courage to look at my dreams again. Head on. Undeniably real. Undeniably mine. And I went for them with a vengeance. I had lost too much time. I had fucked up too many people. I had abandoned myself for too long. Now I had found myself, and nobody was going to get in my way. I was happy as a two-year-old. Bright. Shiny. New. Full of joy and wonder. I was going for mine.

Until the Universe pulled my sponsor out from under me. My financier.

The greenback king. The man... the husband. *Oh, all this isn't ours? You mean I'm not an independent woman? Oh, I guess...I guess...I...Quick! Scramble! Make a living! Now! 'Cause it's all about survival, girl. You know that! Survival Buttons have been activated. Proceed. What is the procedure? Step #1. Survive. Release dreams first. Release dreams first. SURVIVE! RELEASE DREAMS FIRST!*
Damn.

You gotta do what you gotta do. But I wasn't going to do what I had always done: take the short cuts that keep me ahead of the game for a minute until I get kicked back twenty yards behind the starting line, foot up my ass the whole bumpy way back. Then it had always been either run or die. Run as fast as I can for the finish line or kill myself because life is so fucking unfair and that hurts in a place that nobody can touch. Because after fighting my way back from a twenty-year suicide attempt, I just got a big fat foot in my face. Nowhere to turn and nowhere to go.

This time, I did the only thing I have been able to do to take away the pain in the last seven years. I wrote. I wrote *run free*. Never looking back. Never thinking what might have been. Mad as hell. I wrote. And I ran.

It didn't matter that this time I had a place to stay and clothes on my back, food to eat and a car to drive. My options were running out fast and I felt just like I did when I didn't have shit. No options is no options, baby, anyway you look at it. And for me, working as a waitress because my creative talents couldn't bring in money to support my kids, and not being able to pursue my dreams—merely surviving—was having no options.

For me, hopelessness has always meant death. Slow suicide. Instantaneous soulicide. Once you have come back from it and refuse to use the Band-Aids that once helped and hurt you, the choices become much more clear. Life. Death. Illusions of escape. Your weapons are few. Slit your wrists. Deny and Run. This time I faced my fears. If I hadn't gone to work on *Slam* when I did I don't know how long I would have been able to hold on. Or how soon it would have been before I went back to my old ways of killing myself to survive.

That's what *Slam* is all about. Being saved. By the bell. By an angel. By yourself. Being able to recognize that no matter how far down you are you can always get back up because there are signs all around you pointing you in the right direction. Being able to see the magic moments in your life and hear the voice of your spirit will give you the answer. Where to go. Who to meet. What to do. And no matter how you feel, what you think, where you are, you go. Do. Listen. The answers are there for you. Anytime. You want it? It's yours. But it's up to you to tune in.

Slam is about awakening. Awakening from the dead existence of your surroundings, of life on this plane, to come up with the solutions to seemingly insurmountable problems and unanswerable questions. When you are born into something you cannot control, fifty miles behind the starting line, without a system that teaches you how to catch up and move forward—and without anybody in your life who has time to show you, because they are either non-existent or working too hard just to feed and clothe you—you must develop other senses that can give you guidance and knowledge. *Slam* is about picking yourself up every time you get knocked down. Holding on when you don't have anything to hold on to. Moving forward when everything in your life is pulling you back. Reaching for the light when darkness has a pit-bull grip on your ass. Life, baby. Living it regardless of how difficult the path, how steep the mountain, how fast you're sinking. Walk. Run. Climb. Swim. Anyway you can. Ironically, it is in our worst nightmares that we find our richest treasures. Being human, our minds cannot fathom this until we have lived it. Live it. And you get to discover what true strength, bravery and courage really are. You find the heart of your soul every time you rise to the occasion and champion your own cause. You find that in your heart is the magic of your spirit. It is enough to dream and to live from that place because sometimes, though your power seems nonexistent and you think your heart does not hear your cries, your magic lives. Dormant, yes, but alive. Ever powerful. Ever growing. Awaiting the day you rise to meet your glory, knowing that it was each small step, each motion you barely managed, each fear you faced and each inconceivable positive thought and intention you harbored inside that got you to where you now stand. In your power. In your magic. In your dreams.

On some level, we have all lived the essence of *Slam*. We are all capable of living it on a conscious level every second of our lives. This film was put together by people who have, in some way, each experienced this essence. It is only through the grace of the Universe that we were brought together and blessed with the ability to channel this story. The uncanny occurrences. The discovery of past-life connections during the shoot and in the middle of scenes. The profound respect I have for Marc, Richard and Henri, the blessed union I feel with Saul, Liza and Bonz. The Sirius star system, my brother, the men in the D.C. Jail—Joe, Bay, Jerome, Talib, China, Red, Regie, Tyrone—I love you. The energy that connects us all, that never wavered for one moment during the shoot—through script disagreements, Henri's lunches, mid-scene headphone freakouts with Richard on the yard, being thrown out of the jail while shooting the big scene... I can only tell you it felt magical to live this process, manifest it, receive it, and give it with one swift timeless kick from the soul.

It is no accident that out of all of the actors and/or poets in New York I was chosen to help tell this story. I am this story because I have lived it. I have been Ray. I have been Lauren. And somewhere beyond both of them lies Sonja. Many people have asked me how much of my character is me, and have assumed that I am playing myself. I am an actor. I am a poet. I am a writer. I am a spirit. I used all of my talents and parts of who I am to help tell this most important story.

Someday my spectrum of work will speak for itself and the talent will be evident as more than coincidence and a stroke of luck. The same can be said for the other actor/poet/writers in the film—Saul, Bonz, Beau and Liza. I am honored to have been their cocollaborator and to have witnessed this magic moment in their lives as well.

Slam, activated at birth and manifested years later, is a gift from the Universe, from the ancestors, from the filmmakers, from the actors, from the crew—to each other, to the 'hood, to the world, to you.

In a place where few have risen above the darkness, few know the light. My deepest desire is that *Slam* will bring light to those lost in the shadows of their lives. There is magic in this film. Find it. Feel it. Believe it. Use it.

My work in *Slam* is dedicated to my big brother

ROGER WILLIAMS

I love you baby.
Thanks.
Good looking out.

RUN FREE

i feel like my back is up against a brick wall and there's a Mack truck two inches from my face. Every cell in my body is screaming RUN! but i can't. My mind drifts. i think about the last time i ran. Left my baby with two cokeheads on acid. what does it matter that one was my sister and the other my best friend? It meant everything to me then. Anything not to get busted. My brain was busted, frying on the hot concrete of my life run amok. Dripping down the dead body of my soul, collecting into pools of blood at my feet. i'm kicking and stomping and running and jumping, wreaking all kinds of havoc, creating a bloody mess and i am going nowhere. Somewhere in my mind i think i am moving. somewhere in reality i am running. somewhere inside myself i am oh so still. Quiet. Dead. My soul is not rising. My spirit is not lifting. My life is not living. But i am running. Moving through the universe, a whirling dervish with no end, no purpose, no means, no life left to live. And yet, still, i want to go to that place where i can run, run free, my mind tells me. But those two words cannot occupy the same space in reality. run. free. My back is against a brick wall. i got a Mack truck two inches from my face. *Run free, baby, right now, it just looks hard, but it would be so easy. Just turn around and go. Clip all the wires, hookups and hang-ups and then you're home free. You can give birth to an excuse so easily, you'll believe it's always been there. Part of the natural order, made to order by your forever clever mind, constantly protecting you against things you no longer need to be protected from. . .* and i believe. i believe like a holy roller singing sweating preaching go tell it on the mountain speaking in twenty different tongues while diving in ten thosand feet of baptismal water without a life preserver. i believe like my bullet-ridden brother out there somewhere right now gurgling blood through his last breath, spitting out a red ripe prayer so new so sweet so baby fresh so full of truth he thinks it can save his life. Brutal honesty won't knock down the doors of heaven, but it'll damn sure crash the gates of hell. So i believe any and everything that sprouts from my colossally imperfect mind, because in this moment i got a Mack truck two inches from my face and a brick wall kissing my ass. God does not exist in desperation and hope is lying dead somewhere in the sewer down the street around the corner in the alley undrneath the feet of somebody itching scratching trembling jonesing for their next hit and sucking somebody's dick. i got two minutes before i run free or die, y'all. i got two minutes before i smash my face into the grill of a Mack truck, before i get ten thousand bricks shoved up my ass
before i run   free   or die.

John Kirby

HENRI M. KESSLER

FOLLOW THE MONEY

Once we made the decision to make *Slam*, I was prepared to go into debt forever. When we formed Offline Entertainment, we got so frustrated trying to do it the Hollywood way: packaging a movie, getting the stars... and you can't get the money unless you get the stars, and you can't get foreign money unless you have domestic distribution, and domestic sales drive foreign sales and there are agents and optioning and key money, and blah blah blah blah blah, and we got fucking disgusted.

Then, in 1996, Richard, Marc and I were in Cannes trying to sell *Acid Test*, and we'd been out all night and went to see *Trainspotting* at 8:30 in the morning—and it blew us away.

"Holy shit," we said. "These guys made a movie about three Scottish junkies. Who would have green-lit this project if you pitched it? Fuck Hollywood, we've got to do it on our own."

And that's where *Slam* was born. From that point, I couldn't imagine doing it any other way.

So middle of summer '97, I let everyone know it's a go—I planned to cover initial costs on a corporate credit card. But the day we rolled out of town and headed for D.C., I didn't have a fucking dime. I'm totally broke. We're in the van headed south, leading this convoy of vehicles loaded with actors and crew and equipment; I turned to Richard and said, "I still don't have the money."

Here we were headed to Washington to film—it was kind of phenomenal just to be leading everyone down the road, knowing there's not a fucking dime in the bank and that I've just committed to spending roughly a million dollars.

When we checked into the hotel, I put down my credit card and they took it. But I would have to pay cash to get the film; they didn't take credit cards. I'd gotten a letter of credit, based on our backer, David Peipers', financials, and used that as a loan guarantee for the money I borrowed to finance the movie, but I was still waiting on that to post. It was taking time for all the paperwork to fall into place and time was what we didn't have: We'd gotten a go-ahead to shoot inside the D.C. Jail, but we had a limited window—we had to get in and shoot our movie before the whole system was turned over to the feds, which could happen any day now.

So I'm in the hotel in D.C. on the phone to the banks, and to our backers in New York, getting checks cut and money wired—just to get the fucking film stock. And I was functioning as everything from Craft Services to Producer, to Line Producer, to Executive Producer, to Camp Counselor, to—*The Hated One*, Holder of the Purse Strings.

All that, plus setting up the office at the Henley Park Hotel. So obviously I was feeling stress, but I was comfortable with that because my life has always been on the edge. I thrive under stress. I love chaos.

Then we get inside the jail. And I'm still negotiating, trying to clear all the financial bullshit. I'm inside the D.C. City Jail, inside the prison, huddled in a corner on my cell phone, with prisoners all around me, and I'm talking to the bank about the million dollars it has got to post to cover all these checks I'm writing. The cell phone is cutting in and out because we're in a concrete block, and I can't just come in and go out of the jail as I please—you've got to be searched and questioned and all this crap to get in or out of the place and I had to be on the set. But I still had to get the money.

David Peipers was great, handling it in bits and pieces: Twenty thousand was wired, ten thousand was wired, thirty thousand was wired; he was just wiring out bursts of cash as I called from the front line, waiting for the letter of credit to fall into place. I was racing to the banks to get the money, making sure the checks got through....

It wasn't until the day production ended that the loan finally came through. At that point, I sent everyone back to New York. But I couldn't check out of the hotel because the bill we ran up was around $90K and I couldn't cover it on my credit card without the bank confirming to Amex that we had the money in the account to pay for it. So I stayed, hostage to my Amex card, trying to ride out the bank and ride out the hotel.

I told the guy at the front desk, "Yeah, I'm still here, doing business. Sure, sure, sure, keep that bill going. Yeah, I'll take care of everything when I leave. And, by the way, I need this, this, this and this."

I analyzed the bill, had them print out copies of the bill and I went over every line, but basically I didn't have a dime to pay the charges. I would get up in the morning, take a shuttle to New York, go to the bank, work on all the paperwork. Hmm, still can't do it? All right, back to D.C.

Next day, same trip: New York again on a shuttle, to the banks, back to D.C. Finally, after three days, I get the word that Amex had been cleared. I was fuckin' pumped. It was balls to the wall, but we did it, we got our picture done, and that's the name of the game. I casually walked downstairs to the front desk, threw my Platinum card on the counter and said, "Ring it up."

And then I came home.

I decide we've got to get the film into competition at Sundance. Marc is editing away—he's like, "Forget Sundance, we'll never make it."

"No! No!" I said. "Marc, we've got to try, got to submit it. Fuckin' A, man, we're a million on the hook, the interest is compounding, the clock is ticking. We've got a year to pay back the bank. Let's go for it."

We had twenty-eight hours of footage. Obviously there was enthusiasm to see what we had. Oh my God, I'm thinking, do we have anything? Now that I owe the bank a million dollars, do we even have a movie?

We put a postproduction team together. Hired Emir Lewis to edit, Pam Widener started logging the footage. And we just cranked it out. In five weeks, once we had a three-and-a-half-hour rough assembly, we did an initial screening.

People were blown away. We really had a great rough cut. Then Marc and Emir, in one week, cut another hour, so we had a two-and-a-half-hour rough cut, at AVR 3 output off the Avid—but we were past the deadline for Sundance.

Our lawyer John Sloss got us a three-week extension.

Of course, we're editing down to the final minute, the day before we were supposed to get it in, the absolute last deadline. Emir's cranking, I'm watching the clock....

The fucking Avid system crashes.

Ahhh!

They fix it. We're up and running again. Okay. All right. I get the car, find out where I can deliver the cut. I drive 200 miles per hour to get the tape to FedEx to get it to Sundance in time since it was a three-week extension anyway.

I miss FedEx. Oh my god. Missed FedEx! Okay, think about this. What am I going to do? I find out there's a special hush-hush top secret courier division of FedEx, and they'll pick up twenty-four hours a day.

It's like $200, *but the guy comes to wherever you are.*

Ah. Extra time. I schedule a pick-up for 2:30 in the morning, in front of my apartment building. Perfect. I've got a party to go to tonight. So Marc and Emir work a little more on the cut, and as 11 p.m. nears I tuck my first feature film under my arm and head to Chaos nightclub to meet my friends.

"Perfect, Henri," Marc says. "You have to christen *Slam*, take the tape through clubland."

So I went to the club and partied, clutching my tape, among my friends. I almost got distracted, but I made myself leave and there I was on the stoop at 2:30 a.m. when the FedEx man showed up. Off went our two-and-a-half-hour rough cut, AVR 3 to Sundance, three weeks late.

Needless to say, we got into competition—which to me was just mind boggling. It flipped me out that we raised money privately—borrowed money from the bank—shot the movie in twelve days, paid everybody, got it done, made the rough cut, got it to Sundance by the skin of our teeth, last possible photo-finish moment. And we got in! That's when I started to feel really good.

The disciplines I'd developed over my entire life—being in public relations, advertising, marketing, producing fashion shows, music videos and being a nightclub owner—all that experience came right into play making this movie. And now that we were headed to Sundance what was kicking in was the marketing, which I'm pretty savvy at.

I began organizing for the festival. We had the poster blown up, made the *Slam* baseball caps. A crew of about twenty of us showed up at Sundance en masse. I structured it like a nightclub event, building it like a party, like you open a nightclub. And we really caught Sundance by surprise, I think. We came in under the radar and we were there in force.

Our first screening was 8:30 in the morning on a Saturday. The audio wasn't loud enough, they cut off the first shot, and—poor Marc—the guy sitting next to him slept through the whole show. It was atrocious. The one film company that had expressed serious interest in buying *Slam* before they saw it walked out without saying a word to us.

Then Marc and I went up to the Sundance Institute, where Robert Redford held a reception for the filmmakers, and we were introduced to Alfre Woodard. She meets us, she's at the middle of the table, she stood up, looked at us, took a deep breath and said, "Thank you."

And then she starts crying. Right in front of Marc. Tears streaming down her face. "Thank you for making this movie," she said. "It was so powerful...."

The Monday afternoon screening went better. We knew something was up when people stood up after the movie, applauding and crying and thanking us for making such an important film. We thought, We've struck a nerve. After that screening, Trimark stepped up to the plate and we entered negotiations.

Tuesday afternoon, our lawyer John Sloss and I went up to Trimark's house and sat down and just started throwing around concepts and numbers and seeing if we could hammer out the parameters of the deal. Point, counterpoint, point, counterpoint. And it looked like we were sort of in the same ballpark.

We'd been there negotiating for eight hours when I had to go. They tried to hold me there but finally had to let me leave because I had to organize the *Slam* party that was to start at nine that evening.

The party was a total blow-out: people dancing on the tables, Marc's dad, Al, doing the mamba down the Soul Train; we had Saul and Sonja, Bonz, Beau Sia, everyone doing poetry; the music was great. We created a happening, a scene. A woman walked in around midnight and said, "God, this is just like we're in New York."

And I said, "Well, welcome to the Big Apple, baby, can I buy you a drink?"

It was really just an intense energy rush, people dancing, partying and having a great time. Every distributor was there, celebrities were there, the whole scene was there—and Trimark was there. They were blown away.

So I was feeling pretty good, arm in arm with a couple of girlfriends of mine, and Peter Block, the VP of acquisition and business affairs at Trimark walked up and said, "You've got to be in negotiations at nine in the morning."

"What!?" I said. "Get out of here! I'm not getting there at nine." We weren't *that* close to a deal before the party, so what the fuck, let me sleep.

But they said, "No no no, we want to see you at nine."

"All right," I said. "Listen, if you want to see me at nine, I would like an everything bagel, scallion cream cheese, Scottish smoked salmon, lemon capers and sliced onions. Then I will be there."

They said, "You got it."

I'm like, "Yeah yeah yeah." But I committed to being there. So everyone continues to party, we're rocking, just getting going, and at 2:30 a.m. the Park City police came and shut us down.

So we went back to the condo. The whole crew was there hanging out and a friend of mine, Eric St. Michaels, is quietly strumming a guitar and we're pretty mellow. I decided to get comfortable, so I went upstairs to put on these pajamas that John Sloss gave to Marc, Richard and me for Christmas. They're classic flannel pajamas, off-white, with the John Sloss Law logo stitched on the front pocket in a cool shade of blue.

After having a massage, I descended the staircase in my pajamas, putting up with a few Hugh Hefner comments from the crew, and just as I reach the bottom stair there's a knock on the door. Not particularly loud or anything. Marc's friend, Doug, went to answer it, came back around the entryway wall and said to me, "The police are here."

He had to be joking. I stepped outside in my pajamas, it's like 20 degrees out there, and just babbled things like, "Yes, Officer, I know, I know," and "I'm sorry," and "No, you don't want to come in here. Exactly."

And the cop stood there shining his flashlight in my face, and then he looked at my pajamas, and then he looked at the John Sloss Law logo on the pocket of my pajamas. He must have figured I was some wacked-out lawyer, because he just looked at me again, good and hard, dead serious, and said, "Don't make me have to come back."

No problem.

I got to bed about 4:30. Then up at 8:30 to negotiate the deal.

Sloss picks me up. Smart move, Sloss. We go over to the Trimark condo, I walked in, and on the table in the dining room is the spread of a lifetime: every kind of bagel, salmon, cream cheese, veggies, sliced onion. Everything I asked for was there, and more. At that point I knew we were about to make a deal because they were so accommodating. They wanted to create a great environment for us to work in. I had made a simple request and it was carried out with style.

We discussed the deal from the start, point by point, hammering the thing out, back and forth and back and forth and back and forth. They'd say something to Sloss and Sloss would say, "No fucking way, man. We're not doing that. What, are you out of your mind?" Sloss would refuse to budge, Peter Block of Trimark would refuse to budge, and we'd sit there staring at each other. Sloss would take me into a room to talk and say, "Don't worry about this. I know what we want to do. This is what we want to do. These are the points. Do you want to concede to that, do you want to concede to this. This is a good deal, this is not a good deal, but we could do this, we could do that." And so on. He would just fire away at me every possible option, and then we'd make a decision together and go back to the table and hit another snag and break off into conferences again.

Tensions were running high. We had to stop negotiations a few times, just take an hour break—in the condo, mind you. They wouldn't let us leave the premises because they were afraid we were getting counteroffers from other distributors. And we were. My cell phone was ringing; it was other distributors. Sloss's cell phone was ringing and it was other distributors. So there was some heat. While we were in negotiations with them, we were backing ourselves up in case the deal fell apart. And I think Trimark knew that, so they didn't want us to leave. We were held hostage. But it was cool, because it was the nature of doing the deal.

This went on for thirty-six hours.

At last we got down to the final deal point, a royalty on video sell-through, and we were so fucking close, and it was a total stalemate. We just hit a wall. Fuck it. Peter wouldn't budge. John wouldn't budge. They were being very stubborn on it. And all the while, the publicist at Trimark was riding the clock so that we could make the deadline for a cover story in *Variety* announcing the deal in time for Wednesday's big screening at the Eccles Theater.

Finally, I don't know who suggested it, maybe it was John, but someone came up with the idea to toss a coin to settle the point, and everyone agreed. John took out a quarter; I flipped. Trimark called it in the air.

I won the toss.

The deal was done. We sold *Slam* for 2.5 million.

Oh, man, it was amazing. It was always my vision, my dream, to get into the entertainment business, and when I met Marc and Richard three and a half years ago—I mean, Marc and Richard are creative guys. My thinking is pretty abstract sometimes, and not everybody necessarily thinks I'm on the planet when I'm in my abstract head space. But Marc and Richard gave me the chance, and fortunately, knock wood, I was always able to fund my insanity and grow the company.

At that point, at the point of closing the deal and coming back to announce it to David, Marc, Richard and Kim, saying, "Guys, I fucking did it!" that blew me away, because it was like, hey, you backed the right horse. He came home with a winner. I did it. I did my job; you did your job. We're a winning team.

It felt amazing to have this as a team, this camaraderie happening, as opposed to being a solo player. How much prouder could anyone feel?

And that's when the real insanity started for me. I went skiing the next day, on top of the mountain in Park City, Utah. I called my mom and said, "Mom, I'm on top of the world!"

I hung out with Marc and skied all day and met cute snow bunnies on the lift. I don't know, I just felt so fucking... *charming*. It was pretty funny.

I woke up the next morning and we had the *Variety* cover story announcing the whole deal. The press storm started. Lisa West, Marc, the cast and publicist were doing the interviews. I really felt like I had done my job at that point, that I had a little time to chill. So I skied for a couple more days, relaxed, worked off the tension. I was feeling great—as good as it gets.

And then: Saturday night: the Awards. The tension returned. Big time. The evening had come down to the big one, the last, final Grand Jury Prize. Alfre Woodard was presenting it, and she starts her speech, and I couldn't even hear what she was saying, I was that tense.

When you're an entrepreneur and you're growing companies and raising money and this and that, a lot of the shit is by the skin of your teeth. You have to have the right personality to digest and deal with that kind of tension. And I do. I digest it, I eat it for breakfast. But at that moment, the moment of the Grand Jury Prize announcement, I was feeling pretty wired. There was a lot riding on it.

And then Alfre said, "...the Grand Jury Prize of the 1998 Sundance Film Festival is *Slam!*"

Suddenly, I felt so calm. I was calm for the first time in my adult life. Calm. Everything's okay. I felt a calm I haven't felt since I was a kid.

The corporate mantra at Offline, and my mantra for my life—having had a couple of close friends die recently in the middle of all this elation—is, Enjoy the journey.

Life is so precious, so tenuous. For some reason, I am so acutely aware of that now, especially with the onset of all this good fortune. Be happy, enjoy the journey, be a good person and then good things will happen. I really believe that. You know, that karmic cycle: If you're a fucking prick, you'll get pricked right back. Sometimes you have to be an asshole. But not a prick. There's a difference.

BONZ MALONE

DIARY OF A ZEN GANGSTER

Donny Brice

Why should there not be confident patience in ultimate justice for the people? Every place is safe for the one who lives in justice. Be just and fear not.

At approximately 9:30 a.m. on August 19, 1996, I stood before Judge Bell, who was intent on sending away one more wiseguy before he retired at seventy-five. I pleaded guilty to assault in the first degree in the B Section of New York State Supreme Court. The judge's last question to me was, "How do you plan to spend your time?"

"I'm gonna free the slaves," I answered calmly.

The guard grabbed my arm and led me away, through the doorway to redemption, and I went to sleep for four months.

No matter how much has been written about jail, nothing comes close to smelling the stale odor reeking through every crevice from behind the wooden courtroom door. And don't even mention the sliced gelatin meat, smashed together with warm waxlike cheese, that they give away in triple layers. After three or four hours lying in a bullpen of filth, men go for those anthrax sandwiches like rats to raw meat.

I hate jail. Always have, always will. That realization never kept me out of the joint for too long, though. But there was this one time—the last time—I must admit, that was the best time I ever spent locked up.

An old friend named Marc Levin, an award-winning director for HBO here in New York, was always championing the silent stories of the underdog. Before I went to sleep, he asked me if I was interested in working on a screenplay with him and a few others called *Slam*, based on my experiences in and out of the joint. It sounded OK when I was free to walk the earth, but having to go back indoors took me out of the screenplayful mood I was in.

The story was totally believable and very familiar, like the many articles I've written in the past for Tuph Street. Since I couldn't play the lead character, Raymond Joshua, I'd be down for a smaller ad-lib later in the script. Marc and I kept in touch by kite and the knife (letters and phone calls), sneaking in pens so that I could work on the script, my monthly meal ticket, and a cover story for *Vibe*.

It wasn't easy to ball from behind bars and answer stacks of letters, but the more I practiced to become Intellectual Zen Gangster, the more freedom I enjoyed and the bigger I grew as a person.

My funds weren't too shabby either. I entered Six Building at Rikers Island with about $175. I spent three-quarters of that on cowboy cigarettes, began to juggle, and within five business days I had tripled my holdings. Fuck jail! I wasn't lettin' anybody keep me from generating sums! I mean, if you do it right, you could come out of your correctional coma rich! That's how I went in and that's just the way it went. By the end of the first month, Boom! Boom! Boom! I earned enough money to keep my commissary comfortably stocked for the rest of my bid.

So I gave some away to the slaves! Each week, I'd max out my credit limit at 75 bucks a pop. When chow was called, I'd wait a while to start distributing cakes and sweets to my fellow guests. They'd all come back from chow and wouldn't know what the fuck was going on. At night, I went to my S.A.I.D. meetings. You know, the Drug and Alcoholics Anonymous mini-conventions they have every night.

That's where I'd go to share with the group how I made my name, Bonz. By the second month, I had business cards sent to North Module. I never gave them to the slave traders, the ones who sell that poisonous shit to our mothers and children, unless they were ready to join my gang.

They were handed out moderately to other wounded healers like me, whose goal it was to make it in the world when we went home. To my friends and enemies, I was Bzo, the Consigliere of High Council. I talked to brothers, aided in their learning to read, helped them write letters and spoke to them like men. I brought books in from Barnes and Noble, like: *Leading People*, *Leadership Secrets of Attila the Hun*, *Of Mice and Men* and *Mastering the Art of War*. We talked about the fucked-up conditions that black folks, as well as some others, are caught up in. Feeling hopeless and desperate to feed their families, they steal somethin' or sell somethin'.

We developed a bond between us, many of us, and we shared intimate parts of our lives with each other. Those who recognized me, I quickly pulled them to the side. I told 'em that I didn't want to be famous, because being famous in jail isn't healthy. If I was to be recognized for anything, it should be that I did business with strangers as if they were brothers and with brothers as if they were strangers. I regularly sat down with the gang leaders and the guerrillas who were constantly in my midst. They agreed not to blow my horn and until the day I left, January 1, 1997, I was respected, well connected, and remained very well protected.

Behind the brick walls of justice, I finished two columns, a feature, and I cowrote my first film. Indeed, all those nights pretending to use the toilet was worth the back-cracking agony and the risk of being caught with a sharp object. Yet I can truly say that volunteering to mop up piss and stool did wonders for self and soul. I also learned a certain amount of patience, as well as learning to refine a gift. I wasn't some big-shot magazine or scriptwriter. I was plain old Bzo, an inmate but by no means a prisoner. Why? Because I went in knowing an important truth: When freedom becomes outlawed, outlaws become free! Meaning: Freedom isn't out there, in the wind—it's in here, in the mind.

At any given moment, I could have closed my Bible and blown out a razor, giving some wanna-be thug a face full of permanent acne. Instead, Marc came to see me on a visit before my release. He said, "We're thinking about casting Saul Williams as the lead in our film."

I knew then that this project would have a certain glow. I was very fond of Saul and his work and I knew what kind of impact he'd bring to the film.

What made it even better was going to jail. Living amidst cold steel and even colder hearts was a blessing for me. It was what I needed and, ironically enough, it was what the film needed. Like many things in life, the manifestation of our heartfelt dreams is usually due to the help of others.

We filmed for seven days inside a real jail with inmates and C.O.s as co-stars and extras. Originally, we wanted to shoot inside Rikers Island. Fuckin' Giuliani. What a scumbag! He didn't want the world to find out what an unpleasant place New York still is, so jail was the last place he wanted a camera to enter.

Finding a prison was difficult, but we found the perfect city to let us film a story about the kinds of choices black men face every day in America. A place where the program of locking up young black brothers is business as usual: the nation's capital, Washington, D.C.

Slam Pictures renamed the D.C. housing project Dodge City, and I went into character. The story would revolve around Ray, a talented poet who gets busted for sellin' smoke in the 'hood. When his supplier gets shot, a gang war ensues behind bars, which Ray is right in the middle of and so am I, Hopha. I chose to play the prison gang leader because only I would know how to challenge Saul's ideology. As a House Representative for two different buildings back on the Island, I knew how to wear the Rep's Robe.

The day we left to go to Washington was July 22, 1997—exactly ten years from the air date of *What's Going On*, the film on which Marc and I first met. So we started off on this spiritual journey with a sense of completion on our side.

I met Robbie, the driver, about two hours before we launched the project. A lot happened that first afternoon. We were supposed to leave New York at about 2 p.m. By 4, I wasn't sure if we'd get our long-awaited chance to spread our wings after all.

Henri was the Bag Man. He was the only guy on the squad I wasn't 100 percent sure on. The guy's a neurotic, plus he smokes lights. Now there's nothing totally wrong with being a neurotic, but smoking lights? That guy can't be trusted! He kept pacing back and forth, yelling on the phone the whole time while we sat around waiting for the green. Then he bolted out of his office proclaiming victory and yelling, "Let's go!"

I had no idea what I had signed on for. I just knew that Marc and I were connected and that Richie Stratton was a stand-up guy and that if any bullshit were to happen on this trip, they'd have my back. So we all shook hands and gave it a shot and hit the road.

The war wagon train consisted of two Jeeps and a craft services bus that was driven by a Spanish guy. I saw him when we passed by in the Jeep, wearing a shirt around his head like a Saudi Arabian banshee. This kid was definitely from Tuph Street. Not until we stopped for some chow did we speak.

"What are you in for?" I murmured.

"I don't know," he answered and we just started laughing.

"I liked your last piece in *Vibe*," he said. "My name's Carlos and I'm a writer myself."

We hit it off from there. In D.C., we met a blind guy by the name of—what else?—Blind Mike. He was going to be a supporting character, yet an essential element to pulling this stunt off. He had been a resident of the Southeast section of D.C. and was shot in the head, leaving him blind.

The day we arrived, retaliation for Mike's shooting took place. Three people were shot in broad daylight on the summer streets of Southeast. We got there about four or five hours later. Our supporting star had lost a lot of friends to gang warfare.

After arriving at our hotel, I immediately inquired about pornography and if there were any peep shows nearby. Although out of New York, I had to stay in the loop with the chicks. I got into character right away, pulled the bathrobe out of the closet and became Hopha—a mutation of Hugh Hefner and Vincent "The Chin" Gigante.

I only brought with me what I'd need on the set of life: one set of clothes (which I washed in the tub), some Calvin Klein shades, various colored stocking caps that I stuffed in my pocket, May Rosa cigars and a box cutter. The robe was the perfect accessory. I wore that thing everywhere!

Each morning, the cast would go up to the executive suite on the eighth floor, where Henri was housed, and start banging on the door for our measly per diem. It was a ritual. "Feed the slaves!" we'd shout outside of room 814.

Robbie looked like he hadn't eaten in weeks. Some of the crew members looked as if they were dying of scurvy. This was only the second day! I kept sayin' to myself, "This fuckin' Henri is going to make me kill 'im! Cheap bastard! Probably gonna make us eat jail food! I knew I shoulda never bought into this scared-straight crap!"

He gave us the money, though, and everything turned out all right.

The next struggle was deciding where to eat. I truly believe the final conflict will not be between good and evil; it won't come from Sadam's biochemical barrage; it'll be a war between vegetarians and land sharks. If I don't see something that looks remotely like meat, I'm kickin' someone's ass. My stomach doesn't play that shit. With all the time I spent wolfing down that flea-soaked hooch they served in Six Building, I'll kill a muthafucka for a Spam sandwich! Word! Saul had me going crazy with that shit. It took fifteen minutes for us to decide to go our own way. But that would mean having to hit up Henri for more money. He settled it by ordering Continental breakfast for everybody.

Marion Barry had to don a judge's robe, since he's the one who sends Ray to jail. That alone is gonna push your wig back, seeing the mayor of D.C., who was convicted of using crack, went to jail for six months, got released and stole the reelection?! Man, listen. We did our thing out there! I admit, it was painful for me at times to be back in Bars and Stripes©, but this time I brought my own lunch. Everywhere we went, the God of Good Will blessed us without a doubt. From the ghettos of Southeast D.C. to the warden's office to the mess hall—never did a problem arise that we couldn't handle.

It took us ten days to shoot *Slam*. Henri maxed out his Amex card to pay for the equipment and transportation. The cast was on a shoestring budget of a few bucks a day. We went to economically impoverished places and brought a kind of love for community that should be in more films!

As a character, a cowriter and the creative consultant on this project, I, personally, have never had a more shining moment than when I went back to jail!

The greatest feeling came at the end of the shoot. A brother came up to me and said, "When y'all are here, it's like we ain't in jail." I quote and I wrote this because we have made something that few have dared. We freed the souls of slaves and built our own yellow brick road, straight through the ghetto. In the spirit of one. In its own time. The scriptures once again rang true: "For he has gone forth from the prison house itself to become king, although in the kingship of this one he had been born as one of little means."

We went from deadlines, to headlines, on the front line with Offline! What!!

John Kirby

MARK BENJAMIN

SHOT FROM THE HIP

02:22:97 Shooting the HBO documentary on incarceration capital USA, Washington, D.C. Too many black men in jail. Like they say here, "plantation to incarceration." Bad story. Master plan is society looking at black men as predators and wanting to lock them up for the years that they're virile and strong.

03:01:97 My dad died today and I left Washington. The crew discovered Big Mike, a 'hood leader who got shot in the head and blinded.

06:01:97 Marc told me that we had to go into production soon because we will lose Saul and Sonja if we delay. Hollywood will grab them. He wanted to embrace the verb SLAM as his title.

06:02:97 We meet at Blowback headquarters and it is clear that there is no written script, everything is going to be workshopped. Story outline is the MO. Marc, Richard and Bonz are getting the story together.

06:06:97 The idea of making *Slam* is becoming an obsession at Marc's place, over and above everything. I know that Marc has the magic and I will be supportive even if there is no formal written script.

07:03:97 I know that Marc has a bad taste about racism and has to make *Slam*. Al and Hannah Levin are political activists, and Marc inherited their genes. Being Al's cameraman before Marc was ready for prime time gives me a perspective on things. Al and I in the early '80s wanted Marc to come aboard and do TV with us but he was too radical at the time. Things change. Marc has picked up his father's sword.

07:04:97   The political passion about injustice in the prisons is everything for Marc now. I have known this for twenty years. It is all going to come out in *Slam*. Thank God Daphne is helping organize the jail location

07:06:97   We are shooting the HBO doc and prepping *Slam* the movie in D.C., also the Bill Moyers series on addiction, *Close to Home,* for PBS. We spend the days on Moyers and HBO, and do *Slam* preproduction at night.

07:07:97   Richard and Henri could make it real. I know the feeling they have for Marc because I had it when I was the original producer on *Blowback*, the first Levin feature. I later decided to just DP the picture and the rest of the story is folly. Very few people ever saw the pic, but it will one day be re-released—when Marc is famous. At least on this picture I will get paid because Henri raised some money. Not like Marc mortgaging his loft again.

07:09:97   The shoot is coming on, we'll be going into the D.C. Jail, where we are making the HBO documentary. Warden Pat Jackson is giving us a green light for *Slam*.

07:11:97   Today I agreed to shoot *Slam*. This will make the twentieth film I shoot for Levin. My wife Jamie agrees I can afford to miss some other, more lucrative, work. I need the soul vitamins that working with Marc gives me, and he's got a burning need for this one. Four one-hour docs for HBO—delivering entertainment value for Joe 6-pack—will not interfere with this pure passion play Marc is planning.

07:15:97   Shooting today in the 'hood for HBO, I thought about Marc's sister Nicole, whose son Benjamin has a Jamaican father. Every time Marc looks at a black child I feel it could be his nephew he's seeing.

07:17:97   Marc says, "Less is more... dance with the characters... follow me." No problem, bubba... use the doc crew... Tony Hardmon—A.C., David Hocs—sound, John Sims—gaffer. They are the best.

07:20:97   Make my deal: some money and a deferral, all my film equipment on the shoot. Marc, Henri and Richard offered me a coproducer slot with them—with points. I choose cash. Nobody who has a DP on an independent feature refuses to give the DP points if the film flies. This, I think, is a truism.

07:26:97 Shoot starts. I tell Henri that he is a film virgin and will have to prove himself. *Stay out of my way.* I am sure Marc let him know that I can be difficult if bothered. Henri tries hard to be serious and do a good job. After twenty years down the road with Marc, I know that he is an eagle soaring, and Henri is trying to hijack himself on the wings of my eagle. Richard is a very different story. He did his time and is a man's man. Richard is a value-added partner for Marc.

07:27:97 Shoot a great scene in a cell with Saul and a real prisoner, Bay, who starts to freestyle with Saul. Some of my best hand-held work to date, back and forth between the neighboring cells, through the bars, while they're rapping *I had to be strong, I had to be real.*

07:28:97 Sonja today had me in tears. I could hardly shoot the classroom scene with such emotion coming in through my viewfinder. She opened up, telling the prisoners how sad it was that they were born black in the ghetto, and about how her dead brother was really a good guy with a good heart—like them.

07:29:97 Caught a real live Code Blue emergency situation today, guards rioting with the prisoners. A Warden Pat suggestion. We loved her for making it happen.

07:30:97 Saul took his shirt off standing on the banks of the Anacostia River with the sun setting in front of him. The water melted into his silhouette. God was our gaffer.

08:01:97 The scene in the yard where Saul lets go his Public Enemy #1 poem has us aware of just how real racism is for the prisoners. The poem left the prisoners in the yard drop-jawed.

08:02:97 The final frame, of Saul silhouetted against the Washington Monument, was shot at 2 a.m. after an incredibly long day. It gave Marc the visual image he wanted for the ending.

08:03:97 Shot a scene in an alley where Sonja explodes and Saul delivers his "This ain't no metaphor, this is my life" line. It blew me away. Saul and Sonja were everything Marc could have hoped for, and more. My job was easy.

RANDOM NOTES AND TECHNICALS

Shoot for ten days and it is over, and 150 rolls went through without a hitch. Every minute of the shoot was a blessed event. We were on a mission. The Marc and Mark Wild Crew, as Al Levin always called us, was on the move.

On location realism is my goal. The *drama vérité* style Marc wanted was transposed to a feature film. We had done it many times without a script in our documentaries, most notably *Prisoners of the War on Drugs*. To say we had a style syllabus going on in our documentaries is self-serving but true. Filming a dramatic feature inside a working jail was not problematic—I've filmed wars and shot documentaries in ten prisons. It's easy for me. I like being among the blood and guts of real life. In fact, I prefer filming in a prison to working in the paranoid atmosphere of a commercial shoot.

We managed to maintain a natural look in the jail scenes while not bowing to the environment's austere visual limitations. As much as this film is about the unvarnished reality of life behind bars, I was also making a theatrical feature, so of course I was trying to enhance the look. The enhancement was not easy, as I had to balance our unprecedented access with limited technical resources. We never did the usual tie-in or used a feature generator. We were limited to lights that would draw no more than 10 amps each. My kit consisted of three Dedo lights, an Arri compact 1200-watt HMI, a 20-to-40 watt hand-held battery light of my own design and a lot of incandescent photoflood bulbs. During the filming of hand-held scenes where people were walking, I used my hand-held light in one hand and camera in the other.

My refusal to use the high-speed Kodak stocks—and thus shoot wide open on the lens—challenged me a lot. Like most cinematographers, I hate a thin negative, so I was always shooting wide open. Not easy without a focus puller. My assistant cameraman was always in the changing bag loading film because we were shooting like mad. Despite the possible perils of shooting in a penitentiary, I was never concerned about my safety.

The use of the Aaton XTR Prod with time code is a natural time saver for a variety of reasons. Because we were in a real jail with real prisoners and guards as extras—pressed for time, you might say—I knew that I would have to put my arms around a methodology that expedited production. By not slating, we surely enhanced the natural performances: actors could be more focused and nonactors spontaneous. For operational convenience, I used available light as ambient fill whenever possible. Lensing with Zeiss and Canon, usually wide open, I could use Kodak Vision 200T, 250D, 320T and

7245 in locations relative to foot-candles available. Some lighting with a 1.2K Arri Compact and Dedo lights enhanced the unvarnished reality I was aiming for.

Real prisoners were included in sequences that were controlled improvisation. We had few rehearsals and I had to shoot all the takes because our time at the jail was limited. The interweaving of prisoners and actors meant it was imperative that I was always ready to shoot. The whole feature concept of blocking and hitting focus marks was out the window, but Marc and I have collaborated on many prison documentaries; we're used to moving fast and shooting on the run.

Super 16 was the way to go and my Aaton was the camera to use. The use of Aaton time code on the camera and the SMPTE DAT recorder utilized state of the art in syncing video dailies. With an Avid edit we would be media logging so scene takes would get organized when time limitations were less critical. Du Art film lab used the Aaton Link on their Rank to complete the totally unslated dailies.

The use of the tiny Modulus video transmitter Velcroed to the video tap was a way for me to be unencumbered by any BNC cable, which I would have hated since I did a lot of moving around on this 90 percent hand-held feature. I also had my video transmitter fitted with an audio circuit for audio transmission. On board the Aaton I Velcroed a Comtex audio receiver with audio output from the DAT which fed me sound I transmitted as a composite video and audio signal to the GVS-50 Sony tuner/recorder/player. This setup gave my director the ability to see live video and hear live audio from the boom's perspectives and have a recorded 8mm video record of both. The small, four-inch clamshell-style monitor gave the director's video village an intimacy which facilitated the review process and allowed us to move forward at the pace we needed with such a short shooting schedule. The GVS could also output to a larger monitor for review by production.

The only regret I have is that I did not try to shoot this film with the very small 35mm Aaton or Moviecam with variable primes. Next time.

In the end, after winning Sundance and all, I know it is all about the story. As a craftsperson in the service of a director, I am lucky to have worked with Marc Levin. He deserves every day of glory he is getting and I am sure happy I could help him get there.

P.S. Henri is not a virgin anymore.

ROBERT LEAVER

WHEEL MAN

Fionn Reilly

Tuesday, July 22, 1997
I show up at noon. My job description is that of driver. I'm down in the budget for 75 bucks a day. Henri wanted me to do it for 50 but I held out for the big money.

Going to D.C. to make a movie called *Slam*. Two-week guerrilla shoot. I've known these people for a while; I'm not a pro, more like family of some kind. Henri and I test the walkie-talkies and headphones. My first task is to pick up Bonz Malone. He needs to go down to Canal Street to buy a prop. Henri walks out with me and we run into Bonz walking toward the office on West 26th Street.

Bonz has a bag of books on his back, a blue tie and untucked shirt with a jean jacket and long jean shorts. He's wearing wraparound mirror shades and smoking a Newport. Bonz has hard, wide-set eyes and a square jaw. He's done time at Rikers Island and writes a column for *Vibe* magazine. His crime had to do with a billiard ball in a sock, and he has since stopped drinking. In the masthead of *Vibe*, where the writers are listed, he is down as *consigliere*.

The character Bonz will play is an incarcerated gang boss he has named Hopha. He tells me that on this mission he wants to find where the common ground lies, what connects us all. I take him downtown in Marc Levin's Windstar and double park. Bonz jumps out and is back in minutes with a small metal badge that says Marshal, Dodge City. He tells me today is ten years to the day that he first got involved with Marc Levin and Daphne Pinkerson. They were doing a piece on troubled youth and Bonz was one of the characters they found. He stood out. He still does.

Back at the office I am waiting in the Windstar for someone to come down. A car pulls up and an exotic-looking caramel-skinned woman gets out with a ten-year-old girl and an older white woman. It is Sonja Sohn, a poet and principal actress in the film. She hugs her daughter good-bye for a few minutes while giving instructions to the older white woman, who looks to be a nanny of some kind.

Upstairs, in the Offline/Blowback office space, Miles and then Marley are playing in the background. The view is heavenly: clear north to the George Washington bridge, south past the Statue of Liberty and on to the Verrazano.

Dom Chianese sits at a table in a dark suit smoking Marlboros and flying through a crossword puzzle. He's a stand-up comic/performance guy. Dom is downtown with a capital D. His father played Johnny Ola in *The Godfather, Part II.* Tall, lean, with a goatee, gaunt face and Roman nose. A few of us at the table listen as Dom talks about a dream he had last night where he had a huge nose stuffed full of rock cocaine. He misses it so badly. He tells everyone he's an addict. It's part of his ongoing, real-life tragicomedy routine. Dom will be playing a guard in the jail.

The conversation at the table takes many turns. Bonz announces that the big money is in cologne. Millions to be made, millions. It occurs to me I need a scent. I nod in agreement. Bonz stalks off to read more of *The Art of War* by Sun Tzu.

Beau Sia comes in. Beau's a handsome young Chinese kid, a performance poet who will play Jimmy Huang, the murderous son of a diplomat. I hear he's prepping an *Asian Men Are Hung Like Horses* routine. In person, Beau comes off like he's sweet and innocent. His humor is dry and spaced-out. He grew up in Oklahoma and came to the city to attend New York University. I don't think any of these people have acted in a movie before.

Saul Williams shows up. Saul is the star of the film; the whole story centers on his character, Ray Joshua. Saul is stoic, aloof, loose and deeply focused at the same time. He's regal-looking—an African prince. He has a strong, unusual presence and speaks with no discernible accent. His diction is clearer than any anchorman's. He has a crown of dreadlocks and smooth deep black skin. He's the poet from the 'hood, the brother from another planet.

It's close to dusk when we leave. I drive the Windstar with Marc riding shotgun. Marc is the director, our fearless leader.

He has a documentary due for Bill Moyers and another for HBO. Moyers' people are not supposed to know Marc's leaving town for ten days to make his own movie. I'm in the elevator going down to the street with Daphne, Marc and John Kirby (*Slam*'s jack-of-all-trades) when Marc mentions that it seems like Amy, Moyers' series line producer, knows something is up. I realize that I have blown our cover before we even left town. On the phone last night, I told Amy I was going to Washington, D.C., to work on a film with Marc and Daphne. Amy is best friends with my girlfriend. I had no idea this was a covert operation. Then I remember that, unless one hears otherwise, everything with these people is covert.

I tell Marc of my blunder as we reach the ground floor. Marc shakes his head, unable to believe it. Daphne rolls those big eyes of hers and Kirby laughs quietly. I apologize. Daphne gets on damage control with the cell phone. When we stop at Marc's place so he can grab his duffel bag, I pull over, too close, hit the tire hard on the curb and Marc's new minivan hubcap pops off like a bottle cap and rolls down the sidewalk.

"Way to go, Robbie," Marc says. He gets out, shaking his head again.

Marc is slightly irritated, more disgusted by the lameness of my maneuver. I can sense his doubts about my driving. Kirby and I put the hubcap back on. I assure Marc that I am a professional. I can't believe my stupid luck. One does not take pleasure in disappointing Marc, as with all good leaders. He seems to forget about it quickly, not wanting to clutter his mind.

Marc gives the impression he's winging it. He's open to suggestions, not afraid to let you see his process. I assume he has a plan. He barely eats, claims lack of food gives him an edge and helps him to hallucinate.

At last we are out of the city. The sunset is a menacing blast of color, industrial New Jersey landscapes in the foreground. Someone must still have confidence in me because once we are on the highway a joint appears in my hand. Two hits and I am choosing not to speak.

Once it is dark, Marc pulls out his computer and a pad with notes scribbled all over it and says, "Well, guess I better write the script."

The closer we get to D.C., the more tolls there are. The weed is so strong I feel as if I may be forgetting how to drive, but of course I'm not. Like tiny seizures or something. I keep this to myself. I can practically feel Marc's skull pulsing with ideas. He prefers loud music to background jabbering. He types away furiously, then drops his head back, mouth open, eyes shut, head bobbing slightly to the beat.

Marc's eyes open, his mouth shuts and he attacks the computer with a new thought. The hours slip by and I feel the Windstar almost driving itself, but choose not to test this theory. Daphne and Kirby are somewhere in the back, dozing. I'm afraid to take my eyes off the road. I feel like a hitchhiker who has just been picked up and is faking an ability to drive.

We arrive at the Henley Park Hotel around midnight. Valet parking, swanky little Tudor place with a charming restaurant and bar. Up in suite 814, mission control, Henri is chain-smoking cigarettes, rattling off to-do lists to his assistant, Helen Tsokanos. Helen, lovely Greek homegirl from Queens, is under the gun, trying to get things organized and keep up with manic Henri.

Warm Heinekens arrive. We are given room assignments. The actors have already gone to bed. Everyone else is buzzing with anticipation. Marc pronounces his mantra, to be implanted in camaraman Mark Benjamin's head when he arrives. Marc's mantra is: Less is more, dance with the characters, and follow me. The plan is that when Marc is occupied, or negotiating, then Benjamin can grab other kinds of shots. Otherwise, the film is to be shot on the fly, hit and run, documentary style.

I go to my room, a single for now, until David Hocs, the sound man, arrives in a couple of days. I lie awake, still slightly shaken from the weed.

Long drive. My head is soft. The mayor of D.C. is in Zimbabwe....

Wednesday, July 23, 1997
The AC in this place is on Arctic. Outside, the heat is tropical.

Downstairs, in the restaurant, I have my first breakfast. Continental. The regular egg or pancake breakfasts are around 15 bucks. Henri won't go for that.

I'm an hour early for the first morning meeting. The decor is high tone but the coffee is dreck. The *Slam* team assembles in an out-of-the-way section of the restaurant.

Saul arrives in slow mo, listening to his morning music on big phat padded headphones. Others arrive and forage through the pile of continental breads and pour fresh-squeezed juices. Dom is wearing a hat that says ADDICT. He smokes Marlboro Reds for breakfast.

Marc arrives with the producers, Henri and Richard Stratton. Bonz makes his entrance dressed as he was the day before but with one addition: He wears a white terry cloth bathrobe over his clothes. The robe is courtesy of the hotel and has a large Henley Park Hotel insignia over the heart.

Bonz is smoking some god-awful black and tan packaged cigar with a white plastic mouthpiece. He works his way around the room, giving a warm earnest greeting to everyone. He may be completely in character. This bathrobe is to be his uniform and his Vinnie "The Chin" Gigante fashion statement. He has *The Art of War* under his arm. He's wide awake and ready. He feels like the heart of the project.

Richard Stratton has the best music. You ride with him, you're riding with George Clinton, Bob Marley, Van Morrison. Richard is the rock-solid, bad-ass, laid-back ex-con of the team. He's someone you trust and respect right away. Richard and Marc came up with the *Slam* movie concept. Richard has access to Mayor Barry. More importantly, he is tight with the mayor's right-hand man, another ex-con named Roach Brown.

Saul and Bonz take off with Richard in his Jeep to meet with important people in key locations.

Henri and I head to the airport to pick up his personal rental car. We have our walkie-talkies. Henri is in an efficient, official hurry. Amped for *Slam*.

The guy at the Budget rental desk has an X carved into his forehead. Could be a birthmark. Henri is irritated. He wanted a dark sedan to project an undercover appearance. They show no record of his request. He settles for a green Ford Taurus.

Back at the hotel, Saul, Bonz and Richard return in the rain with Roach Brown. The mayor truly is in Zimbabwe attending a conference. Roach is our ticket to D.C. access. Roach got a pardon from President Gerry Ford. He was in for murder, did work in prison teaching and performing theater.

Roach, along with the mayor, had a taste for mind alterations, and he got busted again around the same time the mayor was set up by "the bitch." Roach looks prosperous, calm and dignified nowadays. He says your name when he meets you and he remembers it. It's July and he keeps wishing everyone Merry Christmas.

Big black blind Mike is also with them. He has a hand on Bonz's shoulder to guide him as they file into 814 and sit down. Mike was shot in the head a year and a half ago. Blinded. Gang-related. There was a mock funeral for him to make it look like he was truly gone.

Mike wears sunglasses most of the time. Without the glasses, his eyes look like cloudy, deformed blue-gray marbles. He will be playing a character based on himself. I get him some Fig Newtons. He calls people "lover."

Saul, wet and solemn, squats down by Mike's chair and talks to him. Saul strikes me as some kind of African hip hop Siddhartha. Roach is on his cell phone graciously pulling strings. Saul and Mike come up laughing with a nickname for Mike's character. Booty something.

News of the Chin's trial is on CNN with no sound. Versace's murderer is still on the loose. Bonz is further inspired by Chin and decides his bathrobe will be Hopha's one and only wardrobe.

Henri is on the phone with Tony Cheng, making a deal for a big Chinese blow-out dinner with all of us and two D.C. policemen, known as the Doo Wop Cops, for later tonight.

I go on supply runs with Carlos McBride. Food, film, Staples, etc. Carlos is gung-ho out of Hampshire College, by way of the 'hood in Brooklyn. He's a twenty-something street kid with two kids of his own and a wife of ten years. They live in Amherst, Mass. He dropped out of high school in ninth grade. Always held down legit jobs but did other shit on the side. Got into Hampshire through some program and has one more year to go. He says it saved his life. He tells me stories about bringing his 9mm automatic to school in Amherst, making disrespectful frat boys piss their pants. He's thrilled to be on this project, bouncing off the walls—*Gotta get somethin' goin. Know what I'm sayin?*

Huge meal at Tony Cheng's. Plates of food just keep coming. The Doo Wop Cops are at one end of the table with Marc, Roach and Richard. I guess they sing "Lion Sleeps Tonight," etc.

Dom quizzes Sonja and Saul on their vegetarianism. "Is it physical, or political, or what? I mean for you personally?"

Saul says it's all one and the same for him. Dom seems to enjoy challenging them. Sonja gets irritated with Dom. She says you can't use words to describe where poetry comes from.

"You just did" is Dom's response.

Across from me, Carlos is leaning over to hear Blind Mike's story about his shooting. Evidently, the guy who tried to kill Mike was shot the day we arrived in D.C. This guy weighs 400-plus pounds and has been shot at and hit three or four times in the past but never seriously hurt. His fat protected him. This time they hit him in the leg. Mike, though, got shot in the head. He makes a circular motion around his skull to illustrate the path the bullet took as it severed his optical nerve and blinded him.

Guns guns guns.

Thursday, July 24, 1997
Cunanan, Versace's murderer, shot himself in the head when the cops closed in around his houseboat hideout. Case closed. The celebrity/supermodel world mourns hard for Versace.

At breakfast, the actors stick to themselves. I'm sure they are wondering what the fuck is gonna happen. Richard looks over at them and jokes that they don't even talk to him. Truth is, he is one of the only ones they talk to right now. On the drive to D.C., Bonz told Richard, "I always suspected you were black."

I ask Saul if he knows Beau from NYU. He answers me as if I may not speak English and am partially deaf. He explains with frightening clarity that Beau is an undergrad in creative writing and he himself is in the graduate program for ACTing.

I ask Saul where he did his undergrad studies.

"I went to MOREHOUSE College," he says, staring at me and nodding very slowly.

Bonz and I go from breakfast out into the rain. We're in my chariot, the Windstar. Our mission is to get Bonz photo I.D. He remembered this morning that he does not have proper I.D. Without photo I.D., you cannot enter the D.C. Jail, our location. Bonz is wearing his white bathrobe and wrap-around shades, it's pouring rain southern-style, and we're in a hurry.

I pull up in front of a number of photo places. Bonz jumps out and goes inside to ask if they do photo I.D. I am on the walkie keeping mission control posted on our progress. Everyone is waiting for Bonz to return so we can go to the location. Bonz strides into the photo places with total purpose. The employees don't know whether to fear for their lives or laugh out loud. Bonz means business.

We find a place that sets him up. He comes out and shows me the I.D., still hot off the presses. I break up at the name. Kevin Handsome? I say it sounds like a porn actor's name. He tells me it's his real name and Bonz Malone is just some guy who writes for *Vibe*. I don't know what to believe. Later in the evening, Bonz will refer to himself and me as "Huggy and Hutch." He tells Henri that he reminds him of Oscar Goldman, head of the OSI on the motherfuckin' *Six Million Dollar Man*. Bonz can take over a room whenever he feels like it.

Back at the hotel the scene is calm. Most people are out on scouts for potential actors or locations.

Prop list? Special effects? Shot list? I assume all these components are in the works. Has Henri disappeared for a massage? Nothing much to do for a little while, so I go up on the roof of the hotel, take off all my clothes and bark at passing birds.

Later in the afternoon, I drive Saul and Sonja to Adams Morgan, a groovy neighborhood where they will wander, eat, bond for the love scene.

Back in 814, Marc, Richard, Big Mike and Roach are in a holding pattern strategy session.

Jeremy, a friend of Beau's from NYU, shows up. He is the low-budget special effects punk. He has a distinctly arrogant off-putting vibe. Someone tells me he had a car accident that destroyed his face. His face had to be completely rebuilt. He has a recipe for fake blood. He wears martial arts T-shirts and Beau tells me that Jeremy is a black belt in something.

Daphne and Marc have been videotaping potential actors at the jail. They need guys for the Thug Life crew, Hopha's Union crew, and a Narcotics Anonymous meeting. There are many standouts among the prisoners. Packed into suite 814, we screen the highlights. Sign 'em up by consensus.

I take a ride with Richard to drop off Roach and Blind Mike at Roach's office. Mike tells me about a song he heard, he says it's "so pretty" and he's been trying to find it. He says the song is by Metallica, called "Nothing Else Matters."

Mike tells me he has no interest in vengeance as far as the shooting goes. I assume he knows his guy got shot the other day. Hard to read him with his eyes gone.

Friday, July 25, 1997
John Kirby and Dom stayed up late at the bar. Dom says he told John to "write all the shit he's saying down." The shit being John's *what's wrong with the world, why, and how to fix it* political science rap.

I hear that Saul performed twice last night. Blew everyone away. Already, he is at a place with his work (a term he's not crazy about) where he knows he can go into a room and floor people. He seems supremely confident.

Dom announces to a full table that John got all liquored up last night and gave him a blow job. I am the only one there who finds that funny. In Dom's hands that humor almost works. Below the borsht belt stuff.

People are starting to complain about the Continental breakfast.

Beau and Saul rehearse on the couch in 814. Daphne shoots it with the Hi-8. Beau has a good-sized cold sore on his upper lip. He's concerned about how it will look on camera.

Beau and Saul work on a scene where they first meet in the police van on the way to jail. Beau is a performer, but not a trained actor. Saul gently tries to coach him into a naturalized way of speaking his monologue.

Saul takes off his overshirt and ties his ankle to Beau's with the shirt to give them the feeling of being shackled together. They work on improvs of the scene. A half dozen of us stare at them. It looks like there's a long way to go.

Big static arrives when Henri gives Sonja, Saul and Beau release forms that must be signed before shooting starts. Shooting starts tomorrow. Sonja raises her voice and says the name Henri with an interesting lilt. Henri plays it cool, spells out the facts.

All these actors have spoken-word record deals, lawyers, agents, tours, etc. They need to talk to their lawyers. Beau says quietly after others have semi-stormed out that all he cares about is not making anyone crazy. He will call his lawyer, "Mr. Frank."

Henri makes a pained face. "Not Peter Frank," he says. "Big, fat Peter?"

Beau nods yes. Henri shakes his head, disgusted. He seems to know this guy. Things get ironed out. Everyone ends up chilled.

Henri, Beau and I go to buy wardrobe for Beau. D.C. is clean, soft-core, half full. Beau is actually incredibly innocent. He's trying to get into his killer character, and when he says he's going to kill us all it's almost chilling in its sweetness. He's sarcastic, tentative and curious. When asked if he is ready for his big scene in the jail bullpen tomorrow, his response is a dead-pan, "I wish I was taller."

Beau is nervous. He has to throw a wild tantrum and do a monologue in a jail holding tank full of real prisoners, and he's keyed up. We don't find Beau the right clothes, but Henri finds himself a groovy Diesel windbreaker and a portable public address system, otherwise known as a bullhorn. It will be needed on location. This one supposedly amplifies your voice three hundred feet and plays ninety-four musical favorites. Preprogrammed for your crowd control convenience.

Henri is almost out of cash. Beau and I wait an hour while he berates "Shittybank" for fucking up his $4,000 money transfer.

Henri and I go to buy beer and groceries. Henri is covered in wires and gadgets. Cell phone, walkie-talkie, headset, bullhorn, and a SLAM I.D. laminate on a thin chain around his neck. He's growing a beard, he looks a little insane, not his usual coifed and cruisin' self. A mogul in the making. He is hell bent on *Slam*.

I'm getting to know where everything is in the supermarket. I buy Bonz, or should I say Hopha, two decks of cards that he will never open. He says he may put one deck on the table when it's time to negotiate, but it won't be opened, "'cuz I don't play games."

Across the parking lot next to O Street Meats is the liquor store. I'm one white guy waiting for one Asian guy to get me two cases of Heineken. The Asian guy is ancient and blurry behind four layers of fading Plexiglas. The Plexiglas is speckled with burn marks from cigarettes. Twenty black men and women wait for me to finish my business. It's taking a while. Nobody complains. The place is silent.

Back in 814. Marc, Daphne and others return from a potential location. The location is a war zone housing project in Southeast. They are all a bit shaken by an assault they endured from a 300-pound irate woman. She didn't want them there. Turns out her husband was up for Roach's job in the mayor's office. She wants a piece of Roach. Daphne kept the Hi-8 rolling and, on the videotape, it looks like somebody might get hurt.

A guy named Calvin was in the background. I'm not sure who Calvin is—ex-prizefighter, football player, player in general. He knows Roach, who knows everybody. I guess Calvin is helping us. We won't be shooting at Mrs. Watson's project, though. Marc calls her to try and calm her down and she tears into him again. We can all hear her voice screeching over the phone. Marc is polite and assures her that no disrespect was intended. Her husband gets on the phone and threatens us all if we come back. No problem. We will use another project around the corner where the woman in charge welcomed us with open arms.

Dinner at Tony Cheng's again. A smaller group this time but still a ton of food.

Dom is telling jokes. Saul, erect and dignified, finds meat in his tofu. Dom is once again expressing anxiety about what he sees as *Slam*'s total lack of structure. I tell him that if Marc wanted a real prison guard, he would get one. I tell Dom he should just go as far as he can and let Marc rein him in. Marc is there when I say this and he agrees. Dom likes the idea but he is still unsure.

It occurs to me that this is an awesome collection of experience and talent. This fact does not guarantee success. *Slam* is fraught with potential. It is the night before shooting begins.

Back at the hotel bar. In comes Mark Benjamin—Bengo—the feared, the loved, the cameraman. He has his Du Art T-shirt on with SHOOT FILM across the front. He is buoyant and hyperalert. Ready to go gonzo with his old friend Marc Levin on another adventure. Big greetings all around.

Back in mission control, the crew assembles. David Hocs is there, ready for sound, and Tony Hardmon, the AC [Assistant Cameraman] with the great smile.

Benjamin is brought up to speed. Marc is clearly pumped to have the whole team around him, hours from action.

Earlier today Bonz walked into the jail as Hopha, in his bathrobe, smoking one of his cheap cigars. Saul did a killer poem inside the jail for a bunch of prisoners. At the end one guy said, "That shit made me forget what I was thinking." The line was instantly incorporated into the script that nobody has seen.

Saturday, July 26, 1997
Serious heat. D.C. is a southern state.

Out to the projects, across the Anacostia River. I'm driving the Windstar as usual. Marc points to our destination, a green wooded ridge in the distance. It doesn't look like a ghetto until you get there. The area is green. No concrete jungle here. The box brick buildings are surrounded with lush green weeds and trees.

We park and within minutes the shooting begins. Benjamin is moving among the children like some alien with a camera for a head. He doesn't shoot you in close-up so much as smell you with his camera, sniffing up and down like a bloodhound. His camera is endlessly curious and alive.

Saul is Ray Joshua now. Shots of him hanging with the kids from the project. Pied Piper shots. The kids are thrilled. The circus has come to town.

The ice cream truck arrives and turns on its bell. No sweet little ice cream tunes. Just a harsh electric bell ringing like a burglar alarm. Look! The white guy with all the gadgets and the bullhorn is buying everyone ice cream.

Behind a fence, through some trees, teenage boys with big Afros stare at us without expression. Everyone is out to watch us. The over-thirteen boys and girls hang back while the younger ones come up close. A baby girl falls on her face chasing a rottweiler puppy. She hits pavement littered with shattered windshield glass. She is picked up and brushed off. She barely cries.

The heat is deep. Word is spreading. There's a movie being made here in the 'hood.

A scene is shot under some trees, by a Dumpster, in a vacant lot. Guys in their late teens and twenties throwing dice. Shots of the rottweiler pup chewing on a roll of hundreds. Improv dialogue nobody could write unless you transcribed it.

Saul comes over, only now he's Ray Joshua, and they greet him. He's the local rhymer. Blind Mike is there, only he's not supposed to be blind at this point in the story. From where I stand, guarding some equipment, the scene looks like a cockfight or a barbecue. Only the boom and mic hovering over the gathering gives the movie away.

Daphne is shooting everything with her Hi-8. Kirby is running wild, holding the video tap hookup, trying to keep up with Benjamin, and stealing still photos when he can. This thing is going to be well documented.

Bonz, deep into Hopha, is in the van with the AC cranked, reading more *Art of War* and Dale Carnegie. Some passages he highlights in green, others in yellow.

A little girl named Kenya latches onto Daphne. Her first full sentence to Daphne is, "I got a cousin who's white."

Daphne lights a cigarette in her mouth and gives it to Blind Mike. He smokes it slowly and the whole time he keeps saying, "I can't believe she lit it for me like that. Every time I be blowin' smoke out, I'm blowin' her a kiss."

A woman comes by and tells me, "You lookin' for a ghetto, you in one now. Got anything you want here. Crack dealers, crackheads, crack babies. Heroin, drunks, gangsters. Shoot-outs. Everything."

We go to a basketball court after shooting Ray selling some weed. A pickup game starts with Ray and some other guys. I'm watching this guy run off every few minutes to the street. He does an exchange with a passing car and is back in the game without losing a beat. He seems to be a little wired himself.

A wacked-out crack zombie drifts into our midst. The dealer guy chases him off. He's dealing, using, protecting us, playing basketball and starring in a movie all at once. His son is hanging around. Fat, solid kid about nine or ten. He has a mean look on his face and a handful of rocks that he keeps tossing in the direction of the equipment. We ask him to move but he won't. Ask him to be quiet and he makes noise. His father tries to discipline him but is ignored.

We break for dinner, pile into our vehicles and head off to a nearby cafeteria-style restaurant. It's dusk and the heat is lifting a little.

Saturday night. I tell Dom and Carlos that the whole vibe is gonna change here at night. The place is gonna be buzzin', twice as many people. Word is spreading as we speak.

We follow Walter Woodward to the cafeteria. From my understanding, Walter is in charge of public relations for the D.C. Department of Corrections. He is also a photographer. Big, easygoing dude. Played some pro football a few years back.

Driving back to the projects, I have Blind Mike riding shotgun in the Windstar. I'm blasting Ben Harper. Dom says he plays drums. Mike doesn't believe him. Mike says Ben Harper's singing voice "sounds like Tracy Chapman with bass or some shit."

Mike says everything in a very specific stabbing cadence. The rhythm of his speech is sharp and tight. His sentences are little riffs. He often speaks with a slight smile threatening to appear.

Ben Harper's bass is shaking the Windstar and Mike says, "I got a twenty-dollar bag 'o dope in my pocket. That's why I be scratchin' my nose 'n' shit. Want some?"

He looks in my direction, blind and smiling. All I can see is me puking up my dinner then nodding out when I'm supposed to be guarding the sound equipment.

I look at Mike. This guy is the lead in tonight's scene. He has to reenact his own shooting, probably the worst moment of his life. He got shot in the face and he is offering me some of his medicine. I imagine he has skull-cracking migraines and politely refuse the offer.

A few hours later we have a hundred extras and I'm mixing ketchup and water. Jeremy, the special effects guy with the rebuilt face and bad attitude, couldn't make it. Henri had to fire him after a confrontation of some kind. Beau warned Henri that Jeremy was a black belt, and Henri informed them that he studied five different martial arts and all he remembers are the death blows. I'm trying to simulate blood and I crush up a pretzel and put it in the mix for brain and skull matter. I drip some on the pavement. Bonz thinks it looks bogus.

There are twice as many people as there were this afternoon. The place is electric, crackling, a hot summer Saturday night. People dressed up, hoping to be chosen. Mothers appear with beautiful sons and daughters and ask me how their children can get in the movie.

Tension mounts as the shooting scene is mapped out. The hundred extras are coached on what to do once the gun goes off. Richard asks me to make a bag of marijuana for the dope deal Mike and Saul will do just prior to the shooting. Quarter pound, more or less. Green oak leaves in a big Ziploc with some gaffer tape wrapped around it.

Some guy asks me a question as if he has people nearby waiting for the answer. He told them something was true and now he is going to prove it by asking me. He says excuse me and asks, "People get paid to do what you're doing? To do what's goin' on here tonight?"

"Yeah, sometimes," I answer.

He nods and smiles, says thank you and jogs off.

People look stunned watching us make this movie. It makes them curious and some seem uncomfortable. That we are shooting here raises questions: What do we see in them? Why have we chosen their home for our story? What is it we hope to convey?

A man comes through the parking lot that is now our location. He is the village idiot. Buck teeth, filthy clothes, goofy smile. Retarded. Must be about twenty-five. The people point at him, smiling, some laughing, and they tell me to put him in the movie. He laughs along with them, swings his arms and rolls his head. He is excited. His laughter gets louder. A group of elders is drinking on a stoop, laughing. They call him over.

"Reggie, come over here, baby."

He lurches toward them, then veers off and disappears alone around the back of the building.

The scene is set. Saul is in position. He starts break-dancing to loosen up. Beau joins him. The place is vibrating with anticipation. Richard has the bullhorn. He shouts instructions to the crowd—where to run when the gun shot goes off; don't look at the camera.

Marc is pacing, talking to the actors, looking up on the small hill where Benjamin has the camera set up. Marc has no walkie and the signals are being missed or delayed.

All the pieces fall into place and Marc yells his unique ACK-SHUN command.

Saul approaches Mike and the two greet. Mike gives Saul the bag of prop weed.

The firecracker gunshot goes off and people scream and scatter. Mike grabs his face and falls to the ground. Problem is, the people are laughing as they run. Richard tries to explain it to them. Calvin motions to Richard for the bullhorn.

Calvin is about five foot seven in sneakers, built like a fire hydrant. He is tomcat royalty in this neighborhood. Must be about fifty years old. There are many Calvin stories. How he made money prizefighting and playing football. How he set up an outdoor gym and boxing ring on the hill where Benjamin now has the camera. People from all around came to fight on that hill. The power of Calvin's punches changed peoples lives. His speed on foot when he played football is compared to NFL greats. He has two new Cadillacs and many relations.

Calvin holds the bullhorn out to examine it, then puts it to his mouth, raises a hand, pulls the trigger and speaks. He tells everyone that this is serious. They are listening. He points at Mike and explains that this is the re-enactment of his real shooting.

"This man was actually shot in the head and now he's blind."

Calvin asks for cooperation. He gives the bullhorn back to Richard and the next take is better.

The Doo Wop Cops are there to chase Saul up the hill at the end of the scene. On one take, a cop falls hard running up the hill and people laugh hysterically.

I lie down as a body double for Mike. Marc is ready for the blood. Mike lies down and I open the jug and pour some out onto the pavement. It looks pretty much like what it is. Ketchup and bits of pretzel.

"What is that shit?" Marc says, crouching down, in a hurry. He's pointing at the pieces of pretzel and starts plucking them out and flinging them away.

"It's brain matter," I explain, but he doesn't hear me.

I wonder if Mike hears us. His head is a foot from the phony blood. Maybe he's on a nod.

There's confusion about light, blocking and continuity. The scene is extra-lit by the high beams from Richard's Jeep.

I'm standing near Hocs, who's seated on a crate dealing with sound. A long, thin, intense-looking woman approaches us. She is made up heavily. Skeletal face, perfect teeth. She starts to tell us about her acting ability. Says she has all emotions available to her, then runs down a list, infusing each word with the emotion. I can be angry. Sad. Show lust. Joy.

She has our attention. She sees Daphne shooting her with the video camera and says, "She's cute. Yeah, gorgeous. You ought to put her on top and spin her around."

Daphne keeps shooting. The woman gives us her apartment number and instructs us to come for her when we need her.

A guy tells one of us: "I've lived here twenty-nine years and nothing like this has ever happened around here. This is the best thing that's ever happened here."

Others call it a miracle that we came here to make a movie. Others still look angry and suspicious.

Back in 814, 2 a.m., unwinding. Cold Heinekens. Benjamin appears briefly, dressed only in his briefs. The dozen or so of us applaud him and he stays for a few minutes, but leaves before we settle in to watch our primitive dailies.

What everyone has suspected looks to be true. Watching the video tap from Benjamin's camera, it is clear that Saul Williams is the *Slam* star. He looks like any young man from the projects and at the same time he completely stands out. You wonder who he is. You have to keep watching. In the shot of him leading a group of kids, he strikes me as some reggae messiah. He looks like an urban shaman mystic leading those kids across the parking lot. He has this earthy rural roots vibe mated with the project poet of cosmic oppression thing.

I'm sold. It is 3 a.m. and we're all giddy with exhaustion and thrilled by the first day's results.

Sunday, July 27, 1997
Even hotter today. Dom can't get an image from jail out of his head. Marc had him go to the jail and study guards to get into character. Dom keeps talking about the "kids in cages watching cartoons." All under eighteen and

in for murder. We will be in there with them soon enough.

Now we have another day shooting in the projects. I'm guarding equipment on the hill by the door to an especially rough-looking building. Sweating profusely and doing nothing.

They are shooting indoors. Kids come around and talk to me. A little girl rubs my head. It feels good and my eyes shut for a moment. She asks me for a dollar.

Rottweiler puppy has needle-sharp teeth. The area I am in has trash all over the ground. I start to pick it up with help from a little girl. People pass and I can see they feel vaguely insulted by my actions. I fill a garbage bag and stop.

Two guys approach me with a question. One, possibly retarded, has thick Coke bottle glasses. The other looks like a regular, straight working guy. He says he has a story he wants to tell and he can use his partner's computer. He's very earnest about consulting me. His partner with the glasses nods. He says the story is about his brother. He was in a gang, he was depressed. Something was going on and he wouldn't talk about it. One morning he shot himself in the head.

"It's a story I want to tell," he says.

His partner nods again.

I ask him about his computer and he says, "I'm into the whole Internet thing."

I tell him he should write the story, have his partner type it for him. This strikes him as a good idea. He thanks me profusely and the two of them wander off.

Marc hears Dom sing a bass part with the Doo Wop Cops. Tells Dom he's the wop in Doo Wop.

The day is sweltering. We shoot a big confrontation scene between two gangs in a parking lot. All actors except for Saul and Mike are recruited on the spot.

Tall skinny kid comes around wearing baggy jeans and no shirt. He has an iguana on his shoulder. The iguana is bright electric green with bug eyes and a wrinkled belly. It rests on the kid's shoulder, gripping with claws that look like they are about to puncture the kid's skin. His skin is black and shining with sweat. The iguana's tail hangs halfway down the kid's back. He leans against a car with his arms folded over his chest, watching us. Says nothing.

We finish shooting at the project and go at dusk to eat in a nearby Chinese restaurant. On the drive, Saul expresses concern to Marc about doing a 'hood film. Saul thinks there is some cliché stuff going on and the poetry aspects are being lost. He wants Pink Floyd on the soundtrack and no hip hop. He wants it to be further out there.

Marc listens intently and assures Saul that it will be out there.

At dinner, I am seated across from Bonz. He's in a dark mood. I ask him a question and he looks up from his food with no expression. He stares me down, nods and goes back to his meal.

Outside, after dinner, I lay on the pavement and digest. We steal a scene out in back of the restaurant. Saul running from the Doo Wop Cops down a length of white fence.

Saul runs very fast. I drive the Windstar for a dolly shot. One of the Doo Wop Cops pulls a muscle chasing him and we are done with the scene.

In the Windstar, getting ready to leave, Saul plays me a tape of himself reciting a poem. The poem is accompanied by a sample of The Beatles' "Strawberry Fields." The song is slowed down and is now a lurching hip hop beat on a loop repeating "Nothing is real" over and over again. We both have new appreciation for Ringo Starr.

Later still, and we are near the projects, outside a police station. The van in front of me is bouncing up and down. Bonz, Carlos, Dom and Saul are going wild freestyle-rapping in all directions. Banging on the dash and seats and on empty cans, stereo blasting.

Carlos is completely charged behind the wheel of the van. He can't believe he has fallen into this experience. Nobody can. Spirits are high.

Monday, July 28, 1997
First day shooting in the jail.

Beau does his scene in the police van when he and Saul are brought in. Beau claims he wrote twenty pages of backstory on his character. Way into his role, he spits on one of the guards. They are not thrilled.

Soon it will be time for Beau's *Asian Men Are Hung Like Horses* routine. I'm in the bullpen, locked up with twenty black convicts. I've been recruited to play a white junkie. I sit on the floor in the corner by the stainless steel toilet. The convicts assure me I look like the real thing. I see a roach crawl across the floor and hide under the back heel of a man's boot.

Soon, I have to piss. No big deal. Beau is going wild screaming and acting his ass off. Between takes, I stand up, step between a couple of guys and stand there facing the toilet. Nothing happens. I really have to go, but nothing comes out. Not used to pissing next to twenty strangers. Piss proud?

I go back to my corner and twitch and itch like a junkie, then I get up and try again, and then again, attempting to be casual. Finally, some guy asks me what the problem is. I blame it on all the coffee I drank. Junkie boy can't piss.

When we are done shooting and the cell is empty, I stand and deliver, gallons. Halfway through my release, Daphne is there shooting the event with her Hi-8.

We move on and I'm locked up again with the guys in another area. White Junkie II.

The crew wanders off, leaving me locked up while they grab a scene with a giant bull of a guard who gives Saul a heavy-duty improv rap, warning him about the perils of doing time in the D.C. Jail.

The guard gets all worked up. Marc says, "Cut!" and the guard storms off down the hall, flips out and cracks someone's head open with his fist.

A Code Blue is called: All officers to the scene! The flipped-out cop has to be subdued by five other guards.

I'm locked up at this point and forgotten. I'm somewhat concerned as the panic spreads. The guy next to me is sure he knows me from somewhere. He doesn't seem to have fond memories of me. Hostage situation crosses my mind.

Tension makes me sleepy. Within seconds, all is calm again.

At the end of every day, around dinnertime, the jail pipes in R&B Muzak.

Tuesday, July 29, 1997
We move to another cellblock in the jail. The windows look like melted plastic. There is light but no view outside. The ceilings are dripping some cold yellow liquid onto tables meant for dining. We are invading the dungeonlike quarters of the under-eighteen murderers.

Unlike the rest of the convicts locked up here, these young men have only a sneering, sullen interest in us. They don't ask to be in the movie. They lurk, gangly and jangled by hormones, with near-life sentences breathing down their necks. They are teenagers acting out a rap video with no end and no commercials. Damned and banished for the crimes they have committed.

Some of these guys have dead blank expressions. Others are just as hard but seem to shine with energy and unfettered youth. Not a white one in the bunch. Two of them are famous in the D.C. area. They go by the names of Face and Bay. They are charged with first degree murder.

Bay is raw and electric. He has a long scar down his cheek and jaw line. He wears a blue skullcap and round glasses. Face looks like a baby who would not hesitate to kill. Whatever innocence he has stays buried way down beneath the wreckage. It's like being around a movie star: it's hard to tell if their charisma—the larger-than-life aspect of their presence—is a product of the hype or the effect they naturally have.

Whatever it is, something about them is chilling. Even the hard-core older convicts find them unnerving.

Within minutes of our arrival, Benjamin and Marc have Saul in a cell directly adjacent to Bay. These are to be Saul's first moments locked up proper, in his new home. I set up craft services with Carlos in the day room above where the scene is being shot. Henri is in the corner on the cell phone, trying to explain to some banker in New York what we are doing.

I hear a bass beat, fist on steel wall in perfect heavy time, then the snap of homemade snare drum—a hairbrush wapping on metal sink. Bay's voice cuts in, an eerie pleading threat to the beat. We all stop short and listen. Bay is keeping his own time, rhyming his story to Saul in the next cell. The kid's voice is jagged, cold and mournful. It is insistent, relentless. His beat is deep, in the pocket, echoing all around us. He passes off the rap to Saul, keeps the beat going for him, and Saul jumps in with his own freestyle tale of Ray Joshua's journey. They are meeting for the first time, rap around poetry, telling each other their histories. Everyone is silenced. Henri, jaw dropped, has the cell phone held out for whoever is on the other end to listen.

Wednesday, July 30, 1997

The morning coffee comes from a nearby Starbucks and the gang is amped on the way to jail.

The bottleneck we go through to get into the jail is always tense. Outside never feels bigger than when you are about to go inside again. Through the tiny box room of security, raise your arms, empty your bag, into an elevator, up to North Three, where we have Hopha's scenes to shoot and more Ray and Lauren stuff.

The warden comes around. She wants to call a Code Blue so we can get a piece of authentic action between guards and convicts. She mistakes Bonz for a real prisoner and from then on is strangely fixated on him. There is something sexy about her. Power. Bonz fucking the warden in a jail where he is playing a gang boss would not surprise me at this point.

The Code Blue is called and a mob of guards comes charging down the hall. The prisoners in the scene taunt the guards at the sliding Plexiglas-and-steel door. All of us except Benjamin are safely out of the way. Hard to tell if the guards know this is staged. They burst into the room and there is a full-tilt hand-to-hand rumble going on.

Richard and I freak with laughter and amazement at the instant over-whelming intensity of the scene. Looks like no fists to the face and no weapons but otherwise full-on grappling between huge guys, pumped up on restless rage and lots of heavy weight-lifting. Benjamin is in the middle of the melee holding the camera over his head, hopping around in circles, moving with the flow of the conflict. Marc told him to dance with the characters and fuck if he isn't doing it.

In less than a minute the mini-riot stops and both sides are breathing hard, shaking hands, some bleeding here and there. Everyone seems a little less uptight after a chance to go at it.

The warden nods her head, pleased with the results. She smiles and appears positively titillated by the scene she created for us.

A guard walks by, keys jangling over my head. I'm lying on the floor next to some equipment. It's the bull steroid bruiser guard who freaked out and bashed some guy's head in a few days earlier. Today he's whistling the theme from *Rocky*.

Thursday, July 31, 1997
D.C. is in flux. The United States Congress has opted to invade and take power. Marc says we are on a seam in time. In the jail, there is the feeling that no one is really in charge. A guard approaches me reeking of booze. Word is, federal inspectors are coming tomorrow. This state of affairs, this "seam in time," enables us to shoot on and on in a priceless location.

Sonja is inside the jail with us to shoot a scene of her character, Lauren, teaching a class. Before the scene, we sit down to eat. Below us, in a room separated from us by a thin Plexiglas window, a half dozen of the young murderers motion me to move. I move and realize they want to see Sonja, who sits next to me.

I stand and see that a few of the young convicts have their dicks out and are half jerking off at the sight of Sonja.

I go into the small white-walled basketball gym to eat. I look up on the wall and see a large splattered stain of some kind close to ten feet up. I can tell it's blood but it's impossible to figure out how it got that high up there.

I wander around, walk by a cell. Marc and Daphne are inside, sitting together. Marc is on a cell phone. I hear him talking in respectful tones to someone named Bill. Must be Bill Moyers.

I linger and hear Marc saying, "Don't worry, Bill, we're gonna bring it home."

It is time for Bonz's first scene. I find a place somewhere behind the camera, out of the way. Dom plays a guard on the take. He brings Saul to the cell and announces him to Bonz, aka Hopha, leader of the Union crew, who is reclined on his bunk, face hidden behind the *Wall Street Journal*. "Your boy is here," Dom says and leaves the two alone.

The floor of Hopha's cell is covered with bags of cookies, packs of cigarettes, books, baby powder, whatever a convict needs. Hopha lowers the paper, sits up and welcomes Ray. He is in command, wearing his bathrobe and wraparound reflecting shades, at ease, a killer, a wit and a philosopher. Bonz's Hopha is a warrior, urgent with the knowledge that it is time to become king. There is nothing tentative in the performance, nothing forced. Hopha is seasoned, battle-scarred, a leader in search of power beyond the violence he knows too well. Bonz's preparation is in place and paying off. Exactly as planned, Hopha lives.

In a later scene, Hopha walks and talks with Ray. Hopha carries *The Art of War* under his arm. Out in the yard, Hopha has just witnessed Ray's moment of victory, poetry triumphing over violence. Bonz portrays Hopha as genuinely stunned and respectful of Ray's power, trying to grasp this nonviolent form of warfare that he has read about but never quite believed. Hopha sees something rare in Ray, something he wants to understand, to honor and protect. Like a true king he offers to pay Ray's bail and set him free.

I am a witness to Bonz Malone in the zone.

The time we spend locked up is a unique strain. First, there is the noise. There is nothing in here to muffle or absorb the cacophony of incarceration. The acoustics seem designed to grate on one's nerves. Banging, clanging, echoes of steel crashing. Walkie-talkies squawk, keys jangle. Brutal buzzing sounds. Doors locking, unlocking, then squeaking moans as they swing and crash shut. A distant shriek from down the tier will pierce your eardrum while a simple request from across the room gets lost, bouncing off the walls, and you have no idea what has been said.

Then there is the air. I am breathing stale, dry, pure institutional gas. I am breathing the burps, farts and fury of every soul stuck inside here.

All the clocks in the jail are set at different times. Two hundred new prisoners in and out of here every day on their way to or from court or prison, waiting on trials, sentencing or just doing their time here in the jail. Years go by. Names are carved into cement, written on cell walls—dates, declarations of allegiance.

Ghosts in here. They rage in the corners, in shadows, under the metal bunks. They drift aimlessly among the living dead. Bars can't contain them, but they stay on, locked down in the next life.

At around five, we leave the jail and get glorious golden-hour shots of Saul in the graveyard across from the facility.

Evidently, the graveyard is a national landmark. We find J. Edgar Hoover's grave and smoke a joint on it.

On the way back to the hotel, Benjamin tells Marc that there needs to be a scene to explain why Saul (Ray Joshua) from the 'hood speaks like Peter Jennings. Benjamin feels this must be explained.

I am driving. Marc must think I am completely out of it. He is compelled to tell me when lights change from red to green.

Across the street from our swanky hotel there is a park inhabited by ragged crackhead transvestites. A block away is a stretch of road where fairly attractive female hookers ply their trade.

Wheel Man (far right) and crew on location.

Friday, August 1, 1997

Out in the jail rec yard we stage a fight between China, leader of the Thug Life crew, and another guy. Everyone is shirtless, lifting weights. Marc explains the scene he's trying for and the two men nod, eager and serious. Marc yells "Action!" and they improv a short exchange where China accuses the other guy of wavering loyalty to the Thug Life crew. The exchange turns physical and they are suddenly wrestling, two powerhouse guys going hard at each other, spinning in a tangle, falling hard onto the pavement.

Marc calls, "Cut!" and they stop. Marc gives them an adjustment and they do it again. Something about the scene floors me. I look at Richard and he seems to be moved in the same way. I'm not sure what it is exactly.

Something about the outlet these two guys are experiencing, the expression, the creativity they are exercising and succeeding with, maybe for the first time since they have been locked up, perhaps for the first time ever.

Certainly it is all new for these convicts to collaborate with a white guy director and crew from NYC, stage a mock fight and get praise and thanks for the performance. I think part of the purpose they bring to this is because they know what the film is about. They couldn't have been more cooperative, real, alive, these two young men, serving out their prime behind bars.

Later, still in the yard, Saul and Sonja are upset about the way the big Thug Life/Union crew confrontation scene unfolds. They think it's not realistic. Marc hears what they have to say and does his best to explain his ideas, listen to theirs, and push on—get our shots and get out.

I think the actors can tell a little more every day that *Slam* is their film as much as it is Marc's. They are rising to the occasion.

The sun is sliding fast, about to hit the top of the prison wall, throw the yard into shadow. It is time to stage Saul's big scene where he stops violence with an explosion of poetry. The *Stealing us was the smartest thing they ever did* rap.

It's also the scene where Lauren walks by the yard and sees Ray delivering the poem. She watches Ray, then sees the rival factions stunned into temporary peace by his poetic assault. This is where she gets her hard-on for old Ray. There's a lot to shoot: Ray's close-up, convict reactions, Sonja's reaction and various other coverage.

Golden hour on the yard. Saul does his first take, then another. The guy is deep, double deep, triple deep. Around him, there's frantic planning, positioning, then smooth execution of takes. Saul is far-out serious, sweating, hard-charging on visionary juices, incarceration and love.

Marc pushes the whole team, no huddles now, just call the play and go for it. The sun is slipping behind the tower when out of nowhere the warden shows up. She is pissed off. She shuts us down. Marc tries to understand what's happening. He talks to her, but it's no good. She feels taken advantage of. Someone ratted us out, called the warden at home and told her we were still here, out in the yard with too many extras.

It seems as though some of the guards and prisoners are getting tired of our presence. As far as the jailers are concerned, we're in here making stars of some randomly picked people and mostly ignoring the rest.

We pack up and file out of the yard, down through security, out to the main gate and parking lot. It's so good to be outside. A group of convicts is just coming in from court, stepping out of a van, shuffling on shackled feet toward the entrance.

One guy calls out to us: "What's the movie called?"

Before any of us can answer, one of his comrades yells: "It's called Fuck-All-Y'all!"

I can't tell if we are banned from the jail or not. Nobody seems to know. We head back to the hotel to regroup and prepare for the party scene.

On arrival, it occurs to Marc and Benjamin that we have good golden hour time on our hands and we need to take Saul, find some cool locations and shoot.

We go skeleton crew down the road to a building we have passed that is nine rooms, each with different wallpaper and only three walls. The entire façade of the building has been torn off, exposing the inside, which from the street looks like a giant-sized tic-tac-toe grid.

I suggest we get Saul coming out of the building and I cross the street to do a quick scout. As soon as I enter, I am blown back by the stench of feces, urine and slow crack death.

We shoot Saul walking by instead. The cops show up while I wait with the Windstar. I yell to the crew and we are gone before the cops can get a fix on us. The cops here in the capital seem easier to fluster than NYC's.

We go down to a big park on the banks of the Anacostia and steal more glorious sunset shots. Marc explains what he wants. As Saul walks away from the camera to take his place by the river, where he will stand with hands resting on head, he says softly, "I'm gonna walk on water if you don't mind."

I wouldn't put it past him. Benjamin shoots Saul from behind and nails outrageous wavering stripes of pure gold sun rippling off the surface of the water with Saul's silhouette in the center.

As the camera rolls, we all look at each other and nod. Money shot. Then we get Saul walking across the bridge toward downtown D.C. with more sunset.

I wait with the Windstar in a parking lot by the river. There's a breeze coming off the water. A new red Cadillac rolls by, slow, with the windows down. Al Green's "Let's Stay Together" playing loud and clear, a slick young dude behind the wheel laughing with a lady friend.

It seems like a long way from China and the other convicts at the D.C. Jail, just a couple miles from here.

Later we shoot the party scene where Ray has been invited by Lauren after he gets out of jail. Just a groovy group of real-life D.C. hipsters Sonja knows. Fellow poets. One or two New York imports.

A little boy watches us through a hole in the fence. He and his friends are in an alley behind the house as we shoot on the back patio with torches and sun guns for light.

We are all giddy, tired, wired from all the running around. I have become one with the Windstar after all the driving I've been doing. I've been bouncing a tennis ball against any available wall when I have nothing else to do. Reading Turgenev's *Diary of a Superfluous Man*.

Everyone is in the zone now. It feels like we could just keep going, shooting a story that never ends, for as long as we live. With only a couple days left, we are just hitting that kind of vital looseness that breeds magic.

The party scene goes easily, Benjamin waltzing his Aaton around, weaving, bobbing in close like a curious invisible visitor. People get up and do poems. A tall, beautiful amazon woman does an erotic piece to hoots and sighs of appreciation. Sonja as Lauren does a poem and introduces Ray as her new friend who just got out of jail.

Saul gets up and delivers a gem of a love poem. I'm trying to help out, be available to move equipment, but mostly I just get in and out of the way.

It's well past midnight when we wrap the party scene and take off on another skeleton crew mission. We are headed for the mall to shoot Saul walking alone toward the Washington Monument, pondering his situation.

On the way to the location, a joint appears in my hand and I smoke some, hoping it will wake me up. Saul does not partake, nor does the cameraman.

Saul digs one of his favorite tapes out of his bag and asks me to play it. Pink Floyd's *Umaguma*. I put it on and am instantly transported to a disturbing place. The music is melodic and disorienting, strange samples of natural sounds sped up, played backwards, with echoing drums and strange human voices.

I shake my head and focus on the road. I'm fighting off a combination of euphoria and paranoia. I'm mad at myself for smoking, but I'm definitely wide awake as we pull over at the deserted mall and unload.

Hocs has his sound equipment, Kirby does the video tap, Tony assists Benjamin, Marc directs Saul. I wait with the Windstar. The group walks toward the Washington Monument. One hundred yards away Marc calls out for me to drive alongside the mall and follow them so they don't have to come back to this spot.

I jump behind the wheel and crank up the *Umaguma*. I'm crawling along up the dead empty mall at 2:30 a.m. with all the windows open. It's a still night and I hope I'm providing a soundtrack for the crew. I realize that if they call out to me I won't hear them, so I turn the music down.

I've lost sight of the crew, then I hear them and pull over. They're out in the center of the mall and I can just hear their voices. The sprinklers come on, hundreds of them, watering the government grass.

Suddenly, I remember and I am mortified. I left something back at our first stop. I'm sure of it. I left a piece of equipment on the side of the road. This is bad, very bad. I curse the *Umaguma* and turn it off. I pull over and get out of the Windstar.

"HEY, I'LL BE BACK IN A MINUTE," I yell.

Marc bellows back at me from somewhere out on the lawn. "DON'T FUCKIN' GO ANYWHERE!"

I see someone running toward me. It's Tony, coming up to the Windstar for more film. I tell him what's happened and he laughs. I ask him to tell them I left my notebook back at our first stop, down near the Capitol Building. I ask him what happens if I don't find this piece of equipment. He slides a finger across his throat, laughs again and runs off into the darkness.

I take off, go a good mile or so, all the way around the mall, not a soul in sight, hoping I remember the cross-street we were on. I see a homeless guy walking across the grass toward an object on the side of the road and I start honking, flick on high beams and gun the engine, headed straight for the thing. I pull up as he is about to reach the object; he is startled and backs away.

"This is mine. I left it here earlier," I say, picking it up.

He puts up his hands and walks off. I can't believe it's still there. It's just a cart for Benjamin's equipment, but losing it would have been so fucking lame. Benjamin would have shit. I find out later, when I offhandedly ask him how long he's had it, that he's owned the thing for many years. If I had lost it my name would have been synonymous with outer space. But no, I got it. I am back in the game, sober from the adrenaline rush, and flying with *Umaguma* again, back to the crew. I pick them up just in time at the foot of the Washington Monument.

Saturday, August 2, 1997
What day is it? I'm losing all track of time. Damn. *Slam*. Close to done.

We've been lucky, and the luck is holding. *Slam* wanted to be born. It has a life of its own now.

We've been allowed back into the jail to shoot one more time in the yard. Today is different. The yard is full of all kinds of people. The place is bristling with tension and I stick close to the equipment, sitting right on it. The camera is set up and a basketball is fired out of nowhere at the lens. Tony deflects it. The feeling is not friendly. Guards and convicts alike are losing patience with our presence.

The people we have teamed up with in here are still on our side but the rest are about to get nasty. Some goofy-looking shirtless white guy covered with tattoos and kinky muscles starts doing a twisted little grind dance in the middle of the yard, pointing at the female guards watching him from the door. They howl with laughter, double over, and he keeps humping the air in their direction and smiling.

The warden shows up, lets us know we have exactly one hour to get our shot and get the hell out. Wrap it; you've worn out your welcome. This is the big take, Ray's moment of truth, the key to the film. I thought we got it yesterday, but it turns out we didn't, not the master shot, anyway. The yard is tense, full of movement, explosive. There are bad intentions floating around. It's a whole different mood from the day before. Too many people to keep track of, too many pissed-off prisoners, invisible signals.

We set up and Saul goes for it, fueled by real fear, an actor's secret dream. This time he is on another level, beyond performance, into the realm of survival. Ray is delivering a message as he simultaneously offers and saves his own life. The lines of his poem change to include everyone, even those who mean him harm. It's no longer "stealing *me* was the smartest thing *you* ever did." Now it's "stealing *us* was the smartest thing *they* ever did."

The hour is up. It's time to pack up and leave the jail. We got the shot. Everyone feels like Hopha, who can only shake his head and say, "That shit made me forget what I was thinking."

Out of jail at last. It really feels as though we have been liberated. There is more to do elsewhere; the day rolls along. We grab pickup shots as we head for the big love scene between Saul and Sonja.

Dom seems to be going, or is already gone. He was unable to deal with the lack of structure, and he was offended by the lack of on-camera time he got.

Bonz is still a study in cool focus. Nodding sagely, he repeats his mantra, "Everything is going exactly as planned."

The love scene is set up in the same house where we shot the party. Henri designs the bedroom that will be Lauren's. She gives her input and makes some changes.

Benjamin wants to use some kind of floating-arm piece of equipment to fly the camera over the naked bodies. Marc doesn't think it's important.

Saul and Sonja find their way in rehearsals. All of us outside on the back patio are listening to them on the Comtek mic-headphones. Inside, it's a semiclosed set, but outside I'm having an audio soft-core experience. I can hear every whisper, every wet kiss and brush of skin as if I were right there. Very strange.

I hand my headphones off to someone else, who puts them on and smiles. The scene is taking some time to come together. Listening to the actors trying to improv dialogue on their way into physical contact is painful at times. They are a little nervous.

Slowly but surely they get into it and I take the headphones off again when I hear the real thing. Gotta give them some kind of privacy. Henri is still wearing his headphones. He nods at me with his Cheshire cat grin and gives me two thumbs up.

I see the kid looking through the hole in the fence again. All he sees is grown men standing around wearing headphones and smiling.

Tonight's production meeting is out of control. No going back, no getting off this ride.

Richard's wife, Kim Wozencraft, and their two boys, Max and Dash, arrived yesterday. Kim is at the production meeting in mission control. Looking at the expression on her face, I realize our energy is insane. Those of us here from the start can't see it anymore.

Bonz holds up a hand to speak. "Anyplace where the mayor, who is down with us, loses his power, and we're here doin' something like this? It's time to get the fuck up out of Dodge City."

Everyone laughs, roars, passes more doobs and cold Heinekens.

Benjamin has Henri's ear over on the couch, selling him on the idea of wild shots in the jail that the film must have.

"I need the kitchen, with steam, vats of soup or something, cauldrons with big, ya know... spoons."

Everyone is wild with the possibilities facing us. It's exciting to be here, to capture this on film. But it also means coming face to face with a depressing, disturbing reality.

Sunday, August 3, 1997
Morale remains high, with only a few complaints about craft services.

In keeping with the chronological order of the shoot, it is time to film the morning after with Saul and Sonja. Here they are at an outdoor market buying funky souvenirs, watching kids playing homemade drums on the sidewalk, walking together down tree-lined D.C. streets.

We end up back in the dirt alley behind the party house after searching for a location in parks all over the city. We need a quiet spot for Saul and Sonja to have their big confrontation.

I am waiting out of sight down another, even smaller alley around the corner from where they are shooting. First, I park and secure the Windstar. Then I find my own horrific drama in the alley, far from the camera. A Siamese cat covered in dust writhes around on the ground shuddering, clawing at the dirt, its head stuck or hiding under a rotten overstuffed chair.

Suddenly, the cat jerks its head out from under the chair and gasps for air. Its eyes are rolling in its head and sounds are coming out of its open panting mouth, horrible cries of agony and fear. It pisses itself, and contorts, shivers and shakes as if it were being given high-voltage shocks.

The alley reeks of human waste, the heat is oppressive and the sky is turning yellow and gray. John Sims, the gaffer, grew up on a farm and he thinks we should kill the cat. He looks for something heavy to drop on the cat's head.

Tony comes running around the corner for more film. He looks at the cat and shrugs. "Cats die in back alleys," he says and runs back to the set.

This cat isn't just dying. This cat is possessed by ten tortured devils. I can't take my eyes off it. It's in the throes of death but it won't die. Every time it spasms we are sure it is going to croak, but it doesn't. The most disturbing thing is that every few minutes the cat has a few seconds of peace. It lies there stunned, begins to calm down and then it is run through again with torment.

My ankles start to itch from some invisible bug bite and suddenly the cat sees me and lurches toward me, only to fall again, eyes wide open, filled with terror and confusion. It shudders and twists into impossible positions.

I jump back and scratch at my ankles. I imagine the bite is infecting me with whatever the cat has. I get some water and approach the animal. Its mouth is wide open and I pour a few drops onto the tongue and around the mouth. This sends the cat over the edge. The few drops of water may as well be boiling acid, holy water on a vampire. I imagine what hell the cat would cross over into, how it would tear itself to pieces if it started to rain right now.

Sims has found half a cinder block, but Kirby is here now and he insists on calling the ASPCA. He runs off and borrows someone's cell phone.

Sims drops the block in the weeds and gives up on his mercy killing mission. Benjamin comes around the corner and I immediately tell him he has got to shoot the cat, get it on film. He is mildly interested, mostly just grossed out. Marc won't even look at it. Richard seems drawn to it and strangely fascinated, as I am. Everyone has a very specific and telling response to the cat's suffering. I end up alone, still transfixed.

Down the alley, the scene sounds real. I hear Sonja screaming her story at Saul, from her gut, like a painful birth. I swear the cat will die now, at this moment, with the wailing of a woman filling its ears. But the animal holds on. Does the cat need pouring rain to finally let go? Will it only die in silence, at the end of the scene? Its struggle is pure, the animal programmed to stay alive. I feel dizzy. I need a break.

I walk back up the alley to the street where the Windstar is parked. The sky is heavy now with rain and it seems only a matter of minutes before it opens up.

An animal rescue truck pulls up. I walk over and look inside at the rows of cages. There is a dog in there whose head looks like it got chewed on by a giant pit bull. I see various other cats and dogs, all in bad shape.

The animal guy is in a hurry so I show him to the cat. He has on heavy-duty gloves to his elbows. Without hesitation he walks to the cat, picks it up and takes it to his truck. He gives the animal a shot and it passes out. He tells me it has distemper and won't make it. He is a gentle guy who seems to feel bad for the animals he is trying to help. He tells me he is the only guy in D.C. who does this. A one-man department with dwindling funds.

I go and guard the entrance to the alley. A kid comes up on a bike and asks me what's happening. I tell him they are filming a movie in the alley and I'd appreciate it if he could go around.

"Fuck that. I'm gonna be in that shit," he says and rides by me down the alley right in the middle of the big drama take between Saul and Sonja.

My one attempt at security and I blow it. The kid rides right through the shot and the camera keeps rolling. Marc calls it the homage to De Sica's *The Bicycle Thief* shot.

A few minutes later, I call down the alley to give a rain warning, but everyone is already packing up to go. We all pile into the vehicles and roll up the windows.

The rain starts, a couple of fat drops at first, then sheets, buckets, cats and dogs. It washes away our footprints back there in the dirt alley. It washes away any sign of an animal's suffering. There is no trace of us. The only proof of our presence is the film, alive and well in the Windstar, headed back to the hotel.

Monday, August 4, 1997
Today we leave town. Time to get out of Dodge City. All except Henri, who has to stay on as a hostage because the money is still not in the bank for the film nor the huge hotel bill. He will make it happen, somehow; juggling, smoke and mirrors, balls and willpower.

I drive Saul and Sonja back to NYC, with Helen riding shotgun. Saul and Sonja are giddy and intense. There is not much talk about what has just taken place, not with me anyway. They are high on Marc, high on *Slam*, with just enough doubt—like hot sauce sprinkled on top—to make them wonder what the hell they just participated in.

I drop Sonja off first, and her daughters greet her, full of love. Saul gets out and says good–bye, as distant and serene as ever.

Coda

A few weeks later, I get the call that we are going back down to Washington for some pickup shots of Saul. This time we fly and rent a Windstar at the airport.

The peak of these two days, the last shot of the film, takes place on our final night in D.C. We need the final shot of Saul walking to the Monument, putting his hands against the bars of the gate and looking straight up.

The first time I try to pull over in front of the Monument, a cop comes and tells us to move on. We go back immediately and the crew runs up to grab the shots. I stand below with the rental Windstar, certain the cops will be back.

They never come. I stand there and stare up at the monstrous spire with the two red lights blinking on top like tiny evil eyes. We could strap a thousand pounds of explosives to the Washington Monument, blow it to the moon, and nobody would be here to stop us. Instead, we get the shot, like all the others before. Nobody fucks with us.

When the crew comes back to the vehicles, we break out some cold beers and stand around drinking, there below the Monument, like teenagers in a parking lot.

We are a gang, on a job, and so far we pulled it off. We stole a film in the nation's capital. And I drove the getaway car.

BEAU SIA

John Kirby

K nown primarily for his B-Boy style, Beau Sia hopes to instigate revolution with his debut album *Attack! Attack! GO!* on Mouth Almighty/Mercury Records. He graduated from NYU with a BFA in screenwriting in May 1998. When asked what else he would put in a bio besides his astounding IQ (a whopping 713!), Dr. Sia replied, "Everything that we know now about the laws of physics will be disproved in another twenty-three years. No one is alone. Young, sexy girls, I am here for you. I love you, mom and dad, thank you." Now, it would be silly for Dr. Sia to continue listing all of his great accomplishments or to predict any future accomplishments, so just rest assured that Beau Sia can run the 100-yard dash in 9.5 seconds; Beau Sia knows that without love everything is futile; Beau Sia really invented the microscope.

P.S. Teach a kid how to read.

THE HORSE COCK MANIFESTO

There's a rumor going around
that Asian men
are hung like horses!

I don't know who would think to say such things,
who would want to say such things,
who would sit around and say,
"What can I do now
to tarnish the names of Asians everywhere?"
blurting out the obvious
in such a crude manner.

But some menace, villain, nemesis, enemy, threat
to the Asian community as I know it,
has spread the rumor that

"Asian men are hung like horses!"

and I hate the idea of the fact,
as the word has spread farther than I can control.
My lies seem to be of no use
as I am continually disproved,
and I cannot stop them,
a flood of people going east to Asia,
fucking around the clock with Asian men!

There are women in Sweden
who are crying over their blond-haired,
disastrously blue-eyed beaus' minuscule proportions,

and there are teenage girls in Africa, disgusted
at the lack of feeling
between the legs
when warrior men give them their best,

and there are southern belles gasping for something
more

than the triteness
of redneck penetration,

and this has ruined the ecological, sociological, sexological
breeding patterns of the whole world,
as some nitwit has let out that

"Asian men are hung like horses!"

I don't know why these things happen,
as someone had to reveal that we are great with laundry
and convenience stores,
and someone else let loose how we all know martial arts,
and just recently I found out that everyone knows how
goddamned good at math
we are,
but now
I face the most humiliating release of our culture,
as the woman who has sworn vendetta on us has
claimed that

"Asian men are hung like horses!"

it ends up that I can't take this anymore.
I can't live like this anymore,
with sex five times a day
sex eighteen hours a day,
sex every day,
sex in every fashion known to man this side of the
kama sutra,
all because there is some one-woman organization
dedicated
to spreading the rumor that

"Asian men are hung like horses!"

and I don't want to hear it,
because the pager is beeping off the hook,
and the messages keep piling up,

and the anonymous notes I keep finding
in my coat pockets are getting to be more than these
literary eyes can stand,

and it is always so uncaring,
as it is name, number, place, time

no list of hobbies, interests, or favorite colors.

And this is the marked men that we Asians have become
as the demand increases and we decrease,
no longer able to take the abuse,
phalli rubbed too raw for description.

And now we face the sword proudly
as we do not like it to be known,
that thing.
that horrid thing,
that thing some vindictive whore
must have said at a really big party,
very loudly,

"Asian men are hung like horses!"

I don't know how to act around people anymore,
as eyes glare at my Gap khakis,
and I now fear the day that someone
starts spreading the rumor that

"Asian men are hung like horses!"

because I don't know how we'll go unnoticed again.

I WAS JIMMY HUANG

I was Jimmy Huang. That guy on the screen: That was me on the inside. *Slam* saved my life. I was born into a world of middle-class, suburban privilege—above the law and oblivious to anyone who wasn't. A kid who didn't have to answer to anyone because of who he thought he was in the greater scheme of things. When I saw myself screaming, "Do you know who my dad is?!" on screen, I felt like I was saying, "I'm not black, I'm not poor, so why am I here?" I didn't want to be the only Chinese guy in a jail full of black people. They were all real prisoners. The D.C. Jail made me physically ill. I had never been inside a prison. I spent my entire shooting day fighting throwing up. It didn't become clear to me that the prisoners were real people until after I left the jail.

Saul and Sonja usually spent time together after shooting, preparing for the next scene, so I was often alone in the hotel room, thinking. I would just write in my journal all of the things I had seen and been a part of during each day. There are entries about prisoners telling me how they were going to fuck me, and there are guards' stories about everyone shanking each other, but that's not what I kept writing about. I kept writing about how sad it was to see kids, actual kids, in a jail cell looking at 75-to-life. I wrote about playing basketball with Pretty Tony and Jerome. I wrote about Pretty Tony's expression in the van when he actually got to see people in the real world, especially women. I couldn't stop writing about lying in bed at night and still feeling the shackles I had to wear in the van, and thinking that I was just an actor who could walk away from it at any time, but Pretty Tony, Reds, Joe, Jerome, China and all of them had to live it day in and day out. And what's horrifying isn't the shackles, the food, the Code Blues, or anything like that. What's horrifying is the acceptance of it all. The conditioned nature of the prisoners and the rare moment, joking with Saul, when I caught some kind of fire in their eyes. A little scream that they want to and can be something more. That they can be people and be treated as people—as human beings.

I still have parts of me that I need to work out in this life, moments of prejudice and ignorance, but if it wasn't for my work in *Slam* I would've carried Jimmy Huang back with me to New York. I never knew how fucked up government was until I was placed in the situation I thought I would never have to face. If you think prison is soft and that anyone who's thrown in jail deserves to be there, then you don't know what it's like to be healthy, alive, and left for dead.

ORIGINAL JIMMY HUANG
VAN MONOLOGUE

Lack of control. Do you have a girlfriend? Of course you do. My father has many—white chicks dig my dad. My brother is half-white. The stepmom who made him promised me a girlfriend in the form of a cousin. She said she looked like an angel, but I never knew angels could be so ugly. This world is ugly. Money makes the world go round. My father says money and power gauges success and that everything else is just chance. I personally believe in fate. Reagan believed in fate. That was something we had in common. I thought that was enough.... Where I come from you rationalize everything—even love and especially murder.... Have you ever been yachting? The way this mass of dead metal just lies there in the middle of everything blue and misunderstood by man. No matter how much you try, you can't get some things out of your head. You don't confront them and they stick there forever. Brushing something under never works. Obviously, but who am I to know? I thought everyone brushed things under and that was how the present became the past. But the past remains always and the resolution of it is how you finally create that dull feeling of time. Otherwise you're haunted with memories that shouldn't be there like brown hair gone bad and big lips made blue with choking. I mean, how am I supposed to sleep, fuck hookers or run amok if all I have in my brain is a picture that will never die of a girl that died because the educational system in this country sucks. Where's a fucking moral structure when you need one? Ha! I'd like to find out who's gonna keep this little thing quiet. Shake his hand and say, "Thank you." Damn, I miss Italy. Do you miss Italy?

BOB HOLMAN

Peter C. Cook

BOB HOLMAN KICKS THE HISTORY OF SLAMS

Dateline: Athens, MCCXII BC

THE FIRST POETRY SLAM :
Marsyas vs. Apollo.

> *The man picks up flute, plays, but does not know*
> *Athena invented it an oboe*
> *Apollo's lyre twangs back fervor*
> *Marsy spits a reed-word curver*
> *Boss God antics pick and droll*
> *Shakes of Olympus! dance crowd's soul!*
> *Human vs. God, Music vs. Po*
> *The winner only Judge Goldy Midas know*
> *"Don't give a damn!*
> *   Close the book—SLAM!"*
> *'Pollo reaches down*
> *   Will hand off his crown!*
> *The joke's the dream!*
> *Vice is verse-a, Marsyas' butt-a scheme*
> *Midas's ears turn into an ass's*
> *Marsyas decides to invent sunglasses*
> *Better to see the Muses huddle*
> *Suck up to the King, a cloying cuddle*

Changing the scores, inverse decision
Separate "co" from "laboration"
Add competition to the play!
Tie Marsyas to a tree—flay away!
This subject becomes favorite, "Suffer for art"
Find it in the Forum, learn it by the heart
Corrupting power builds own image
Poetry escapes for a new pilgrimage

Flash Forward! Tokyo, 905 A.D.:
Excitement banners and a rushing hush today as Ono no Komachi (Left Team) and Shikishi Naishinno (Right Team) squared off (*rounded off,* my Lover giggled) in Round One of the *Uta-awase* (Slam). Komachi, Most Famous, must have place of honor. Her poem caused blushes and sighs and I saw a pear blossom fall—up!

First fall
asleep
to make him come
Must I dream
to bring him home?

[Reader, please write score here: _____]

Next, Shikishi, daughter of Emperor Goshirakawa, delved into act of memory, conjuring:

To forget
what only you and I know
when you are gone
the months pass
the years.

This sweet fuzzball of mental gymnastics made my Love swoon[1]

[Reader, please write score here: _____]

---

[1](Entries based on the competitive anthologies of women court poets in Japan, 905–1314. Further reading: *The Thirty-six Immortal Women Poets,* translated/edited by Andrew J. Pekarik, Braziller: NY, 1991.)

Flash Way Forward!
July 20, 1986
Marc Smith, construction worker, poet, working with a guerrilla gang of
performing poets, needs to come up with another "act" and tries a competi-
tive reading he calls the Slam. At the Get Me High, a dingy soulful boite on
Chicago's North Side, Slam arrives, kicking and screaming, full of Contra
Verse. Soon thereafter the troupe and Slam troop over to the Green Mill,
where to this day Sunday nights are devoted to the brawling art of Poetry
Slam, the Greatest Po Show on Earth.

The Slam Migrates to the Nuyorican Poets Café (1987–89):

August 20, 1988
The idea of opening a poetry café had been snipping my braincells till I
couldn't think. It was at Miky Piñero's wake in '88 that I approached Miguel
Algarín, who'd founded the Nuyorican Poets Café with Piñero and Lucky
Cienfuegos in 1974, with the idea. The next day, Roland Legiardi-Laura,
Miguel and I started the work of reopening the Café .

September 5, 1987
A year earlier I had read in *The New York Times* about a poetry phenomenon in Chicago. This was the first I'd heard of the Slam, of founder Marc
Smith and of the Green Mill, where Slam took root. The *Times* piece excited me—understand, at this point any piece about poetry was amazing. Not
yet Extinct, most certainly Endangered, the Art of Words was a footnote in a
painted-in corner, hungering to be an asterisk. This Slam thing harmonized
with my feelings, my vision for a new café: There was something fresh as
rock 'n' roll, something funny and simultaneously in-your-face raucous. Art
sans pretense, poetry that could play with the elitist idea of itself. Slam res-
onated with the multiform poetics I'd strived for while working at the St.
Marks Poetry Project and NYC Poetry Calendar in the '70s and '80s, the
performance-based aesthetics I'd found at the Nuyorican Poets Café and at
the Poets Theater Festivals I produced at St. Marks and La Mama, and the
full-blown audience interactivity (hecklers wanted!) that Pedro Pietri and I
had made the dominant theme of our "Double Talk Show" and the roving
reading-celebration of the oral tradition we called "Poets in the Bars."
Understand that at this point in time there was no network of poets outside
the academic circuit, and even at the home turfs of alternative literary cen-

ters such as St. Marks, Beyond Baroque and the Detroit Institute of Art and Intersection, there was little notion of spoken word and performance.

I was hooked by Slam. In September of '87, my wife Elizabeth had a speaking engagement in Chicago and the whole family went. I was there on a Sunday night, and made the pilgrimage to the Green Mill. The host, in a tux, did a great job. A poet erupted from the bar at one point—was this all part of the performance? A great night, some great poetry. And it wasn't until years later, one caffeinated morning at the Busy Bee, that Marc Smith would tell me of the crisis that stuck him in the hospital that night in '87, kept him from being at the Mill, and changed his life totally.

My life was also changed that night. Having seen a Slam, I knew even more clearly this was the programming I could bring to a new café. It would haul in a bunch of poets, provide heckler grist. It would be the collision of art and entertainment. I wanted to ride this bronco, to pull poetry through the lasso to freedom. It was cheap. Fun. And pricked the ear for poetry. Audiences would hear a variety of poets, would be tuning their ears to the poetry they liked, would be judging the judges. Slam!

By this time if you don't know what a Slam is, your name must be Ray Joshua and you must be a poet from another planet. But just in case you ARE, please follow this Footnote Trail![2]

---

[2] Footnote to the Future: OK, what is a Slam, anyhow? The mock Olympics of Poetry, the Poetry Slam provides access to poetry for those who learned in school that poems are impenetrable word clots requiring a master's degree to comprehend but still felt there was a magic in language. Some could even be found sneaking into the closet with a flashlight, jotting lines that didn't come close to the edge of the page.

I loved poetry when I was growing up, but the idea that I would ever meet a poet, let alone become one, never entered the picture. When the Beats appeared in *Life* magazine, when Maynard G. Krebs appeared on *Dobie Gillis*, the idea of becoming a beatnik was appealing. I was already writing poems; now I started writing Beat Poems: "Onion Soup" went like this: "Onion soup/Onion soup/Onion soup." My mother sewed strands of black yarn onto a plaid hot-rod cap; when I was a hippie my own hair would flow down below my shoulders. The idea was to be Beat, cool and opposed to the hypocrisies of bourgeois U.S. Midwest life. But my burr haircut and Midwest uptighty kept me under lock and key. Slams do not promulgate a lifestyle or detailed political agen-

Slammin' the Nights Away (1989-96):

Halloween, 1989
Nuyorican Poets Café reopens after a seven year hiatus with Slams every Friday at 10 followed by an Open Room and a Sunrise Slam with scrambled poems threatened after that. For the next seven years, I would be volunteer Slam Host from 10 p.m. to 4 a.m. Fridays, and sometimes we went to Chinatown (Wo Hop, of course) after that.

November 3, 1989
First Café slam winner is Jim Brodey (*The Heart of the Breath*, Hard Press), who crashed at the Café when Tompkins Square becomes too unfriendly. Nina Zivancevic, Tamra Plotnick and John Ferris are his co-po's.

November 10, 1989
Slammers are Paul Beatty, Tito Lespier, Barb Barg and Lee Ann Brown. Steve Cannon is a judge, and takes up his reign as the Only Paid Heckler in New York. The Professor gives each and every poem a one, because poetry is Number 1. Paul Beatty wins, too, although his performance is antiperformance. Paul's poems become a launch pad, help lift poetry and the Café into orbit.

November 24, 1989
I have a reading in New Jersey, so Miguel takes over as host. Raoul Santiago-Sebazco becomes so disenchanted with his score that he condemns the whole enterprise in a flowing Spanglish aria and vanishes. Miguel raises his eyes to the heavens, begging for Bob to return to this madhouse.

---

da. What you learn from Slam as form you could learn from that apocryphal scene at the beginning of *Dead Poets Society* where Robin Williams begins his poetry class by attempting to graph a poem's greatness with form across the bottom and content down the side and, when the class is thoroughly flummoxed, lets them in on the secret that poems must not mean but be, as Archibald MacLeish said, and has the students rip the introduction advocating the rate-a-poem system from their textbooks.

Slam wants to rip the poetry rating system from the hands of the university-trained experts and hand it out ad lib at Slams to whoever walks through the door, to return poetry to people's daily lives by doing the impossible, which is always poetry's job: realizing the imagination. To liberate words from the dictionary and have them breathe in readers' minds. Who wants to go to a poetry reading and watch someone hide behind a podium, a tome, mutter words that barely make it past the lips?

There's a lot of air between the lips and ear, and the young poets who hang out at Slams want to fill space with language, entertainment, thought and love.

December 15, 1989

Low point of Slam. No heat, grand total of nine winter coats huddled in attendance, Slammers have to score themselves. At this reading I premiered my Slam DisClaimer, which would serve as the Invocation for all Slams for years to come, and forever after let it be known that The Best Poet Always Loses:

We begin each SLAM! with a Disclaimer:

As Dr. Willie used to say,
We are gathered here today
because we are not gathered
somewhere else today, and
we don't know what we're doing
so you do—the Purpose of SLAM!
being to fill your hungry ears
with Nutritious Sound/Meaning Constructs,
Space Shots into Consciousness
known hereafter as Poems, and
not to provide a Last Toehold
for Dying Free Enterprise Fuck'em
for a Buck'em Capitalism'em. We disdain
competition and its ally war
and are fighting for our lives
and the spinning
of poetry's cocoon of action
in your dailiness. We refuse
to meld the contradictions but
will always walk the razor
for your love. "The best poet
always loses" is no truism of SLAM!
but is something for you
to take home with you like an image
of a giant condor leering over
a salty rock. Yes, we must destroy
ourselves in the constant
reformation that is this very moment,
and propel you to write the poems
as the poets read them, urge you
to rate the judges as they trudge

to their solitary and lonely numbers,
and bid you dance or die between sets.[3]

Bob Holman, Host

March 23, 1990—First-Ever Grand Slam:
Paul Beatty wins in a jampacked café full of hopes and poems, dreams and
streets. Eryn Trudell, Denise Bell, Anya Achtenberg and Bruce Isaacson must
bow to Paul, who awkwardly dons a crown and faux fur cape by artist
Orlando Lobelo. We never try that again. Paul's prize is a book. His own
book. An edition of *Big Bank Takes Little Bank*, designed by Mike Tyler, published by the Nuyorican Poets Café Press imprint, paid for by me with a
poetry grant I received from the New York Foundation for the Arts. Paul will
represent New York at the first-ever National Poetry Slam in San Francisco in
April 1990. He will travel cross-country to read two poems, and lose.

Grand Slam Champs from the Nuyorican Poets Café:
1990–96
1990 Paul Beatty
1991 Willie Perdomo
1991 Reg E Gaines
1992 Dana Bryant
1992 Tracie Morris
1993 Peter Spiro
1993 Regie Cabico
1994 Tish Benson
1995 Xavier Cavazos
1996 Saul Williams

---

[3] DisClaimer can be found in *ALOUD! Voices from the Nuyorican Poets Café*, edited by Miguel
Algarin and Bob Holman, and in Bob Holman's *The Collect Call of the Wild*, both published by
Henry Holt, with thanks to Jack Macrae and Kim Witherspoon.

The arc originating at the Café's first slam on November 3 of 1989 and concluding with the triumph of Saul Williams/Ray Joshua in 1996, defines a perfect seven-year cycle. Not only did the total number of poetry readings in the country increase dramatically during this period, but the percentage of nonacademic readings soared and, indeed, became predominant.[4] Groups like Dark Star, the Pussy Poets and the Green Card Poets became popular; collaborative poems were common. Sonja Sohn, one of the Green Card Poets, stunned audiences with her poem "The Player," and steadfastly refused to Slam. Sonja could electrify the house like nobody else, but said she had other work in mind. She wanted to be in film....

The Grand Slam champs were more than winning Slammers—they were great poets, too. Beatty parlayed his first book into a second from Penguin, and a first novel from Knopf. Perdomo published his first book of poems with Norton, the cream of the academic publishers, and tipped in with a CD, bringing text and spoken word together in a revolutionary manner. Reg E Gaines went on to release two CDs on Mercury Records and to write the book for the Tony Award–winning Broadway play, *Bring in da Noise, Bring in da Funk*. Dana Bryant toured the world with the band/moveable musical feast Giant Step; released her album, *Wishin' from the Top*, on Warner Brothers; published her book, *Song of the Siren*, with Boulevard Books. Tracie Morris can be seen in *The United States of Poetry*, and wrote the book for the Ralph Lemon dance piece *Geography*, presented at the Brooklyn Academy of Music. She has been hosting the Performance Series at the St. Marks Poetry Project. Peter Spiro is also in *The United States of Poetry*, and his plays were produced at the Nuyorican and other venues. He continues to teach poetry in Brooklyn. Regie Cabico was national winner of the MTV/Lollapalooza Slam and on the 1998 National Slam Championship Mouth Almighty team. He cofounded the Poets Theatre at the Asian American Writers Workshop, and published his book, *I Saw Your Ex-Lover Behind the Starbucks Counter*, with Anne Elliott's Big Fat Press (Anne being another slammin' poet). Tish Benson has produced her one-woman show,

---

[4] Mirroring my own work that had occurred within this seven-year arc: producing, with Josh Blum, *Words in Your Face* for PBS (Mark Pellington directing); editing *ALOUD! Voices from the Nuyorican Poets Café* (Henry Holt) with Miguel Algarin; creating Nuyorican Poets Café Live Touring Company, which evolved into Washington Square Arts (thanks to Jessica Baker and Robby Fahey); seeing *The Collect Call of the Wild*, my book of collected and new poems, published, also by Holt; *The United States of Poetry* PBS/ITVS series with Josh Blum and Mark Pellington; NuYo and Mouth Almighty Records with Bill Adler and Sekou Sundiata; and my own CD, *In With the Out Crowd* (Hal Willner, producer).

Three Bean Stew, and toured extensively. Xavier Cavazos visited Thailand as an Official Poet and now tattoos poems directly on flesh. Which brings us to...

April 23, 1996
It's Grand Slam #10! and who should wander in but my dear buddo, Marc Levin, and his luvverly wife Ellin. We are old pals, having met as CETA artists back in '77. CETA! The largest federally funded artists project since the WPA, a grand experiment that, at least for Marc and Ellin and me, and Pedro and Roland too, and Kenneth King and Ed Friedman and so many others, set us off on Lives as Artists in the Public Sphere. But, back to the Café the fateful night when Saul Williams bested Jessica Care Moore, Beau Sia, Mums da Schemer, Carmen René, Jamal St. John, Ercuement Aytac (who qualified by being the National Slam Champ of Austria), with an introductory poem by Jaap Blonk, the great Dutch sound poet. Williams had been an astonishing presence at the Café , the beginnings of the NEXT Generation, which would settle in at the Brooklyn Moon, releasing the great CD *Eargasms*. Taylor Mali was keeping score. Bonz Malone, who had been my cohost at many of the rAP mEETS pOETRY events that Bill Adler and I put on at Fez and S.O.B.'s, was there. In fact, this sensational night was a live mirror refracting the outraged reality you'll find in the movie *Slam*, rashomonized by the prismatic disjunctures that would lead to the human, and therefore seemingly inevitable and painful, dissolution of The Scene, and its consequent growth. Saul Williams, Jessica Care Moore, Beau Sia and Mums da Schemer would represent the Café and New York at the National Slam in Portland, Oregon.

---

[5] Among the many non-champs who must get a bio in a footnote: Steve Cannon, the Only Paid Heckler in New York, whose Gathering of the Tribes Gallery and magazine was the ancillary antidote to the Café. Edwin Torres, NuyoFuturisto, whose CD, *Holy Kid* from Kill Rock Stars (producer Jordy Trachtenberg) is the real *auténtico*. Mike Tyler, who conceptualized the scene and published two of his own books in the process, *From Alabama to California*, from Art Cannot Be Damaged Press (A Share Book—if you want to keep it send him $20; if not, leave it somewhere); and *From Colorado To Georgia*, published by the Carlton Arms Hotel, where Mike is poet in residence. Everton Sylvester, lead dub poet for the Brooklyn Funk Essentials, represented in *The United States of Poetry*. Dael Orlandersmith, whose one-poet shows *Monster* and *Beauty's Daughter* have both played Off Broadway and toured nationally. And Hal Sirowitz, the Jewyorican, another poet in *The United States of Poetry*, whose book *Mother Said* (Crown) was the best-selling poetry book of 1997.

End Game? or, Next Step in Evolutionary Consciousness?

Imagine a world where we speak poetry.

Ray Joshua lives there, and the touch of his voice enlightens. Lauren Bell understands the pain of the force needed to wrench us out of our human shells into the next step in the evolution of consciousness. Jimmy Huang lives there too, but he lives there alone, a brutal loneliness. Hopha is all process—he intuits that Joshua can lead us to Poetopia, but the smoke that rises from the flesh of the beast is thick indeed and Hopha, don't forget, has all the cigars.

Slam is a raw poem of a movie. Overcoming impossible odds, handing in a three-hour rough assembly three weeks late at Sundance and then not only getting accepted into competition but winning the Grand Jury Prize—this is the stuff of dreams, of poetry. Indeed, the cast is all poets. At Sundance, they gave poetry readings after screenings to audiences in tears after seeing the hard-hitting film. At one reading, Ally Sheedy bowed in awe to their word power. The multiculti cast and their linguistic skills gave Sundance a whole new basis, and the result: *Slam* and its poets will play in your local theater, the soundtrack is full of famies, and this book rests in your hands' eye.

Poetry? What's going on here?

As a poet, I'm often asked to explain the phenomenon of poetry's increasing popularization. Actually, I'm not asked "Why now?" so much anymore—the current rise in poetry's status is generally accepted as beginning with MTV's *Spoken Word: Unplugged* shows in 1992 and '94 (although those programs were more like "Poetry Plugged" than Un-). Actually, the reopening of the Nuyorican Poets Café is a more potent benchmark—or Marc Smith's first Poetry Slam at the Green Mill. But why stop there? Take a time-traveling trip to Tokyo, 905 A.D., or twist the dial further into the past to the First Poetry Slam Ever where the human Marsyas challenged Apollo.[6]

Because to begin the movement as the press defines it is to accept the self-fulfilling prophesy of performance poetry as fad; to reveal the origins of the art is to comprehend its vitality and strength. The poetry movie *love jones*,

---

[6] Thanks to David Lehman for this insight.

and now *Slam*, the advent of spoken-word record labels like Kill Rock Stars and Mouth Almighty/Mercury (where I work), are signs poetry is moving beyond the hype of MTV into a central spot in the culture. Like Superman molecularizing through a lead wall, Poetry is inexorably easing out of its academic corner and into the heart of the country.

(Here, Poet as Critic Steps to Plate!)
Slam's victory at Sundance marks a critical move for the art. Poetry's value is completely tied to its integrity, and in *Slam* it is the poem that defines the terms. Saul Williams and Sonja Sohn, the star-crossed fiery loves at the center of this story, are both seasoned poets in the New York spoken-word world, as are fellow members of the ensemble Beau Sia, Bonz Malone, Liza Jesse Peterson, Taylor Mali and I (I appear at the end of the movie in my traditional role of host at an *actual* poetry slam). Washington's DJ Renegade, New York's Jessica Care Moore and Beans, and New Orleans's John Sinclair all put in cameos. All of the poems you hear are the writings of the poets themselves. Indeed, all the words in the movie are the poets' own: This movie was completely improvised.

Imagine a universe of wordslinger gangs and verbal assault squads and you get a flavor of the heat that the language in *Slam* contains. We've got ourselves a Richter 10 here: The poem that Ray Joshua (Saul Williams) uses to quell a jailhouse gang battle is his own; that's Saul Williams' soul speaking. The passionate struggle of Lauren Bell (Sonja Sohn) to keep her new love grounded while he demands Poetopia Now is of the moment, a poem straight from the heart's mouth.

Slam does not move seamlessly like most movies—it lingers, lurches and leaps breathlessly—more like poetry than film. Levin and crew go for Truth, not Chronology, which sometimes makes for repetitions and odd disjunctions. But the barrage of emotions that this film touches doesn't "make up for these lapses"—rather, it puts you in another universe, where film, like literature, works to move you, not to put polish on sheen. The poets in *Slam* speak a poem through film, they do not sit on a piece of plastic waiting for the pan across a furled eyebrow.

The documentary sensation is undeniable. The walls of verisimilitude come crashing down: In one absolutely extraordinary sequence, Williams jams on a freestyle duet with Bay, a seventeen-year-old convict who will find out within a few weeks whether he is behind bars *for life—in real life.*[7] The unbelievable pain of this poem tilts the whole film into a zone never before reached: We are exploring the inside of a soul here. This is the Realm of the Poem.

Slam is the recipe for a movie for a new millennium. There has never been a movie like it. The pain of the prisoners, the reality of the poetry, the brilliance in this go-for-broke production is that it just starts with changing your life. *Slam* is out to change the world.

---

[7] To find out what's up with Bay and other poets in *Slam*, drop me a line: poetry.guide@miningco.com

LIZA JESSE PETERSON

Donny Brice

Liza Jesse Peterson, actor/poet, poet/actor, graduate of Georgetown University, classically trained at Stella Adler and the National Shakespeare Conservatories for acting, Philadelphia-born Libra-Cancer-Gemini vessel of art, seeker of truth, trumpets information from transmitted inspiration, wrote, bound and illustrated her first book of poetry at age twelve. She continues to write, teach, perform and activate on scaffolds, in classrooms, on TV, in films, on CDs and in book; no telling where she's due to shape-shift next. Currently Liza teaches poetry workshops as a poet-in-residence in New York City public schools. She also teaches fifth and sixth graders at a Brooklyn inner-city afterschool program. Through intense brainstorming and collaboration with her Brooklyn students, she wrote an urban folktale, *The girl who think she all that,* an Urban Angels production. Peace out to her first one-woman show, *Chiron's homegirl healer howls,* and her first collaborative play with three other women, *Supernova,* both due to land in theaters soon.

She loves and misses her mom—big kiss, hope she's proud and smiling!!!

THE MOTHERSHIP

January 1997—Sundance Film Festival
Where do I even begin to begin? So many levels, so many revelations, questions, my mind is moving much faster than my hand. So much joy, excitement, pain, trauma, confusion simultaneously happening, all I could do was hold on to each hour to get me to the next hour to get me through the day to get me to the next day to get me through the week.

Here I am with my peeps, my fam, witnessing a spectacular dream come true right before my eyes and no sooner than we land in Utah and I unpack my bags at the condo, I go to open my mouth to say something and ZIP!! No voice, no fucking voice, only a crackling whisper would emerge. This can't be happening to me, not now: God, ancestors, spirit—this is not the time to take my voice away from me. My voice means everything to me, if this is about some lesson can we get to it after my performance, this pain is next in line to my mother dying, what the fuck are you doing to me? Did I bring this on, is this some cloaked internal sabotage or some higher karmic/cosmic lesson I have to learn?

I couldn't speak, I couldn't be heard like I am used to being heard, but I was determined to perform so I said (in the midst of pain and trauma) fuck it, speak with what you got, and all I had was a deep, deep drag queen doing Grace Jones octave coming out. TRAUMA!!

Ally Sheedy was like a golden kernel on the day when I had just asked the creator why was I here—what was the point? And after this one particular screening and Saul's hypnotizing performance Ally leaped up with intense passion praising the movie, praising Saul and then asked me to please, please perform the ice cream poem. I was so in my sabotage that I thought someone put her up to it to make me feel better since I was feeling so—whatever, ha, ha, ha, ha I was really tripping.

And of course my voice started coming back on the last fucking day! All this juxtaposed to witnessing the magic of a film that is so powerful because of its passion, truth and far-reaching healing power. Every time I watch a screening I get blown away—it's a classic and I'm honored to be a part of it and contribute my vibration to it, and plus my peeps represented and truly kept it real.

Bonz is a trip, I love him, he cracks me up, leave it to him to go snowmobiling with us in a three-piece suit, no coat, sneakers, goggles and a stocking cap and he mowed down three trees!! Hahahah! It was the funniest shit I have ever seen. I laughed so hard I couldn't breathe. Sonja, bless her heart, came over to me and whispered, "Shhh, don't laugh so loud, you know the male ego." That just made me howl even louder—what a blast!

The shit is on, everybody represented and we've only just begun, floodgates are open, my spidey senses tell me.

Oh, how about the night before the award ceremony, I had the most incredible dream. I looked up in the sky and saw three stars shining bright in the formation of a pyramid, I was taken aback because I had never seen a constellation in that formation. The stars got dim and when they got bright again there was another pyramid/triangle formation next to the first one. Both constellations got bright, then dim, bright, then dim until I realized that I was looking at the underbelly of a spacecraft and I yelled, "Oh shit, the Mothership!" and then I woke up. That was a sign.

ALL I REALLY WANTED WAS AN ICE CREAM CONE

Umm, Umm, Umm, Umm, Umm, Umm, Umm, Umm
Ice cream, Ice cream, I want some Ice cream
Umm, Umm, Umm, Umm, Umm, Umm, Umm, Umm
Ice cream, Ice cream, yeah, I used to be an ice cream fiend.
See, it all started when I ordered a large scoop of Rain
Forest Crunch with extra walnuts
"would you like a cup or a cone, miss?"

Cup or cone?
Hmmm? Cup or cone
Cup or cone and now I'm in a zone where I have to
make a wise choice between a cup or a cone.
See it's more fun with a cone
because I lick the tip and crunch and munch the cone
Then I lick the tip again and crunch and munch the cone
'til there's only one sip in the bottom tip of the cone
and then I pop it in my mouth and grin
because I like that game.
But the last time I had a cone in public, men associated
my lick to their dick and said mean things and made
the milk curdle in my gut
So, I stopped ordering cones a long time ago.
Fuck it, I had it in a cup

So I've got my large CUP of Rain Forest Crunch with
extra walnuts dance...
(you know) HEYYY, UMPH UMPH, HOOOO,
UMPH UMPH, HEYYYY, UMPH UMPH,
HOOOO, UMPH UMPH, HEYYY...

"Hey, hey, hey, slim. I'd like to stick my dick in that cup"

The rage welled up
The milk curdled in my cup
As he grabbed his nuts making the hairs on the back of
my neck stand up
I realized I was facing a degenerate beast from hell who
was sent on a kamikaze mission
to ruin my day,
curdle my cream,
and make me have to draw!
So I drew my blade and it cut the roof of my mouth as
it somersaulted out.
YOUR MOTHER SHOULD HAVE ABORTED
YOU AFTER CONCEPTION AND THANK GOD
FOR ABORTION BECAUSE SEEDS LIKE YOU
DON'T DESERVE TO BE NURTURED IN A
WOMB BUT BELONG IN THE BELLY OF A SUR-
GICAL HOOVER AND SAVED AND PRESERVED
FOR AN EIGHTH GRADE FROG DISSECTING
CLASS AND THROWN AROUND THE ROOM
LIKE A FOOD FIGHT AND THROWN UP IN THE
CORNER OF THE CHALK BOARD ROTTING
AND CRUSTIFIED FOR DAYS 'TIL YOU FLAKE
TO THE FLOOR AND THE JANITOR SWEEPS
YOU UP AND AWAY FOREVER FUCK YOU
PUNK!
AND FUCK A CONE!
AND NOW BECAUSE OF YOU FUCK A CUP!
MATTER OF FACT MOTHERFUCK BEN AND
FAGGOT ASS JERRY!

I retreated back to headquarters

breathless from surviving yet another day of battling
the slings and arrows of outrageous motherfuckers in
the street.
Temples throbbing
'Til I spotted a Baskin-Robbins
and yeah, I stopped to contemplate a milkshake in a
paper bag
When all I really wanted
Was an Ice Cream Cone.

JOHN KIRBY

THE POLITICS OF *DRAMA VÉRITÉ*

Fionn Reilly

The slums of Washington, D.C., are hidden in plain sight, fronted by Masonic palaces whose marble veins course greed and deceit. You can't make them out on television; the Networks keep the cameras tight on the cherry trees to soothe citizens stuck to their sets chasing Prozac with Budweiser as their jobs are free-traded south. And while some Americans may suspect that corporations run the world, not many imagine that Rome itself is crumbling.

At dusk the Monument looms, a Klansman's hood rising out of the consume-and-die concrete block projects of D.C., its twin red lights like demonic eyes pulsing the codes for hate and avarice. It is the guardian of the law, sword-arm of the ruling class, held high over the sprawled body of the poor. I can see it plainly now, having broken away from the White House tour.

Have the powerful grown so careless? I had thought the maintenance of legitimacy demanded that at least the Capitol and surrounds be kept looking immaculate, that our elected representatives were image-conscious enough to ensure that the seat of justice was always swept clean of class-war casualties. But there it lies, not a half-mile away from the nation's pinnacle: Simple City. At the entrance to the ghetto, graffiti on a dull brick wall proclaims: *You have now entered the war zone.*

Perhaps America's public officials are secure in the thought that we're too busy watching the game to notice their single-minded service of capital and their criminal neglect of our civic spaces and services. And so here in D.C., while the institutions of government work to make the rich richer than ever (we can report a robust economy), the poor are kept at bay by tuberculosis, dead-end jobs, dope, death and prison.

Into this reality steps *Slam*.

The filmic concept for *Slam* is *drama vérité*, a marriage of the documentary style that Marc, Al and Daphne have developed over the years, with a theatrical thru-line. Each element extends the other: Documentary provides the reality of existing situations and people; dramatic writing and acting offer otherwise unavailable moments of reconstructed truth (lovers in communion, guards on the take, gang kids taking shots to the head). The most remarkable thing this union creates is a democratic, collaborative process that is capable, at its best, of painting the clearest possible picture of the world that film can provide. As in drama therapy, most of our actors are the real thing. And the professionals who've been cast in *Slam* have a deep connection to the world being captured on film. The collaboration between them occurs on the nonset of the ghetto and the prison—genuine life locations as opposed to prefabricated sets. During the filming of *Slam*, real prisoners participating in the movie are asked *How would this happen? What would you do to the new guy?* And they act it out, pulling from their experience. The kids in the projects show us their lives in Southeast through a living medium: our journeyman actor, Saul. A modern-day Odysseus wending his way through the razed landscape of late-capitalist millennial America, Saul becomes among other things a device to draw moments of focused reality from the people on the real-world set and string them like beads onto the thread of the story.

Like a moving epiphanal feast, the presence of the moviemakers in the prison and the ghetto asks of everyone participating: *Why and how are people living like this, in poverty and prison, in estrangement? And what can we do about it?* The truth is in the collected questions and answers of the ensemble. During production, I am continually astounded by the willingness of people who have nothing or have lost almost everything to *represent,* to fill out the arc of the story provided by Marc and Richard with *themselves,* who they are or have been. They are just a few of the frustrated; there are a million stories like theirs right here in the naked capital.

Drama vérité is the cinema of freedom; it is the filmed voice of real people. The characters collaborate on the story of their lives, each adding their individual testimony to the tale. This method, this revolutionary aesthetic, stands in defiant opposition to the top-down storytelling of a single studio screenwriter, to Nielsen-point plot imperatives, to the re-creations of docu-drama and especially to the co-optive corporate categories of edu-tainment and info-tainment. It defies the tendencies of hyperindividualist Hollywood to create *Rambos* out of reality, fantastic tales of the hero against all, isolating the viewer in a "me against the world" mind rut. Real change is made by *groups* of people, as all stories in the lived world are made by the interaction of individuals. *Slam* tells the story of Washington, D.C., in a way that bank-bought studios never could, because it is in their interest to obscure the nature of reality, to tell lies of isolation, to deny the collaborative nature of existing, struggling and winning.

Drama vérité, because of its populist method, automatically stands opposed to hierarchy and rails against structures of class, race and gender. It states that means are ends in and of themselves; it is the intersection of emancipatory method and content, theory and practice. When regular human beings are given, or better yet *take,* democratic control over the unfolding story of their lives, the result—in film as in life—can strike fear into the hearts of those who attempt to rule by obfuscation and force.

Film, most costly of the arts, has for a moment handed over the means of production to real people. Given more such opportunities, *drama vérité* can unite disparate voices, can speak truth to power with alacrity, and can finally reclaim reality from the image-makers who would control it.

Slam
Poets

DJ RENEGADE

DJ Renegade (Joel Dias-Porter) was born and raised in Pittsburgh. Upon his graduation from high school he enlisted in the air force. After leaving the service he became a professional disc jockey in the D.C. area. In 1991 he quit his job and began living in homeless shelters, while undergoing an extensive Afrocentric study program. He also began to write poetry, and to participate in poetry slams. From 1994 to 1997 he competed in the National Poetry Slam, finishing fifth, fourth, third and then second in the individual competition. His work has been published in *Callaloo, Asheville Poetry Review, Red Brick Review, GW Review,* and in the anthologies *Revival: Spoken Word from Lollapalooza, Catch a Fire* and *The Black Rooster Social Inn: Poetry and Art of the Black Rooster Collective,* which he also edited. In 1995 he received the Furious Flower award from James Madison University. He has performed his work on *The Today Show,* in a commercial for Legal Jeans, and in the documentary *Voices Against Violence,* on BET's Teen Summit. Currently at work on a CD of jazz and poetry called *A Desperate Wrestling of Tongues,* he is informally educated, and a member of Writers Corps D.C.

DIMINUENDO IN BLUE

Brothers and Sisters,
Today I'm preaching from chapter 107, verse one
of the royal Blue Book of Ellington.
And on the third day the good Duke
told a story as old as blue-green algae.
How Love is the Devil in a tight blue dress,
eyes flashing like a bluefish,

tongue poisonous as blowfish.
It'll have you at the crossroads,
black as a blueberry,
blue as a Jay,
with all your feathers in disarray.
Don't you know Love will leave you
navy, wavy, baby blue,
sleeping in a doorway on the avenue,
blue as two frost bitten fingers.
Can I get a witness.
Brothers and Sisters,
It will make you melancholy
as a muted trumpet,
bluer than a cloudless sky,
bluer than a Viking's eye.
Love will leave you strangled
with a blue ribbon tangled in your beard.
Can't you see through these shades of blue,
something's stuck to your shoe,
and it ain't money.
There's a blue moon rising,
it's gonna leave you St. Louis Blue,
thin as bamboo,
in a leaky canoe,
with all your bills past due.
Love will leave you
with a Leadbelly,
blind as a Lemon,
yellow as the Sun's House.
Do you hear me
Brothers and Sisters,
Love will torment you
with a blade of bluegrass,
'til you're hot under the blue collar,
a blue chip on your shoulder,
and an indigo joke stuck in your throat.
Please read this whole blue note
and come in out of the blue
gap between clouds,

or you'll be sour as bleu cheese.
Love hurts like a thumbscrew,
lasts like a tattoo,
locks you into a rubber room with a view,
blue devils dancing in your brain,
a blue heron flying through your veins.
Makes you sing the Blues in 12 bars
that overcharge for the same sorry drinks.
Raise a hand if you feel me.
Brothers and Sisters,
Love is a bluebottle fly
flitting between purple and green,
wings raggedy as a pair of old jeans.
Merci beaucoup,
Love is Winnie the Pooh
doing Voodoo in corrective shoes,
it tracks a trailer through your bruised heart
leaving blueprints marked in the snowy part.
Love is salty as cashews,
crooked as corkscrews,
bitchy as a blue crab,
itchy as a new scab,
scientifically proven to lower your IQ,
Love mails all its letters
with the postage due.
Now, let the church say Amen.

SUBTERRANEAN NIGHT-COLORED MAGUS

(3 Moods in the Mode of Miles)

Subterranean means underground
        deep, profound
wasn't Miles one deep brother
        deep as a mine shaft
        decrescendoing to the motherlode
        blue blowing undersongs
Miles on tenor trumpet

ten or eleven levels deeper
than the next cat
painting all up under the canvas
making it bleed All Blues
out the other side
Blowing subterranean solos
underground rhythmic resistance
visual virtuoso
battling musical mafiosos
burrowing under they skin
Miles, son of a dentist doing rootwork
with a hoodoo horn hollering Bebop toasts
He Petey Wheatstraw
Satchmo's son-in-law
a Signifyin Junkie jumping cold turkey
out the Lion's mouth
Shine below the deck of the Titanic
blueing up the boilers
Miles could blue like Bird
freight like Trane
early like Bird
night like Trane
wing like Bird
rail like Trane
Rumbling underground.

Nightcolor is blacker
than a million miles of fresh asphalt
wasn't Miles a deepblack brother
black and fluid as floating smoke
black as the sky round midnight
black as a tire turning for miles ahead
black kettle stewing a Bitch's Brew
so black, he was Kind of Blue
Miles, slick as black ice
cool as snow
sweet as black cherries
On the Downbeat like a blackjack
a black jackhammer

black Jack Johnson
black jack of all trumpeting trades
Miles, Jack of Spades
was our Ace cuz he played
nightcolors
Deepblack, tripleblack
shinyblack,
cinderblack
ashyblack
quarterblack
multi-media-megablack
All shades of Miles
shifting harmonic gears
in his chromatic Ferrari
Blowing Blue Moods
with his black turned
to the audience
speaking coolly
in the colors of night

Magi are priests
spell-wailing wizards
wasn't Miles a deepblackmagic brother
Magus, Magus? ask minders
of the metronome
Miles is secular they say
but we know you spiritual
a soloing sorcerer with E.S.P
Lord have mercy
you Rev. Miles tonally testifyin
from the Book of the Blues
blowing muted magic
as chapter and verse
Making a joyful noise
unto the Lord
or anybody hip enough
to dig the scene
You Magi Miles with crazy styles
even sported a Tutu

Miles, 1.6 sacred klicks of cool
    5,280 feet doing
    the East Saint Boogie
    moody as any Monk
    you were Live and Evil
    but In a Silent Way
Your subtle hands
    cast Milestones through
    the stained-glass tradition of Jazz
    cast sharp notes like flat seeds
    cast molten-blue music
    into spells
conjuring in the key of We.

TAYLOR MALI

Although all of his degrees are in English, Taylor Mali teaches history and math at the Browning School in New York City, which is exactly as it should be. Mali first started competing in poetry slams in graduate school. Already a classically trained Shakespearean actor, he was immediately drawn in by the raucous, competitive nature of slams.

"To be honest, most poetry bores the shit out of me," says Mali. He prefers a form where accessibility and entertainment invariably win out over more traditionally dense and textured verse. "At its best, poetry is the most powerful distillation of feeling and imagery you can conceive. But if you make an obscure literary reference and your audience doesn't get it, whose fault is that?" Does Mali ever read poems with obscure literary references?

"I would prefer not to."

LIKE LILLY LIKE WILSON

I'm writing the poem that will change the world,
and it's Lilly Wilson at my office door.
Lilly Wilson, the recovering like addict,
the worst I've ever seen.
So bad the whole eighth grade
started calling her Like Lilly Like Wilson.
'Til I declared my class a Like-Free Zone
and she could not speak for days.

But when she finally did, it was to say,
Mr. Mali, this is... so hard.
Now I have to... think before I... say anything.

Imagine that, Lilly.

It's for your own good.
Even if you don't like...
it.

I'm writing the poem that will change the world,
and it's Lilly Wilson at my office door.
Lilly is writing a research paper for me about how gays
like shouldn't be allowed to adopt children.
I'm writing the poem that will change the world,
and it's Like Lilly Like Wilson at my office door.

Lilly's having trouble finding sources,
which is to say, ones that back her up:
They all argue in favor of what I thought I was against.

And it took all four years of college,
three years of graduate school,
and every incidental teaching experience I have ever had
to let out only,

That's a real interesting problem, Lilly.
But what do you propose to do about it?

That's what I want to know.

And the eighth-grade mind is a beautiful thing;
Like a new-born baby's face, you can often see it
change before your very eyes.

I can't believe I'm saying this, Mr. Mali,
but I think I'd like to switch sides.

And I want to tell her to do more than just believe it,
but to *enjoy* it! That changing your mind is one of the
best ways of finding out whether you still have one.
Or even that minds are like parachutes,
that it doesn't so much matter what you pack them with
so long as they open at the right time.

I want to say all this but manage only,
Lilly, I am like so impressed with you.

So I finally taught someone something,
namely, how to change your mind.
And learned in the process that if I ever change the world
it's going to be one eighth grader at a time.

JESSICA CARE MOORE

Jessica Care Moore took poetry to the masses in 1995 when she made her first record-breaking appearance on the nationally televised *It's Showtime at the Apollo*. Mesmerizing her audience, this young female voice made Apollo her-story by being the first five-time winner.

Currently a Harlem resident, she began her poetic journey hitting the open mic scene in her hometown of Detroit, reading her work at popular spots like the PourMe Cafe and on mainstream radio stations. A trained journalist and writer for Fox News and several local newspapers in Detroit, Jessica left the comfort of home and headed for New York City to become immersed in the growing spoken-word circuit. It was a move that would change her life.

"I know people have preconceived notions about what poetry is and where it belongs. I say it belongs everywhere and as artists we can't limit ourselves to one type of audience."

Jessica took New York by storm, exploding on the scene in a matter of months, hoping to add her Motor City voice to the sea of talented artists. Her dynamic voice has since been heard at poetry events all across the nation, and captured on numerous spoken-word CDs. Her poetry has appeared in the *New York Times*, *Bomb*, *Rap Pages*, *African Voices*, *Stress*, the *Metro Times*, *Vibe* and the anthology *Seeds*. Jessica has her own publishing company, Moore Black Press, which published her first book of poetry, *The Words Don't Fit in My Mouth*, in August 1997. Her second book, *The Seventh Octave*, is in stores now.

THE SWEETEST REVOLUTIONARY

My evening gown is guerrilla green
I make offerings of myself before the first of every month
'cause there are bills to be paid
instead of getting laid I prostitute verbs manipulate whispers
defined as words
saying shit we've already heard
but not quite like that

See, I know she-poets who'll
squeeze nippled hard headed trees
at their knees
just so their men will name them honey
haikued hips dripping 17 syllables of sweat
drying you off with sunset breath
still he ain't feeling you yet?

Tongue-tied you travel on top of yellow bees
hiding your real sting 'cause he likes the quiet type
cool yeah right-right right-right
you search your belly adjust your skully
hoping to find some sexy sentence hiding between revolution
and rhyme making

Damn he's throwing my poem off
got the nerve to sit in the front row/on my front porch/on
my living room faux Asian throw rug/In my bathroom/on
my mahogany paisley throw/down on my bedroom futon
I'm trippin'

But he blends so well with the pillows
there are reasons I'm not supposed to look at brothas like you
telling me I betta write harder/talk louder/sing protest
lyrics/keep my stomach flat/wear my hair in a politically
correct style/smile and wink between oppression/Then
outdo the main poets/was his confession
Like I'm wearing leftover pink frilly prom dress lace
under my brown kufi

got a six pack of gunfire in my garter

I'm a bowl of mashed potatoes from scratch cooking martyr
Yeah, a war torn Detroit born bush baby
when you unbutton my belly telescope tenderoni
a turkey bologna with two knife slits fried in butter bitch
one of them deep hoes
those abstract poetic tricks
you wanna get with
when the café rhetoric smoke clears
got true fears of feline lick cleaned culture kitty cats that
you meow at
when the jeans look tight as we weigh in on invisible scales
on stage

How many pounds of black rage can your love - handle?

Still miracle our way wearing brown sandals carrying seeds
on our sultry
saddles flipping the pancake spattle shaking the snakes off
baby rattles
got to be head wrapped when we haiku/You love the way
I seduce with
my blues
even if I cry when I sing?
'Cause baby we can do ANYTHING excuse has abused us
into believing
we cannot fine china break cause we eat earthquakes
during snack break
double dutch during dramas of who dun it
when I know the most wanted by first names
meditation on solar plexus erects us into blue candle light
perfection a hot
bath water affection nourishes our naked nature numbed
by unnatural
nine to fives that need more than calgon to make the ugly
of the world
wash away

Make our black butterfly spirits feel simply make-it-
through the day

okay

wings wobble and weaken as the star-spangled banner
swings billy
clubbed choruses and horses the voices of our children's
throats forced to
sing slave to grave dreams that die when fire works don't
burn our names
in branded flames
and you steady throwing me what's up baby game at my
frame?
admit to trying to get my flirt on while I file my nails down
for the frontlines or the free throw

whichever comes first

There is a thirst in wanting to let you drink my hot cocoa
mango lips
that can't convince you that my work is never done
and my night oil races a sun showing up on my doorstep
with long-stemmed doubt

-For the sweetest revolutionary-

When the vase lacks spiritual base politically imprisoned
passions petals
can't grow broken hearted it seems so romantic and cute to
get started
but I need to finish my next book
containing complete thoughts not part time wants
knowing Marvin Gaye died the night before his birth
Is why I hurry and you worry that my life work may kill me
before you ever get a chance to kiss my face
when I really just need my voice hugged
my spirit loved
and a little time to work being a woman

into my busy schedule
america offers advil in place of menstrual huts
so we press our ear lobes against our ovaries
listening for our children's footsteps cramping our style as we
keel over on concrete tile painting on smiles
so no one will know
we really want to fly south for the winter
with the rest of the black eyed birds
leaving white stained relief on curious teeth
looking up our winged skirts
You blew your purple silk breath of fresh air into my fertile
sand-colored belly
And now the dust got in your eyes so you can no longer
find the sexy in
me between my knees
talking bout "Get your poem on baby" You a fine
revolutionary lady
wanna wade me in the water but not help me raise our
daughter?
Imbalanced we dance with americanized feet that never
remove shoes
and don't know how to walk one block with laundry bas-
kets on our heads
Instead we wed dollar signs fornicate for dimes corporate climb
trying to get work on time blowing kisses at positive rhymes
that can't get you a deal
So it's hard for us to deal

For REAL

I'm the MC's wife in search of an angel to untangle vocal
cords wrapped
around my neck plugged into misogynous microphones
making me bob
my membrane to my own gang bang
You think I don't matter
So my voice turns to matter
Squeezed so small It no longer occupies space
Yet It's still here

Hiding in the center of black holes in my panty hose
So loud clear nail polish can't cover it up
I'm pregnant with potential but I birth silence
And just 'cause you slap me on my ass doesn't mean I'll
scream
For you

My private is braided into pigtails decorated plastic
barrettes and yellow rubber bands
The little girl in me is afraid
But the woman in me will kill you
While cooking breakfast
That's that Scorpio shit
You get caught up on wanting to *ménage-a-trois* my
metaphor five six
Time a lady third eye invade me
We drown in lyrical libations never played on radio stations
Hands grow impatient

and I want to be sweet for you baby
but your spit no longer drips liquid sugar
teeth are rotting and falling as I speak
to my spirit alone with my things to do list
standing on my spine before realizing your feet are too
heavy
for my back so I simply erase your name from the paper
wet the dead tree with my tears in hopes to grow a dozen
more of you so afraid
To let me show you how a real woman could
help you find the man in you
My wholeness will guide you to the half of you
you thought you didn't have
so you only offered the little that your body allowed
And in the end it's never enough
'cause
I wanna smell like it taste like it feel like it walk barefoot
inside it wrap it around my waist wear it in the shower take
it home with me share it with my girls play an Aretha CD
to it eat it sweat it believe it

African dance to it wash my face with it hold it love it
grow it out my stomach rock my addidas with it let it run
down my back lick it live it shake a tambourine and say an
amen because of it steal it if I have to melt chocolate on top
of it just want it to be sweet baby sweet like you like we
can be
like revolution

JOHN SINCLAIR

New Orleans–based poet and saxophonist John Sinclair managed the avant-rock band MC-5 and was chairman of the White Panther Party—later the Rainbow Peoples Party—a revolutionary organization formed in November 1968.

In July 1969, Sinclair was sentenced to nine and a half to ten years in prison for possession of two marijuana cigarettes. He served twenty-nine months in maximum security before the Michigan Supreme Court overturned his conviction and abolished the existing marijuana laws.

Sinclair also served as director of the Detroit Artists' Workshop and the Artists' Workshop Press.

In his distinguished career as a music journalist, record producer, educator, lecturer, scriptwriter, radio personality and award-winning broadcast producer, Sinclair has worked as arts editor and editor-in-chief of the *Detroit Sun*; president of Strata Associates, a grassroots community-arts consulting firm; founder and executive director of the Detroit Jazz Center; concert producer, booking agent and artists' manager; freelance journalist, educator, lecturer, poet and performer.

Sinclair's publications include two collections of journalism,

Music & Politics (with Robert Levin) and the underground classic
Guitar Army; five books of poetry; and numerous articles and
liner notes. He has released four CDs and has appeared with his
ensemble as John Sinclair & His Blues Scholars at venues around
the country. He currently broadcasts two weekly programs for
WWOZ-FM in New Orleans and is founder and owner of a
record production company, Big Chief Productions.

"SPIRITUAL"

for Linda

what is jazz, but spirituals
played thru saxophones
& trombones,

spirit voices
thru metal tubings
& the terrible repetition

of the formal premise, *viz.*
trance-like
at its best, or boring

when the spirit doth not move,
oh what is blues
but spirituals with a line

removed,
that is structurally,
& in content just a prayer

to the gods of daily life,
to ask the blessing
that the body of another

may lay warm in the bed

beside you at night, and the rent
be paid, and a meal

on the table, with the sheriff
far away
from the scene of the crime, oh

what is jazz but the registration
of the human personality
in relation to the spiritual,
stripped of literal meaning
but full of sound & portent,
direct as the voice of the gods

detroit
september 15, 1985
after john coltrane

© *1985, 1998 John Sinclair. All Rights Reserved.*

BEANS

Born in the first city of hip hop, the Bronx, Beans started off as a DJ in high school for a group called Rhymistics. He soon changed to rapping because it was "cheaper than a pen and paper." One of the most refreshing artists to emerge out of New York's cutting edge poetry/rap scene of the early '90s, Beans honed his unique blend of hip hop and poetry at the Rap Meets Poetry series at New York's Fez under the Time Cafe. "Before I came to the poetry scene I was surrounded by people who weren't willing to experiment and do different things in hip hop," he says. "Fez was a spawning ground for some incredible shit. It opened a whole new world for me." Beans is best known for his unique polyrhythmic deliveries and his blending of seemingly disparate topics. He was an integral part of the seminal spoken-word collectives, Soup, As Is, the Boom Poetic, Greg Tate's Women in Love and Mack Diva. He collaborated with Vernon Reid on *Mistaken Identity*, High Priest's "Disorientation," and occasionally finds himself improvising with *Slam*'s music composer, DJ Spooky. As a member of the Anti-Pop Consortium, Beans continues to wage war against the pop mind-set he sees overtaking hip hop. On his latest self-titled LP, Beans sums it up: "Not to think initiates Destruction/ Degradation for demographics on mass-scale."

CREVICE IN THE CLOSET

Close the door—lock it—I couldn't face the mirror
feeling inferior, trapped in dark interior, as clothes neat
but complete was not the person so he grows in the
dark—'cause his real life a worse one. Born on the 3rd
of July when the stars in his eyes twinkle dim
when his pop's fate is grim Raised with a brother, sister,
momma found the answer when God grabbed my pops
by the arm—a-leg of cancer now these events shock the
boy back by leaps and bounds now this once sound 10-
year-old-boy's life is shifted when a drifter drifts on ply-
wood tries to take his father's place in fatherhood—Put
his foot on pop's throne, his mom he wants to bone, her
daughter maybe next if he could get past her brothers
now shit is gettin' tense without sign of potential 'cause
decisions have been made and over mom he's influential
That lazy niga rides the smoke, rising to the end of
fable, throwing joints like pots and pans for scraps of
kitchen tables sayin to herself, "Stop the fightin' fellas,
PLEASE!" for her own security mommy's dissin' me for
P-E-A-C-E with word that cut her eldest son deep
down to size to make him realize relatives is relative if
they ain't got their own as his presence takes up space I
want to bash him in his face YOU KNOW WHO YOU
ARE! You never cared about my mother put more

pride into your car telling me I'll never make it but I
didn't throw a fit so I just told you to your face that I
think you're full of shit now I walk with heavy loads
bottled up I hide inside, emotions lose their motion
started screaming from the closet
Now I remember pops was 5'4"—he useta chain-
smoke, read a book a night, and taught his eldest how
to draw. He delivered sis right in the living room in the
boogie bronx and loved Gladys Knight's tunes but a
snot-nosed kid and report card grids DON'T MIX spe-
cially when you're a bully bashin' heads with stones and
sticks. So when he got mad, my black turned white—
from the fright and fear—of the belt on his waist—hit
the rump of my rear in the
rear of his leg was the stain of Agent Orange over years
that results in a pimp limp dependent on a crutch, leaving leg sedated that eventually was amputated, diagnosed as cancer, leading to therapy—my life stories pur-
gatory as sickness had its stitches and knits my family a
unit out of bad health, no wealth, or a clue so all I do is
watch him decay before eyes
and hope the big guy in the skies hears your pleas but
he's too busy with the world to hear a desperate son—
on his knees especially that Sunday as his eyes opened
wide, when he turned to his maker, and kissed his family good-bye but the next day was school thinking pops
was getting better as mom burst in my room with the
news of no surprise as she held me in her arms, and
told me that your father died.... But he knew it all
along and bottled up, he hid inside it, emotions lose
their motion and started screaming from the closet
Whether it's right or wrong, my daddy's gone—That's
on the REAL! mommy's in man's place got 3 kids and
payin' bills without support perish the thought the fort
was stable in tip top shape was home sweet home
worked her fingers to the bone—by her lonesome as
she was able to dish the cards that life had dealt who
mostly felt the burden of our stomachs churnin' in the
early morning yawning but a new day was dawning and

every dog got his day so she held her head up so her children had no limits but the sky—"BOY! speak when you spoke!" she was strict like no joke swingin' on my upbringing because she pushed a kick in the tush—DAILY 'cause that's what some of us need and it worked like a charm giving props to my moms but I got no more tears with these feelings bottled up for years so now I fold my cards on the table, in light of the land, then place my hand on the knob to turn but not to look back inside it, emotions lose their motion as I step out of the closet

© 1994

The
Screenplay

"And we are Public Enemy Number One."

SLAM

by
Marc Levin
Bonz Malone
Sonja Sohn
Richard Stratton
Saul Williams

Offline Entertainment Group
601 West 26th Street
17th Floor
New York, NY 10001

FINAL DRAFT
January 13, 1998

FADE IN:

EXT. WASHINGTON, D.C. - WIDE SHOT - SUMMER - DAY - MUSIC: DJ SPOOKY'S "GALACTIC FUNK"

HOLD on the Capitol. PAN LEFT to the Washington Monument, then DOWN, past coils of concertina wire and prison gates, to reveal —

EXT. YARD - D.C. JAIL

Filled with prisoners hanging out, working out on weight machines.

CREDITS roll over a D.C. MONTAGE:

RAY JOSHUA, young, black, lanky, walks down a busy Washington, D.C., street with Capitol in background.

PRISONERS in shackles.

Jail yard filled with PRISONERS.

PEOPLE in D.C. pound the pavement.

Ray plays basketball with BOYS in the 'hood.

Ray makes a drug deal.

BIG MIKE and his CREW shoot craps.

Ray writes in his journal.

PRISONERS walk down jailhouse corridors.

Prison cell doors SLAM shut.

END CREDITS.

TITLE FADES UP as Ray, walking through projects in D.C. (Dodge City) is flocked by a group of YOUNG KIDS. It's clear Ray is their hero. He gives them high-fives, plays with them as they walk along the sidewalk.

RAY
(as music FADES OUT; playing with the kids)
Can't nobody get me, can't nobody get me.
(falls into stride)
Can't nobody get me.

CUT TO:

EXT. DODGE CITY - DAY

Ice cream truck pulls into the projects, its BELL RINGING like a burglar alarm.

KIDS swarm around the truck, Ray in the middle of them.

> RAY
> *(counting hands)*
> One, two, three, four, five, six, seven, eight...
> *(to the vendor)*
> Okay, thirteen chocolate—

> KID
> *(shouting in the background)*
> I want chocolate!

> RAY
> You gonna get yours, everybody gonna get theirs.

> KID
> I want chocolate!

> RAY
> *(hands out the ice cream)*
> All right, there you go.

CUT TO:

EXT. DODGE CITY - DAY

Ray's hanging out on the stoop with KIDS.

> KID #1
> You got a rhyme or something?

> RAY
> *(imitates him)*
> I got a rhyme or something?
> *(breaks into verse)*
> I kick rhymes autom-atic
> (MORE)

                    RAY (cont'd)
Addicted to change like leaves
My black is gold like bees
So sting Ray on a sunny day
While the little kids sit out and play—or converse.
Getting ready for the ice cream truck—

He fumbles the rhyme. The kids crack up.

                    RAY
                (to Little Troy)
You wrote something?

                LITTLE TROY
No, I just know a little something.

                    RAY
What you got?

                LITTLE TROY
                    (timid)
I got a little something.
My name is Little Troy
And I'm known as a big boy.
                (a moment)
I gotta put some more at the end, though.

                    RAY
                (quietly)
I'll help you with it, if you want.

                                        CUT TO:

EXT. DODGE CITY - LATER

Ray comes around the back of a building with CUZ.

                    RAY
So yo, what's up with Keisha?

                    CUZ
Yo, chick is bugging. She keeps hitting me.

Ray cracks up.

> CUZ
>
> Look, I need something to get my head right, you know what I'm saying. Share some blessings with me?

> RAY
>
> Yeah, I got you.
> *(reaches into his pocket)*
> Medicine for you.

> CUZ
>
> Please. Please.

> RAY
>
> *(hands him the weed)*
> This is my prescription.

> CUZ
>
> *(hands Ray the cash)*
> Ah, that's what I'm talking. This is that Maui-Waui, right?

> RAY
>
> This is the truth. So help you God.

> CUZ
>
> So after smoking this, I'll understand some of that shit you be talking about in your rhymes, right?

> RAY
>
> *(laughs)*
> Probably not.

They shake hands, embrace, say good-bye. Cuz walks away; Ray holds back a minute, waiting for the coast to clear.

EXT. DODGE CITY - LATER

Under a shady tree, amidst debris and old furniture, BIG MIKE sits on his throne holding court, his CREW huddled around him in heated conference, everyone talking at once.

                    BIG MIKE
          Look! Hold up, though. Ain't nobody coming up
          in Dodge City like that, man, know what I'm say-
          ing?

                    CREW MEMBER
          If I have to go through there, somebody gonna be
          like Biggie and Tupac.

                    MIKE
          Look, man, you handle your business, don't let
          your business handle you, you know what I'm say-
          ing?

They start shooting craps.

Ray approaches the craps game.

                    RAY
          What up, y'all.

They greet him, shake hands, embrace.

SERIES OF SHOTS of the craps game.

Money changes hands.

Ray rolls dice.

                                        TIME CUT TO:

The craps game still in session, Ray approaches Big Mike, leans down to him. They shake hands.

                    RAY
          What up, man?

                    MIKE
          Hey, what's up?

                    RAY
          What's going on?

> MIKE

Yo, I got some good things I'm trying to invest in, you know.

> RAY

I hear you.

> MIKE

We gonna make it big.

> RAY

That's it. You know I'm writing every day.

> MIKE

Every day. You gotta give me that, man, 'cause I'm going with you on that, you know what I'm saying?

> RAY

So you gonna start the label?

> MIKE

Yeah, I want you to do that record label, 'cause I got the money invested in it.

> RAY
> *(smiles)*

A'ight.

> MIKE

I got the money invested in it.
> *(a moment)*
I want you to do me a favor.

> RAY

What's that?

> MIKE

I got this new chick, right. I want you to give me a little good shit to tell her, you know, some slick shit to say to her, you know what I'm saying?

Ray laughs.

> MIKE
>
> I'm serious, man, I ain't bullshitting. You got to do that for me, man.

> RAY
>
> You gonna get me to write poems and shit?

> MIKE
>
> Man, look, I don't want to read the junk, I just want to remember something.

> RAY
>
> I think if I write it, you better read that shit.

> MIKE
>
> I don't want you writing no heavy poems and shit. I ain't gonna be sittin' there singing to the bitch, I ain't no R. Kelly or nobody, you know what I'm saying? I want you to sit there and give me a little something.

> RAY
>
> A'ight.

> MIKE
>
> It's like that. You my man. Look out for me.

> RAY
>
> I got you.
> *(they shake hands)*
> Yo, I'm running low. You look out for me?

> MIKE
>
> Yeah, I got that, I'll look out for you. But look, come back later on. Meet me at Dodge City around 10:30, and I got you.

> RAY
>
> A'ight. And I got you then, too.

They shake hands and Ray gets up to leave.

DISSOLVE TO:

EXT. DODGE CITY - DUSK - MUSIC MONTAGE

Ray stands on a hill in the projects writing in his journal as behind him the sun begins to set. Intercut shots of Ray writing with DREAMY IMAGES of young women and men hangin' in the 'hood. The images are of different texture, like a video playing in his head.

Ray walks farther up the hill, looks out over the sprawling capital city under an orange horizon. He continues to write.

More IMAGES: women in the 'hood.

The CAMERA takes in the wide expanse of Washington, D.C., from Ray's vantage point. Lights are starting to shimmer on and around Capitol Hill as dusk turns into night.

DISSOLVE TO:

INT. UNDERCOVER COP CAR (MOVING) - NIGHT

Two UNDERCOVER COPS, heavyset, graying, veterans, cruise the 'hood.

> COP #1
> It's gonna be a hot one tonight, boy. I can feel it, man.

> COP #2
> I'm getting too old for this shit, man.

EXT. UNDERCOVER COP CAR - NIGHT - SAME TIME

Car makes a turn.

INT. UNDERCOVER COP CAR (MOVING) - SAME TIME

Cops continue their patrol.

> COP #2
> Tell them to get some additional units, because
> they've been acting kind of silly, you know what I
> mean? These young boys, you know, that rap
> music they got is driving them crazy.

EXT. DODGE CITY - NIGHT - SAME TIME

Ray walks through the dark streets on his way to meet Mike.

> POLICE DISPATCHER (O.S.)
> *(from the police radio)*
> Come in, EC-1.

> COP #2 (O.S.)
> *(into police radio)*
> Let all units know to be heads up.

INT. UNDERCOVER COP CAR (MOVING) - NIGHT

> COP #1
> You remember that song, "What's Your Name?"

> COP #2
> Oh, yeah, yeah.

> COP #1
> Remember that one?

> COP #2
> Yeah, yeah. Hit it.

They break into SONG.

> COPS
> *(singing)*
> "What's your name? Is it...?"

They mess up the lyrics and stop singing.

> COP #1
> You remember the song, man?

> COP #2
> No, I remember.

> COP #1
> It's, "I have seen you before," goddamnit.

COP #2

So how does it go?

COP #1

"What's your name/I have seen you before/can I walk you to your door..."

COP #2

All right.

COP #1

Jesus Christ, man, you talking about you know the damn song.

COP #2
(finally)

All right, hit it.

They start SINGING again.

EXT. DODGE CITY - NIGHT - SAME TIME

The SONG continues on the TRACK as Ray walks.

COPS (O.S.)
(singing)

"What's your name? I have seen you before ..."

INT. UNDERCOVER COP CAR (MOVING) - NIGHT

COPS
(singing cont'd)

"What's your name? May I walk to you to your door?"

EXT. DODGE CITY - NIGHT - SAME TIME

CLOSE ON: Ray walking.

COPS (O.S.)
(singing cont'd)

"It's so hard to find a personality with charms like yours for me, ooh-ee."

On the SOUNDTRACK, the SONG segues into RAP MUSIC (BUSTA RHYMES' "TURN IT UP") as Ray walks by.

EXT. DODGE CITY - WIDE SHOT - PROJECTS

It's a hot night in Dodge City. Crowds of people, mostly kids and teenagers, sit around the stoop and parking lot. Ray arrives at the scene, approaches Big Mike.

                              RAY
          What up, nigga.

                              MIKE
          What up.

CLOSE ON: Big Mike hands Ray a bag of weed.

                              MIKE
          Here you go. Be careful with that.

                              RAY
          A'ight.

                              MIKE
          Everything all right? Look, I want you do what I
          asked you to.

                              RAY
          I got you. This is what you're going to say. You
          massage the universe's spine/The way you twirl
          through time/And leave shadows on the sun.

Mike laughs.

                              MIKE
          You are a bad motherfucka, man.

                              RAY
          You like that?

                              MIKE
          Yeah, man. Give that to me again.

> RAY
> You massage the universe's spine/The way you
> twirl through time/And leave shadows on the sun.

> MIKE
> (laughs)
> That's all right, though.

GUNSHOT RINGS OUT. Mike goes down. KIDS SCREAM and scatter.
MUSIC UP.

Ray stands suddenly alone, Mike on the ground next to him, bleeding from
the head. Blood pools on the ashphalt at Ray's feet. Ray bends down, reaches out to Mike just as the undercover cop car SCREECHES into the parking
lot. Ray bolts. The cops chase him up the hill as more COP CARS arrive.

Ray darts out from a clump of brush, runs along a white fence with the
undercover cop in hot pursuit.

Ray slows to try to vault the fence. The cops grab him, cuff him.

Cops escort Ray back to the chaos of the parking lot: A crowd presses to see
Mike's body, cops try to hold them back.

INT. UNDERCOVER COP CAR (MOVING) - NIGHT - LATER

The SIREN is on as the cops take off with Ray.

EXT. COP CAR

They race through the streets.

> RAY (O.S.)
> I didn't do anything. It's just weed.

> COP #2 (O.S.)
> It's just weed?! It's illegal weed, man. What makes
> you think you can use drugs in our city?

INT. COP CAR (MOVING) - SAME TIME

> COP #1
> (holding on to Ray in the backseat)
> What's your name, man? What's your name?

Big Mike is gunned down.

> RAY
>
> Raymond Joshua.

> COP #1
>
> Raymond what?

> RAY
>
> Raymond Joshua.

EXT. COP CAR (MOVING) - SAME TIME

> COP #2 (O.S.)
>
> Buddy, let me tell you, you're in deep shit.

EXT. POLICE STATION - NIGHT

The cops lead Ray into the station.

INT. POLICE STATION - BULLPEN

Ray, handcuffed and shackled, sits on a hard steel bench, stares out into space. Busted.

DISSOLVE TO:

EXT. COURTHOUSE - DAY - ESTABLISHING SHOT

PAN front of courthouse as:

> ### COURT CLERK (O.S.)
> *(POUNDS his gavel)*
> Matter before the court, number 47 on the lock-
> up, United States versus Raymond Joshua.

INT. COURTROOM - DAY - SAME TIME

Marc Levin directs Mayor Marion Barry Jr.

The JUDGE is on the bench. PROSECUTOR is at lectern addressing the Court. Ray stands beside the prosecutor.

> ### PROSECUTOR
> *(typical blue suit, smug)*
> Your Honor, the defendant was apprehended flee-
> ing the scene of a shooting. A man was shot in
> the head during a drug transaction in which this
> man was involved.

JUDGE

My God, what a way to start a Monday morning.
Here you have the Congress taking a lot of power
from the city council and the office of mayor, and
the board of education and the people of
Washington... and then we have Mr. Joshua.
Without getting into whether you're guilty or not,
I just know that these drugs are killing our communities. Mr. Prosecutor, what's the government's
position on bail?

PROSECUTOR

The government feels that this defendant poses a
substantial risk of flight, Your Honor. He was
apprehended fleeing the scene of a shooting. We
would like to see the bond set in the amount of
ten thousand dollars surety.

Ray gives the prosecutor a look of cool disdain.

JUDGE

This court will enter a plea of not guilty on behalf
of Mr. Joshua, and the proceeding's adjourned until
Monday morning at 11 o'clock. Thank you, gen-
tlemen.

PROSECUTOR

Thank you, Your Honor.

Prosecutor returns Ray's look.

EXT. POLICE STATION – DAY – MUSIC UP

Ray stands in line with other PRISONERS, all in shackles and handcuffs.
The men are loaded into a Department of Corrections van.

INT. D.O.C. VAN – DAY

Ray sits next to a young Asian-American man, JIMMY HUANG. The van
doors slam shut behind them. Two CORRECTIONAL OFFICERS sit in
the front seat.

JIMMY HUANG
(shouts)
Turn on the fucking air conditioner! A.C., motherfucker! Give me some fucking A.C.!

C.O. #1
Shut the fuck up!

JIMMY HUANG
My name is fucking Jimmy Huang! Get me the
fuck off this van! Hey! You! Up there in the
front! I shouldn't fucking be in this van, man. You
know who my dad is? Shit! It's hot in this fucking van!

RAY
(to Huang; calm)
You scared?

JIMMY HUANG
(glares at him)
Shut the fuck up.

MUSIC comes up as Ray gazes out the window, lost in thought. The van
makes its way through the city, monuments shimmering in the window
behind Ray like alien monoliths.

Jimmy Huang's restless, sweating, mumbling to himself. Ray, beside him,
starts to rap.

RAY
(quietly, to himself)
Thinking of a master plan. It ain't nothing but
sweat inside my hands, so I dig into my pockets—

JIMMY HUANG
(can't stand it anymore)
There's an emcee in the van! There's an emcee in
the van! Great! Another black rapper!

Ray stops, stares at him, starts his rap again.

> RAY

Thinking of the master plan. So I walk up the
street, whistling this, feeling out of place 'cause
man do I miss, a pen a paper, a stereo, a table...

> JIMMY HUANG
> *(over Ray's rapping; starts quietly, grows louder)*

Would you shut the fuck up, would you shut the
fuck up, would you shut the fuck up would you
shut the fuck up would you shut the fuck up
would you shut the fuck up...!

The two go at it, face to face. Ray refuses to stop.

> JIMMY HUANG
> *(finally; to the van at large)*

Would you get this guy to shut up!

EXT. D.C. JAIL - DAY - LATER - MUSIC UP

The van arrives. There's the guard tower. Guards push buttons at a control
panel. Gates open. Van pulls in. Gates close.

INT. VAN - SAME TIME - MUSIC DOWN

CLOSE ON: Jimmy Huang and Ray.

> JIMMY HUANG

I'd like to find out who's gonna keep this little
thing quiet... Shake his hand and say thank you.
Damn! I miss Italy.
> *(turns to Ray)*

Do you miss Italy?

Ray thinks about it. Appraises Huang.

> RAY

You ever listen to Wu Tang?

EXT. VAN - LATER - MUSIC UP

Prisoners are herded out of the van and up the stairs into jail. Climbing the
stairs, Jimmy Huang spits on a C.O. (Corrections Officer).

INSIDE the jail, shackled feet, piles of shackles.

CLOSE ON: Ray as he enters.

EXT. JAIL - LATE AFTERNOON/EVENING - TIME TRANSITION - MUSIC CONTINUES

A sudden, almost eerie windstorm blows through the trees outside the jail.

SHOTS of the jail with the sky changing color behind it.

INT. JAIL - INTAKE

The clatter of GATES and cacophony of VOICES. Ray and the others file into a bullpen.

INT. BULLPEN - LATER

Ray greets PREZ—full face, wire-frame glasses—with the handshake. They know each other from the neighborhood.

> RAY
>
> What up, Prez?

> PREZ
>
> What's up?

> RAY
>
> You heard about Mike?

> PREZ
>
> Yeah, I heard about it. So what happened?

> RAY
>
> I don't even know. I can't call it.

> PREZ
>
> You know, the word in here is, watch your back.

INT. BULLPEN - LATER

Ray's on the bench, head buried, waiting it out. Jimmy Huang, drenched in sweat now, approaches a group of prisoners in the corner.

Ray begins POUNDING A BEAT on the bench, trying to deal with the time.

In the corner, Jimmy Huang is pressing his luck with some PRISONERS.

> PRISONER #1
>
> Yo, what's wrong with you?

> JIMMY HUANG
> *(explodes)*
>
> What's wrong with me?! What's wrong with me?! I shouldn't even be in this fucking jail, man! I don't want to be in here. I shouldn't be in here with you motherfuckers! Get the fuck away from me? I should get the fuck away from you?! Fuck you, motherfuckers...!

Ray regards the scene.

> PRISONER #2
> *(on toilet)*
>
> Hey man, y'all need to shut up. I ain't tryin' to hear all that. Someone just get me some toilet paper!

Prisoners surround Jimmy.

> PRISONER #3
>
> What's up?

> JIMMY HUANG
>
> Get off of me.

> PRISONER #3
> *(menacing)*
>
> What's up.

> JIMMY HUANG
>
> What the fuck do you want with me, man! I'll fucking get all of you. I'll kill you.

Prisoners move on Jimmy, but Ray slips in and breaks it up, pulling Jimmy free and over to the bench, forcing him to sit down.

>   RAY
>   Sit the fuck down, man. Just sit down. Sit down,
>   a'ight?
>   *(holds him on the bench)*
>   What's your fucking problem, yo? You about to
>   get fucking killed up in this piece.

>   JIMMY HUANG
>   *(crazy)*
>   Yeah, I guess I am.

Ray stares at him.

>   PRISONER #1 (O.S.)
>   Coming to America is a motherfucker.

>   PRISONER #2 (O.S.)
>   Somebody needs to get me some toilet paper over
>   in this motherfucker.

>   RAY
>   What the fuck you trying to do? Why don't you
>   just sit down, a'ight? If you're not supposed to be
>   here, then you won't be here. Give it a second and
>   you'll disappear.

Jimmy Huang sits, trying to comprehend this, dizzied by what's happened.

>   C.O. (O.S.)
>   Hey, Mr. Huang! Let's go.

>   JIMMY HUANG
>   *(smiles)*
>   That's me. I told you I was out of here, man.

He shakes Ray's hand, gets up to leave.

The gate opens for him. The two guards from the van are there to greet him.

> GUARD

Time to go.

> JIMMY HUANG
> *(smart-ass)*

I told you guys.

Ray watches as the guards each grab an arm and lead Huang down the hall.

> GUARD
> *(to Huang)*
> You remember when you spit on my buddy?

They've arrived at the door to the officers' bathroom; the guards tug him toward it.

> JIMMY HUANG
> *(realizes)*

What? Nooo...!

It's too late. The guards haul him kicking and screaming into the bathroom. The door shuts and we HEAR the sounds of Huang getting the shit kicked out of him.

INT. BULLPEN - SAME TIME

Ray, standing near the cell bars, hears everything.

INT. VISITING ROOM - LATER

Ray meets his LAWYER, a suave, fast-talking public defender who's been here a million times before.

> LAWYER
> I'm your attorney. I've been assigned by the court
> to represent you. I'm a public defender. I've been
> asked by the prosecutor to see if we can cut a
> deal—which means, plead guilty or cop out.
> Let me ask you this, are you guilty?

> RAY
> *(baffled)*

Of what?

LAWYER

Of possession of the marijuana.

RAY

What... I mean, I don't know.
(searching)
I can't get a trial or something?

LAWYER

Well, you can get a trial. They call that cop or
rock. You can take the cop—we plead—or rock,
which means we take you to trial. But if you lose,
you're looking at ten. Mandatory. Ten. And you
have to do 85 percent of ten. Which means eight
and a half years.

RAY

(can't believe it)
So wait, if I try to fight it, I have to serve more
time for just trying to fight it?

LAWYER

If you get found guilty, you would. And usually—
(he pauses, gathers himself)
The success ratio of convictions in drug cases is
about 90 to 95 percent. If they lock up ten people, nine, nine and a half go to jail. But the
chances of beating it is like... trying to throw a
snowball into an elephant's mouth, man, at a hundred feet. You can't make it.

Ray doesn't want to hear this.

LAWYER (cont'd)

You are in trouble. You are a victim of—you're a
casualty of war.
(sizing Ray up)
You got two options—three: You can plead guilty
to a simple possession, which is two or three years,
you do eighteen months.
(MORE)

> LAWYER (cont'd)

You can go to trial and run the risk of doing ten years if you get found guilty. Or, you can cooperate, which means you can rat, snitch, blow the whistle on whoever you want to blow it on in order to get out.

> RAY
> *(stunned)*

Cop—cooperate, which I'm not gonna do. You say I can't even fight it 'cause I'll serve more time. This doesn't make any fucking sense. None whatsoever, man. It doesn't make any sense at all. There's niggers out there doing mad shit! My man is down, you know. They shoot my man, they're running free! There's niggers out there selling all types of shit and I got a quarter pound of weed and you're telling me I got to serve five to ten years and there's not shit you can do for me?! I don't have any choices?! Fuck this ol' casualty of war shit, man! I'm saying, I'm just out there surviving. What can I do?

> LAWYER
> *(sympathetic but helpless)*

I know it sounds like a lot of time, but most guys get a lot longer than that, man. The best I can do is try to get you two to three. Even if you were innocent I could only get you two to three. You are a victim, brother. You're black, you're young, you come from the Southeast, you're in the inner city... you don't have a chance. Your best chance now is to see how little time can you get before you get back to society. It ain't about beating it. When they lock you up, you dead.

INT. BULLPEN - D.C. JAIL - LATER

Ray sits waiting.

GUARD
(opens the gate)
Raymond Joshua, step out.

INT. INTAKE - D.C. JAIL - LATER

CLOSE ON: C.O. LUCAS

C.O. LUCAS
(bristling, angry)
When you're in this building, I want you to stay
alive, so listen carefully to me. Nobody in here is
your brother. I don't care if they're as black as you
are or as light as daylight—they are not your
brother. You mind your business, son, and you'll
stay alive...

The C.O.'s stern lecture continues over a

SERIES OF INTAKE PROCESSING SHOTS:

C.O. LUCAS (V.O.)
Every day somebody gets shanked in here. Every
day, somebody gets beaten up in here...

Ray's handcuffs are removed.

C.O. LUCAS (V.O.)
...We got predators in here, son. We got people
that will cut your throat—for nothing at all but a
pack of cigarettes.

Ray's fingerprinted.

CUT TO:

C.O. LUCAS
(to Ray)
...You mind your business in here, son. Do you
understand where you are...?

CUT TO:

Ray is led into the strip search room. He sits on a bench, waits. Around him, OTHER PRISONERS are stripping, standing in line.

Finally, Ray's name is called. He enters the room, strips for the guard, stands before him naked, follows instructions.

> STRIP SEARCH C.O.
> Open your mouth. Lift your arms. Lift your
> tongue. Lift your balls. Turn around and spread
> your cheeks with both hands at the same time.
> Show me the bottoms of your feet. Turn around
> and face me, bend over at the waist, run your fin-
> gers through your hair.

CUT TO:

Ray's up against a wall, he's given the I.D. slate, waits for his mug shot to be taken. Over this we HEAR:

> C.O. LUCAS (V.O.)
> Your number is going to be given to you. It's a
> sequential number. It's not a random set of num-
> bers, son. That number means something, son. It's
> your number... It's your number now.

FLASH—the mug shot is taken.

BACK TO:

> C.O. LUCAS (cont'd)
> (growing even angrier)
> You know what that number represents, son?
> 276,000. Now listen carefully to me and you'll
> understand a little bit about what makes me so
> angry. We only have less than 500,000 people in
> the District of Columbia, son. And only 70 percent
> of them are black. Now what's 70 percent of
> 500,000? Do the math! We got about 350,000
> black people in D.C. Of the 350,000, half of them
> are female, aren't they? Well, what's that? Do the
> math, son, the math! Less than 175,000 people are
> males like yourself.
> (MORE)

> C.O. LUCAS (cont'd)
> Not all of them are over 21 years of age—half of
> them are kids. Now how the devil have we got
> only 75-, 80,000 adult males in the District of
> Columbia, and this number is 276,000? Figure it
> out for yourself! We've exhausted the 21-year-
> olds, the 20-year-olds, the 19-year-olds. And we
> working on 18. We are moving on down the line,
> son; by the time we cross 300,000, we'll be down
> to 16- and 17-year-olds.

As he speaks, we SEE line after line of prisoners—all black, all young—
streaming through intake, herded into bullpens.

> C.O. LUCAS (cont'd)
> We're wiping out our race here in Washington,
> D.C., and here you are in here playing your silly-
> ass little games. Well, we got something for you,
> son! Welcome to the D.C. Jail. You might make it
> out of here, you might not.

CUT TO:

Ray, in a blue jumpsuit, bedroll under his arm, is escorted by OFFICER
DOMINICK down the corridor and into his cellblock. The incessant
shouting and clatter of jail invades the SOUNDTRACK. Ray's led to his
cell. The gate closes behind him. He throws his bedroll onto the bed,
buries his face in his hands.

FLASHBACK SEQUENCE: (MUSIC MONTAGE)

The shooting scene in eerie slo-mo.

The cops chase Ray....

Ray arrested.

We HEAR sirens, see the faces of prisoners pressed up against their cell gates
as we come BACK TO:

INT. RAY'S CELL - THROUGH THE BARS

Ray sits on his bed reading his paperwork. Suddenly we HEAR an intense
rap bass beat coming from the cell next door. Ray looks up toward the

beat. In a moment, the beat is joined by a voice—an angry, soulful, gangsta rapper. Ray listens, gets into it. His head sways to the beat. He moves to the corner, sits at his desk to get closer to the sound. Closes his eyes.

PAN RIGHT to the next cell to reveal BAY, sitting at his metal desk, POUNDING A BEAT on it and RAPPING.

BAY

...Niggas better run
If they don't catch up,
They just get fucked
By my motherfucking....

PAN BACK to Ray, listening.

CLOSE ON Ray, eyes closed, lost in the beat.

BACK TO Bay... then to Ray...

Finally, Ray joins in, takes over the rap.

RAY

Yo sun, as in solar, simply
Because we are, we be
The rising stars and sun that never set
Word up, black
Wanna make a bet, black
I got the formula
Throw me in the sky and I'll warm you
Get your sun block
Throw me in a cellblock...

Still RAPPING, they both make their way to the cell bars, Bay POUND-ING THE BEAT on the wall the whole time. It's the most alive we've seen Ray—verse is where he lives. The CAMERA moves back and forth almost steadily now.

RAY (cont'd)
Indeed, I got the science you need
Lessons more ancient than Greece
Apollo never my creed, my creed
(MORE)

RAY (cont'd)
Obatala will battle you, so bring your troops if you
want to
Satellites in the sky, some selling clouds on the
corner...

CLOSE ON: Ray and Bay as they RAP. The symmetry and rhythm are the culmination of two centuries of slave chants, prison work songs and blues: a modern, hip hop slave song for the '90s. And as long as they can hold it, they're free.

RAY (cont'd)
...But we livin' for the land
From the soil to the sand
And the water in the sea be the essence of me
If you ain't ready for this fruit then put it back on
the tree, uh—
Now God, give me the strength to bend back
these bars
Got the locks of Samson, I'm Sam's son
He's my father
Tried praying to father's, but holy ghost, I miss my
motherfucking sanity
Never been here and never planned to be
But my own plans had plans for me
And now that man's hands got plans for me
And now that man's hands got plans for me
And now that man had plans so I jetted and ran
The mic cord pulled me back
I shoulda dropped it from my hand
and left it at the scene of the rhyme.
Now we're all serving time
Even my prose is on probation
Refugees ain't only Haitian
Come on, fucking shit, come on, keep it going
now.
(As Bay picks up the rhyme, Ray sings a rhythm to keep it going)
Ba bam, ba bam bam, ba bam bam
Ba bam, ba bam bam, ba bam bam...

                    BAY

Now what the fuck, you're fuckin with a psy-
chopath nut
Put on my fucking glasses and 'bout to go bust a
nut in your ass, motherfucker
As I blast in your motherfucking gut...

                    RAY
              (under Bay's rap)
Ba bam, ba bam bam, ba bam bam...

                    BAY

...Put a motherfucking mask on your face
You shoulda never fucked with a nigga from the
base
So now I'm packing steel,
keeping the shit really real, motherfucka
You ducked trying to hop up in the truck, got
blocked down
So motherfuckers really want the judge to under-
stand my motherfucking deal
I'm packin' steel
Slam-dunk it like Shaquille O'Neal

                    RAY
              (under Bay's rap)
I had to be strong, I had to be real.
I had to be strong, I had to be real.
Ba bam, ba bam bam, ba bam bam.
I had to be strong--
              (they both finally fumble it; laugh)
That shit is dope, yo.

They put their hands out through the bars, touch, a long shake and slow
slide of hands.

                    BAY

Damn. You got some talent with you, man. That
shit was tight, mo.

They hold the handshake for a long moment, then slowly let go. Each returns to his own world.

INT. CELLBLOCK - LATER

Chow time. GUARDS and PRISONERS distribute food trays to the cells.

INT. DAY ROOM - LATER

Ray enters with a food tray, joins a group of PRISONERS at the table—the THUG LIFE CREW, rapping a beat on the table and freestyling. They stop Ray as he approaches; stand to challenge him.

> TALIB
>
> What's up, partner?
> *(slides Ray's tray away from him)*
> I know you don't want that shit.

> RAY
>
> *(weary; in no mood for this)*
> Come on, nigga, I ain't trying to be playing this shit—

They start pushing each other.

> TALIB
>
> What's up, partner? What's up?

> RAY
>
> *(moving for the tray)*
> Come on, yo, I ain't eaten all day. I ain't trying
> to play—

CHINA, their leader, stands up, gets between Ray and the food tray.

> CHINA
>
> It's my motherfucking tray. I'm eating this tray.

> RAY
>
> Nigger, you don't know me, I ain't about to sit
> here and let you eat my shit.

> CHINA
>
> I ain't got to know. You ain't gonna eat, unless I
> say you gonna eat. This is my motherfucking tray.

Kim Wozencraft

China (top left) and the Thug Life crew.

                    CHINA (cont'd)
                   (stares him down)
    Any problems?

                        RAY
                      (shrugs)
        Nah. If I don't eat...
          (leans down, sends the tray crashing to to the floor)
        ...don't nobody fucking eat.

All hell breaks loose. The gang attacks Ray and starts beating on him.
Above them, in a neighboring room, a curious ONLOOKER takes in the
scene—another prisoner, calm, composed, watching closely through the
windows.

INT. GUARD'S STATION – SAME TIME

C.O. DOMINICK and another GUARD react to the fight.

                     C.O. DOM
                   (on the move)
        Oh shit. Here we go!

BACK TO:

The ALARM is sounded in the control room and soon a SLEW OF GUARDS race to the scene. It's an all-out brawl, guards and prisoners all over each other on the Day Room floor.

Ray, on the ground in the corner, winded, nose bleeding, looks on.

EXT. JAIL - TIME CUT - NEXT MORNING

ESTABLISHING SHOTS of jail.

INT. CELLBLOCK - LATER

C.O. Dom approaches Ray's cell.

> C.O. DOM
> *(looks in)*
>
> Hey!
> *(raps on the bars)*
> Wakey-wakey, hands off snaky.
> *(to the control room)*
> Open 20!

Ray's cell door opens.

> C.O. DOM
> *(smiles in at him)*
> How ya doin'? Grab your shit, we're leaving.

Ray grabs his shit, follows Dom out. From the next cell, Bay sends a farewell.

> RAY
> *(back to Bay)*
> Peace, Black.

Ray and Dom make their way down the cellblock.

> INMATE (O.S.)
> *(from another cell as Ray passes by)*
> Keep it real, man.

> RAY
> Mm-hm.

ANOTHER INMATE (O.S.)
Some get by but they never get away!

FOLLOW Ray and Dom as they continue through the cellblock, down the stairs and into another block. They stop at an open cell.

C.O. DOM
(to Ray)
All right, first cell to your left. Stand right here.

Inside the cell, the floor is covered with goods—an in-cell commissary. A prisoner, HOPHA, reclines on the lower bunk, face hidden behind an open newspaper.

HOPHA
(voice from behind the paper)
Yo, where the fuck my paper at!

C.O. DOM
(leans in)
Your man's here to see you. I got 32 ready for him.

CLOSE ON:

The newspaper moves aside to reveal Hopha, an obvious leader, very cool, cigar stuck in the corner of his mouth, studying Ray from behind dark shades.

HOPHA
(finally; nods)
What's happening.

Ray doesn't know what to say.

HOPHA
Come on in, man. Take a seat.

CUT TO:

INT. HOPHA'S CELL - LATER

The shades are off now. Hopha and Ray sit across from each other. Hopha's in a clean white robe over his prison blues. We may or may not remember him as the curious onlooker from the Day Room brawl scene.

John Kirby

Bonz Malone as Zen Gangster Hopha.

HOPHA
(extends hand)
I'm Hopha. What's going down?

RAY
Mike told me a lot about you.

HOPHA
He told me a lot about you too, man. So what the
cops is telling you, man. I know they been trying
to ask you questions about Mike.

RAY
Yeah, they asked me a few questions, but I don't
know shit, you know, so I just told them I don't
know shit.

HOPHA
(nods; a moment; eyes him)
You sure you ain't tell them nothing?

                    RAY
I didn't tell them shit, yo.

                    HOPHA
See, this is the problem here. People think you
did.

                    RAY
What.

                    HOPHA
Tell them something. That shit that happened, you
probably don't know nothing about this, but
you're the center of attention now.

                    RAY
What do you mean?

                    HOPHA
Everybody wants a piece of you, man.

                    RAY
How's that?

                    HOPHA
Because they think you set Mike up.

                    RAY
I didn't do that shit! I know I didn't do that.

                    HOPHA
I know you didn't fucking do it. But they don't
know that shit. They coming for you, man. You
got every motherfucker in here ready to take a
piece of your ass, and if I take the fucking veil
down, it's going to fucking happen. You stepped
right into the frying pan now. So be ready to
get down.
              (re the department store on his floor)
                   (MORE)

> HOPHA (cont'd)

Hey, you want some treats? I got some sweets.
Some cookies or something? Here, let me hook
you up, man. Take some of this.

> *(starts handing him stuff)*

Yo, where the guard at! Where my fucking newspaper at! That sonofabitch. That nigga bring me
some shit, too.

> *(keeps loading the stuff on Ray)*

I ain't saying you're sweet—want some baby powder? Here, take some Kool-Aid. Take what you
want, man. Take what you fucking want. You
home, man! You home, baby! You know what I'm
saying?

Ray can only laugh.

> HOPHA (cont'd)

You home here now. You with us. Word. Let the
boys know that we got a new member now.
Everything's going to be a'ight now.

Ray doesn't respond. He starts flipping through a book Hopha's handed
him.

> HOPHA

You like that book?

> RAY

> *(quotes a passage)*

"Most of all, I must see to it that I do not lend
myself to the evils which I condemn."

> HOPHA

> *(mulls it over a moment)*

Yeah, well, you know what I say about that? Stay
the fuck out our way. That's all I got to say about
that shit. You know what I mean? Hey, I love
people, but I don't tell 'em that shit, you know
what I mean? And when it comes to me and
mines, I defend mine very well. Fuck that.

RAY

I want to get out of the game, man. For real.
That's all I want.

HOPHA

Ain't no way out of this, man! Ain't no way out
of this, man. If you move into records—if you
move into shit with us, man—you taking the game
with you. It's all in sync, man.

RAY

I ain't trying to be a part of the whole game, gang
bullshit. I'm trying to write—I need a pen and
some paper. A pen and some paper—

HOPHA

Listen, listen, fuck that. I don't want to hear that
shit, I don't want to fucking hear that shit. Nigga,
you are in jail, man. Bottom line. You down with
us. There ain't no coming out of this shit. This
shit's the same shit on the fucking street. The beef
ain't gonna stop for you. Who the fuck is you.
You gonna stop this beef? You can't stop it. You
help us stop it.

RAY
(lost)

I'm trying to think straight, man. I need a pen
and a pad.

HOPHA

I hear you, man. I hear you. It's gonna be all right,
you know what I mean? It's gonna be all right.
(hands him a pad and pen)
Just waiting till you got here.

RAY

Guess you all gonna have to make me Secretary
of State.

> ### HOPHA
> Or Secretary of Defense. How's that?

Ray gives Hopha a look

> ### HOPHA (cont'd)
> What, you don't like that? Minister of Defense,
> then. Minister of Information— but can fight,
> you know what I mean? 'Cause you gonna have
> to fight, cuz. Make no mistake about it. This is
> jail.

EXT. YARD - DAY

Thug Life crew hangs out at the weight machines, China holding court,
manically lifting weights as he rallies his crew. He's chiseled, angry, danger-
ous.

> ### CHINA
> Man, we got to handle that. When he come out,
> we got to take care of that. It's motherfucking
> personal. It's personal. 'Cause you know that
> nigga we beat down? You know he down with
> Hopha, right? Yeah, they going against us, 'cause
> ain't nothing gonna stop this motherfucking drug
> game, you know, stop none of my motherfucking
> business. 'Cause we ain't having that shit. It's
> Thug Life for life!

                                            CUT TO:

> ### CHINA (cont'd)
> I got the word he's down with Union crew now.
> We gonna get him. Yeah, he down with Union
> crew. And I don't like no bitch-ass nigga cutting
> into my motherfucking business! You get what
> I'm saying?

His crew's right there with him.

> ### THUG LIFE CREW
> Yeah, we get you. We down with you.

CHINA

Fuck that. If I got to push the steel in the motherfucking nigga We gonna do that!

INT. RAY'S CELL - SAME TIME - MUSIC UP

Ray's at his desk, writing, deep inside it.

BACK TO:

EXT. YARD - LATER

On the other side of the yard, Hopha's rounding up his crew.

HOPHA

We got some problems. See them niggas over
there? You know what I'm saying? Yeah, I see
them. Man, there's a difference with us and them,
man, you know what I'm saying? We organized.
That bunch of stupid motherfuckers, man, they
can't handle no business. We already did that drug
shit, and that fucking hand-to-hand bullshit. We
want cake, B. Don't you want cake? We want
fucking cake, man! If y'all want some cake, man,
we do this shit, make this move-on these motherfuckers, man... I don't give a fuck what happens.

INT. RAY'S CELL - SAME TIME - MUSIC UP

He's deep inside his verse, pen moving furiously, oblivious to the world outside.

EXT. YARD - LATER

The tension's building. Thug Life and Union crew face off across the yard,
SHOUTING at each other.

HOPHA

Even your own man don't fucking like you, faggot!

THUG LIFE

Hey, fuck you!

> UNION

Yeah, fuck you all!

> HOPHA

If you was fucking smart, you'd be over here too.
We wouldn't have to be doing this. We wouldn't
have to be doing this!

They keep SCREAMING at each other.

> HOPHA
> *(throws up his arms)*
Fuck these niggas, man! Lay back, lay back.

Back on the Thug Life side, China faces Talib, who's threatened to break
ranks.

> CHINA

You decide who you want to be with.

> TALIB

Fuck Thug Life.

They start to fight, tackle each other to the ground and punch and wrestle
furiously on the concrete yard.

> BACK TO:

INT. RAY'S CELL - SAME TIME - MUSIC UP

Ray's lost in thought, pen in mouth... words and scrawls all over his page...
The CAMERA manages to make out a few lines... Mother sun to be
slain... like Lazarus...

EXT. YARD - HIGH SHOT - LATE AFTERNOON - MUSIC

The yard fills with prisoners. It's a blistering hot day. Prisoners roam
around the yard like caged animals.

SERIES OF SHOTS of China on his side, Hopha on his. A palpable tension fills the rec yard.

EXT. JAIL - SAME TIME - MUSIC CONT'D

A young woman, LAUREN BELL, calm, beautiful, dressed in casual, colorful garb, knapsack on her back, books cradled in her arm, approaches the visitor's entrance, waits to be buzzed in, enters.

BACK TO:

EXT. YARD - SAME TIME - MUSIC CONT'D

SHOTS of prisoners playing basketball, lifting weights, hitting the speed bag. Tension mounts.

INT. VISITOR'S ENTRANCE - SAME TIME

Lauren signs in.

LAUREN
(to Guard)
Is it hot enough for you out there?

BACK TO:

EXT. YARD - LATER - MUSIC CONT'D

Prisoners play Ping-Pong, volleyball, hit punching bags.

INT. VISITOR'S ENTRANCE - SAME TIME

Lauren walks through the metal detector, removes her bag. The guard frisks her.

LAUREN
(knows the routine)
Just my keys in my front pocket...

EXT. YARD - LATER - MUSIC UP

Ray enters the yard, looks around for a place to go, feels the tension.

CLOSE ON: China doing stomach crunches with a vengeance.

Ray starts to pace in the middle of the yard, creating some kind of wall around him.

China's crunches get faster and faster...

A GUARD keeps watch from a guard tower...

Hopha approaches Ray.

Officer Dom and the Thug Life crew.

> HOPHA
> *(re China)*
> You see him there? I want you to do the right thing.

> RAY
> What the fuck is the right thing? I'm saying. What is the right thing?

> HOPHA
> The right thing is the right side.

> RAY
> The right thing is for me to just be my fucking self. Do you know what I'm saying? Do you know what I'm saying?

> HOPHA
>
> Look around, man. It's hard to be yourself in here, man. My crew gotta know where you standing at. I know where they standing at—

> RAY
>
> What the fuck, this ain't no rite of passage or some shit—

> HOPHA
>
> You see that line? You see that line? Ain't nobody gonna cross that shit.

Hopha's crew stands tall and proud in a long line.

> HOPHA (cont'd)
>
> You see them lined up? We got our shit locked over here. Ain't nobody coming over here and fucking with this shit. There's a place for you over here. If not, go the fuck over there with your friend, then!

TIME CUT TO:

Ray sits alone on the sideline, eyes on the yard. MUSIC UP.

China rallies his crew.

Hopha organizes his crew.

Ray watches from the sideline.

On the Thug Life side, China, surrounded by his crew, readies to attack.

> CHINA
>
> It's going down today. It's going down today. Yeah. He gots to go. He gots to go.
> *(passes a blunt around)*
> Pass that joint. I want everybody high. Everybody. I want everybody high. It's the Thug in us. It's all good.

SLO-MO MUSIC UP. A PRISONER punches a steady rhythm on the speed bag, his chest muscles rippling in the hot sun.

Ray moves to the middle of the yard, sits on the ground, watches, waits. China starts toward him, menacing. Ray is like a cornered animal – he sees China coming for him. He's surrounded. He stands suddenly and forcefully.

As China moves in for the kill, Ray faces him and explodes into verse. They all stop, shocked, mesmerized, as Ray lets loose the passion and heart of his verse.

RAY

I stand on the corner of the block slinging
amethyst rocks
drinking 40's of Mother Earth's private nectar
stock
dodging cops
'cause five-oh be the 666
and i need a fix of that purple rain
the type of shit that drives membranes insane
oh yeah, I'm in the fast lane
snorting...candy yams
that free my body and soul
and send me like Shazam!

Never question
who I am
God knows

and i know God personally
in fact, he lets me call him me

In the corridor, Lauren catches sight of the scene in the yard. She moves toward the door to watch.

RAY (cont'd)

yeah, i'm sirius B
Dogon niggas plottin' shit, lovely
but the Feds are also plottin' me
they're tryin' to imprison my astrology
to put my stars behind bars
my stars in stripes
using blood splattered banners
as nationalist kites

Ray is unstoppable, BELLOWING the poem at them, for them, about them.
They watch and listen, stunned.

> RAY (cont'd)
> but i control the wind
>
> that's why they call it the hawk
> i am horus
> son of isis
> son of osiris
> worshipped as jesus
> resurrected like lazarus
>
> but you can call me lazzie
>
> lazy
>
> yeah, i'm lazy
> 'cause i'd rather sit and build
> than work and plow a field
> worshipping a daily yield of cash green crops

Lauren's still frozen in the door, watching.

> RAY (cont'd)
> stealing us was the smartest thing they ever did
> too bad they don't teach the truth to their kids
>
> our influence on them is the reflection they see
> when they look into their minstrel mirror
> and talk about their culture
> their existence is that of a schizophrenic vulture
>
> yeah, there's no repentance
> they are bound to live an infinite consecutive
> executive life sentence
> *(in China's face)*
> so what are you bound to live, nigga
> so while you're out there serving your time
> (MORE)

> RAY (cont'd)
> i'll be in sync with the moon
> while you run from the sun
> life of the womb
> reflected by guns
> worshipper of moons
> i am the sun
> and we are public enemies number one!
> one one one!
> one one one!

He storms off, disappearing before anyone knows quite what has happened. Both crews are left standing silently, awed by the power of his words.

> HOPHA
> *(finally, dazed)*
> I forgot what the fuck I was thinking.

The gangs back quietly away from each other, disperse. Ray has won the battle—using the word as his sword.

Ray heads into the jail, passing—but seemingly unaware of—Lauren, still standing in the door. She follows him in.

INT. CORRIDOR – SAME TIME

Lauren runs after Ray.

> LAUREN
> *(catches up to him)*
> Are you all right? Are you okay?

> RAY
> *(caught off guard)*
> Um—yes.

> LAUREN
> I just saw what you did out there. Do you need
> any help?

> RAY
> No.

He's confused, shaken. He starts to walk away. She follows.

                    LAUREN
          My name is Lauren.
                    (extends her hand)
          Lauren Bell. I teach writing here.
                    (after a moment)
          Where did you get that from?

                    RAY
          I'm sorry—

                    LAUREN
          The poem that you did out there. Did you write
          that?

                    RAY
                    (baffled)
          Yeah.

They're interrupted by a GUARD.

                    GUARD
          Excuse me, is everything all right—
                    (to Lauren)
          Are you okay?
                    (turns on Ray)
          What are you doing out here in the hall?!

                    LAUREN
          Yes, I'm fine—

                    GUARD
                    (to Ray)
          What dorm are you in?

                    RAY
          North three.

                    LAUREN
          He's just talking to me—he's on his way to —

GUARD

He is not supposed to be out here. North three?
Let's go, right now. Right now! You have no right
out here, let's go!

She starts to usher Ray down the hall.

LAUREN
(shouts after them)
All right, you're in North three? I'll put in a
request for you. You have to tell the C.O. that you
want to come to class and they'll let you come
down.

Ray and the Guard disappear into North three.

INT. CELLBLOCK - LATER

Thug Life crew is hanging out on the tier, POUNDING A BEAT on an old
bunk bed.

INT. DAY ROOM - SAME TIME - BEAT CONT'D

...while Hopha and his Union crew are hanging out in the Day Room. The
Thug Life beat continues through the whole SEQUENCE.

HOPHA
(on his soapbox)
I've been searching myself, man. I know you all
have too. The world is fucking leaving us behind,
man. What Ray said was right. I didn't agree with
his methods, you know what I'm saying—

PRISONER #1
What the hell was that?

HOPHA
I still don't fucking know entirely, man, but what
that nigga did out there was just fucking fascinat-
ing.

Marc Levin directs Bonz Malone (Hopha) and the Union crew.

INT. RAY'S CELL - SAME TIME

Ray stares out his cell window.

INT. CELLBLOCK - SAME TIME

Thug Life kills time on the tier, bored and angry, POUNDING A BEAT on the metal bunk.

INT. RAY'S CELL - SAME TIME

Bent over, he stares at the floor.

BACK TO:

INT. DAY ROOM - SAME TIME

Hopha's crew is somber, reflective.

HOPHA
(thinks a long moment, then)
I ain't fucking coming back here. Fuck that shit. I
want you all to know that. I ain't coming back here!

INT. RAY'S CELL - SAME TIME

He paces back and forth... an animal trapped in a cage.

                    HOPHA (V.O.)
          Like I say, I love you all...

                                        BACK TO:

INT. DAY ROOM - LATER

Hopha throws his arms about as he speaks. He's pumped, headed into a rampage.

                    HOPHA
          ...But I'm telling you the way it fucking is! Them
          motherfuckers outside this glass don't give a fuck
          about us! We started off fighting, and we gonna
          end up fighting, but how we fight is the fight.
          That's the way it goes. If I'm gonna die for some-
          thing, I'm gonna die for something that's worth it,
          dig?

He embraces one of his crew members.

INT. CELLBLOCK - CLOSE SHOT

Thug Life hands POUND A BEAT on the bunk.

INT. RAY'S CELL - SAME TIME

He's on the floor, back against the wall, face buried in his hands.

And the BEAT goes on.

                                        CUT TO:

INT. CLASSROOM - NEXT DAY - CLOSE ON LAUREN

She stands at the front of the room addressing the prisoners.

                    LAUREN
               (holding a book)
          We've been discussing the chapters as we've been
          going along. But now we finished the whole book...

A dozen or so PRISONERS, ranging in age from twenties to forties, sit listening with respect, intent on participation in the class, eager to learn, eager to express themselves.

> LAUREN (cont'd)
> ... and what I want to know is, what came to your mind last night, when you were lying in your cell and you were reading the assignment... what was the first thing that came to your mind?

TIME CUT TO:

The class in mid-discussion...

> JOE
> ...I mean, sure, I know I want to stay off the street, and I know I want to be a positive person to my family. But I know that, me personally, if the situation arose where it was either starve—or my children starving—or doing the right thing, then you know, it's trey ball, it's got to be—or Monster Cody got to do what he got to.

> RON
> I do not agree with Joe. Sadly, too many of our brothers got the mentality of Joe, and say, because of this and that, I'm gonna put this in my hand and use my family as an excuse... when all the time, like you said, you got to be responsible for you. So you could use your family as an excuse for why you shot some motherfucker, to take some money—fuck no, you still coming to jail.

> JOE
> I don't know if you know this or not, brothers, but we are capitalists. Whether we're capitalists on a small scale... but we live in a capitalist country and that is what we are. We are born to learn how to capitalize on whatever it is... it's about money.

> LAUREN
>
> So what Joe and John are saying is there are not
> enough resources out there to help you change
> your life. Is that true?

Ray enters the room and finds a seat. Lauren sees him, smiles. He looks back at her.

> JOE
>
> We just happened to be born our color and we're
> at the bottom of the ladder. You understand?
> Now, if I could make it out and have me some real
> dough... yeah, then it wouldn't be like that.

TIME CUT TO:

> LAUREN
>
> All right, you all ready for the poetry reading?

Prisoners respond enthusiastically. Ray can't help but smile.

> LAUREN
>
> Ron, you ready?

> RON
>
> Yeah.

He gets up, rubs his hands across his face nervously.

> RON
>
> The name of my little piece is called "Why."
> *(takes some paper out of his pocket;*
> *unfolds it; clears his throat; reads)*
> I shot three motherfuckers
> And I didn't know why
> I guess I just wanted to see something die.
> You see, I bought this gun for a few rocks
> Just to get even, so I thought, with those
> shit-eating cops.
> Holding the cold blue steel in the palm of my hand
> Not quite sixteen, yet totally a man.
> (MORE)

                    RON (cont'd)
My only plan was money in my hand
I wore Falacci, Gucci, Nikes and Eddie B.
I was the coolest motherfucker in Southeast D.C.
School? What the fuck, that was a thing of the past
Getting paid, school and all that other square shit
could kiss my ass.
Mad at my bun, toying with my gun, tipped on
over to my favorite pool room just to have some fun
Rips was at full blast, so I chalked up my cue,
ready to kick some ass.
I played a few hours, beat all the old-timers and
was about to go
Until one of three 'bama motherfuckers stepped
on my toe.
A split second later, whip-bam it was on:
The ass-kicking begun.
I ducked a few pool balls and eased out my gun
Ratta-tat-tat and that was that.
Three was whacked.
Ten years later:
As I sit in my jail cell about to cry,
I'm thinking, I shot three motherfuckers—
And I don't know why.

The class APPLAUDS.

                    LAUREN
Mmm...Very nice poem. Thank you, Ron.

In the back, Ray writes in his pad.

                    LAUREN
I don't know if all of you guys know, but today's
my last day here.

The class groans, mumbles, hit hard by this news.

                    LAUREN
                (starts to break down)
I'm gonna miss you guys.

CLASS
We gonna miss you too.

LAUREN
It's so wild that we had this conversation today,
because they have cut this program.
(starts to tear up)
And it's just brought home the fact that it really
isn't about rehabilitation anymore, you know. You
were right, Joe. Like I was trying to tell you earlier, yeah, it's gonna be hard when you leave here.
It's gonna be real hard. It's really fucked up that
you were born in Southeast, in the ghetto. It's really fucked up that you were born black. It's really
fucked up that you had the hard time that you had
in your life. Whatever your story is, whatever it is
that brought you here in your life, that shit is really
fucked up. But if you keep shoving the anger and
the pain and the frustration down, and you keep
saying that's all right, fuck it, I'm gonna do what I
gotta do and you don't let it come out, that keeps
pushing it down, that is your prison. You gotta let
that shit out, because once you let that frustration
out, it doesn't hold you back anymore. It doesn't
lock you down. And then you can stand up with
some courage and you can say okay, yeah it's fucked
up, but I am not going to live like this. I am going
to take my destiny into my own hands. That's the
only way to go now. I grew up with guys just like
you all. All of you all. My brother was sitting in
your seat. My brother's not here anymore. He
grew up in your era, Joe, in your era, Ronald.
When everybody wanted to be a Superfly.
Remember that? It was all about a being Superfly,
or the Mac, remember that? Now it's all about
being a gangsta or OG.
(tears streaming)
He had a good heart.
(MORE)

> LAUREN (cont'd)
>
> Just like you all. I know you all are good guys.
> The people out there, they see your face in the
> paper, they think you're monsters. I know you're
> good guys inside. My brother had a good heart...

Ray is quiet, can't quite look at her.

> LAUREN (cont'd)
>
> I know your dreams. I been there. But chasing
> them—thinking you can achieve them by selling
> drugs... that's just a part of the trap, y'all. That's
> just a part of the trap. And yeah, you right,
> Ronald, the cycle just keeps continuing. Who's
> gonna stop it? Y'all got to stop it. Y'all been in.
> Y'all can go back out, change your life, and show
> the young brothers that they don't have to come
> back in here like this.
> *(a moment; quiet)*
> Freedom isn't out here, it's in here.
> *(points to her head)*
> You can be free any time you want. Any time.
> *(strong; almost a whisper)*
> Never give anyone the power to take away your
> freedom. That's yours. It don't belong to nobody
> but you. Remember that.

She's spent.

> LAUREN (cont'd)
>
> I'm not gonna go on and on. Besides, my tissue's
> falling apart.

TIME CUT TO:

Lauren embraces the guys on their way out... they make last-minute
exchanges.

> RED
>
> We gonna miss you.

LAUREN
(hugs him)
I'm gonna miss you too, Red.
(hugs another)
And I'm gonna miss you, too.
(and another)
And I'm gonna miss you, too.

JOE
Give me a hug.

LAUREN
All right, all right.
(moving toward the door)
Richie, give me a hug, baby.

They walk by Ray, who remains in his chair, still writing.

JOE
(to Lauren)
You gonna be okay?

LAUREN
I'm gonna be all right. You gonna be okay? I'm
gonna be fine after that poem you wrote me.

CLOSE ON: Ray's pad, his pen moving swiftly. We catch glimpses of his
verse: "...wings... of catharsis..."

LAUREN (O.S.)
You gonna write me?

She's at the door, seeing the last of them off.

LAUREN (cont'd)
All right, take care, baby.

She starts back toward her desk. Ray is standing by his chair.

LAUREN
(sees him; plays it cool)
Ray... you hangin' back for a minute?

                    RAY
Um-hm.

He follows her back to the desk.

                    LAUREN
So what did you think of the class?

                    RAY
                  (smitten)
I think you're a wonderful teacher.

                    LAUREN
Well, thank you, Ray.

There's an awkward moment.

                    LAUREN
                  (finally)
Ray, what are you doing in here?

                    RAY
I sold weed. I sell weed.

                    LAUREN
So you just happened to be—I don't know, I don't
know.

                    RAY
I got caught.

                    LAUREN
Yeah, I know you got caught. I know you got
caught. I know you got caught, I know.

                    RAY
I mean, it's that simple. It's not—I mean...

                    LAUREN
What, are you in school?

                              RAY
        No.

                            LAUREN
        So you sell weed for a living, that's it? And you
        write poetry.

                              RAY
        I never really thought of myself as writing poetry,
        you know. I write.
                           (a moment)
        I'm really here on a petty weed charge—
        although... I've been told that I have to cop a plea,
        and if I do, I may be looking at like a couple of
        years. But I don't know. I don't know—

                            LAUREN
                          (decides)
        Just stay in touch.
                         (regards him)
        Just stay in touch. You never know. You never
        know. ...I gotta go.

And she does, leaving Ray alone by the window.

INT. JAIL - TIME TRANSITION

PRISONERS walk down corridors, pushing trays, dragging their feet.

                      HOPHA (V.O. THE CUT)
        You got me thinking. You remember that book
        that was in my cell? *The Art of War*?

INT. CELLBLOCK TIER

Ray and Hopha pace the tier, talking.

                              RAY
        Yeah.

HOPHA

Guy's name is Sun Tzu. Some old Chinese guy, a
long time ago. The man said it's about learning to
lead people, it's about being able to win wars
without violence. You know what I mean? He
wasn't no sucker, now—he'd get ready to get
down. But he won wars from the beginning
without ever having to use violence. He said that's
where real power is. Shit bugged me the fuck out,
I thought what the fuck is this nigga talking about.
I mean, I thought about it—but how many people
really do that? How many people really do that.
You did that. I'm telling you, man, you got a hell
of a lot more talent than maybe even you know.
And you got a hell of a lot of decisions. I can't
help you with the decisions, man, but I'm always
there for you.

RAY

I've made my decisions. You can see. And there's
no fear in my heart no more, there's no fear! I
don't give a fuck.

HOPHA

I'm scared every day, but I'm not afraid. You dig?
To me there's a difference. To you there's a difference. You showed that. You gonna be a great
man. You got great things to fucking do. And one
of them is passing this to an old friend of mine.

He hands Ray a Dodge City Marshal badge.

RAY

What's this?

HOPHA

This is something a friend of mine gave me a long
time ago. I'm gonna get you out of here. I'm
puttin' up—

RAY

You gonna get me outta here?

HOPHA

You not listening to me, man. I'm putting up bail
for you.

Ray breaks into laughter, hugs Hopha.

HOPHA

I'm gonna put up the bail for you. If you do this
piece of work for me, I'm here.

FADE OUT:

FADE UP:

INT. D.C. JAIL PROCESSING

Ray approaches the gate.

GUARD

What's your name?

RAY

Raymond Joshua.

GUARD

(opens the gate)

Okay, you're being released on cash collateral.
Take your suit off and put it in the basket.

Ray strips, carries his shoes into the release room. A GUARD hands him
his box of belongings. Ray empties it.

RAY

Yo, where's my shirt?

GUARD

It got lost, shit happens.

(throws him someone else's shirt)

Here, take that. You going home anyhow.

CUT TO:

Ray is escorted through Processing.   C.O. Lucas appears at the gate next to him.

> C.O. LUCAS
>
> Hey, Ray, this is your last time in here, right? I want you to take something out of the door with you when you leave. Those six digits on that band I told you about? They'll be here waiting for you if you ever come back. Now get your ass out of my jail.

CLOSE ON Ray's wrist band being cut off.

> GUARD
>
> Door!

The door opens. Sunshine pours through.

EXT. JAIL - DAY - MUSIC UP

Ray exits, lifts his face to the warm sun. He's escorted to the gate by two OFFICERS.

> GUARD (O.S.)
> *(from the watchtower)*
>
> What's your name?

> RAY
> *(shouts up)*
>
> Raymond Joshua.

> GUARD (O.S.)
>
> Your number?

> RAY
>
> Two seven four zero zero one.

> GUARD (O.S.)
>
> Okay. Officer, what's he going out on?

> GUARD
>
> He's going out on cash collateral.

> GUARD (O.S.)
Okay.

The gate opens. Ray's released into the street.

The gate closes behind him. The officers head back toward the jail.

Ray walks toward the cemetery across the street, jumps the fence, walks through the graveyard, pauses at a monument, looks out at the concertina wire surrounding the jail.

MUSIC MONTAGE #3. IMAGES of the neighborhood, the jail and the shooting scene flood his mind.

BACK TO Ray in the cemetery. Above him, the sun filters through the trees, begins its descent.

FADE OUT:

FADE IN:

EXT. EDDIE'S APARTMENT - DODGE CITY - DAY

The group of kids sitting outside on the fence see Ray coming and flock to him. He's still wearing the clothes he left jail in.

> KIDS
Hey, Ray. How you doing, Ray? What's happening?

> RAY
Nothing much.

> KIDS
Where you been at the last couple of days, Ray?

Ray doesn't answer, heads straight into the building.

INT. APARTMENT BUILDING HALLWAY

Ray raps on Eddie's door.

EDDIE opens the door.

> EDDIE
Everything cool, man?

                              RAY
      Yeah.

INT. EDDIE'S APARTMENT

Eddie lets Ray in.

                             EDDIE
      So how they treat you in camp, man?

                              RAY
      A'ight.

                             EDDIE
                      (motions to a chair)
      Sit down, man. Hold on a second, I got some-
      thing for you.

Ray sits, waits. Eddie disappears into the back room. After a moment, Ray
looks up, can't believe what he sees.

Eddie leads Big Mike out of the bedroom, eyes wrapped in bandages, gait
unsteady. Ray bursts into shocked laughter, jumps up to embrace Mike.

                              RAY
      Oh, shit! Oh, shit! Yoooooo!

                             MIKE
      What's up, man? What's up?

Ray laughs and can only hug him.

                             MIKE
      I'm alive, man.

                              RAY
      I cannot believe this shit.

                             MIKE
      You been a'ight in there?

                              RAY
      Yeah, I been cool. I been great.

MIKE

Well, I'm a'ight. But you know what? I'm blind
now, man. I can't see shit. Somebody in Dodge
City's gonna have to take care of that.

RAY

Take care of what?

MIKE

Man, I'm hurtin'. And the only thing I can do to
feel better is to know that someone else is hurtin'.
What we gonna do is handle this.

RAY

Handle this how, nigga? What the fuck are you
talking about?

MIKE

I got a motherfucking bullet in my head, and
whoever put it there, they going to pay. Now is
you with that or what?

RAY

We've been doing this for years. For what? I
don't understand it. I understood it before, but I
don't understand that shit. 'Cause you know
what? When I was inside, I realized something. I
was blind for a long time.
(regards him)
I see now. And I see that this shit has to end.
There's not shit you can do. There is no one you
could shoot—not even the fucking doctor—that
would give you your fucking vision back. There's
nothing—no one you could shoot. You could shoot
the sun—and everybody else would just be blind.
(changes tack)
I spoke to your man inside.

MIKE

You what?!

RAY

I spoke with your man. Hopha.

MIKE

What'd he say? What'd he say?!

RAY

He said the same shit I'm saying. That this shit is silly. He don't want any type of retaliation.

MIKE

Man, that's bullshit.

RAY

It's not bullshit. It's not bullshit.

MIKE

Man, Hopha ain't say nothing like that. He know Dodge City sticks together no matter what. Anybody in Dodge City go down, motherfucker's being dealt with.

Ray reaches into his pocket, takes out the Marshal badge, puts it in Mike's hand.

RAY

What's this.

MIKE

What is this? Where the fuck you get this from, man?

RAY

Your boy. He knew you wouldn't believe shit I was telling you. What the fuck are we retaliating for? We don't need this shit anymore.

MIKE

So what are you saying, Dodge City is breaking up?

RAY

What the fuck are you talking about, this ain't the Temptations or some shit. We ain't breaking up.

Walter Woodward

Lawrence Wilson (Big Mike) and Saul Williams (Ray Joshua) in Dodge City.

MIKE

What makes you think me and you can go talk to somebody that tried to kill me—and tried to kill you. The fucking mayor can't even talk to these people. The government can't even talk to these people.

RAY

I ain't talking about the mayor, I ain't talking about the government. Nigga, I love you. I love you. I just don't want to see you go out like a million other niggas before you.

MIKE
(starting to give)

Man, I'm scared.

RAY

I know you're scared.

MIKE

Can you help me out, man.

> RAY
> *(hugs him)*

I'll help you.

> MIKE

Help me, man.

They hold the embrace for a long time.

EXT. DODGE CITY - HIGH SHOT

Ray leads Mike through the projects. The kids are shocked to see them, stand back in awe. It's an eerie image, like Christ leading the blind. They approach their crew, embrace.

> CREW 1

Man, I'm trying to get back. I'm gonna punish one of them niggas, man.

> CREW 2

They blind you, I'm trying to blind one of them other niggas. Fuck that shit.

> MIKE
> *(tries to talk to them)*

I understand, I understand...

> CREW 1

They drew first blood, baby, they drew first blood. And they know me. They know all us. They know how we go.

> MIKE

I understand that but—

> CREW 1

Pow pow, baby, pow pow. Live by the sword, die by the sword, you know what I'm saying?

RAY

Pow pow. For who? Who the fuck you fighting
for? What are you fighting to protect?

CREW 1

For my man. For my man. For Dodge City.

RAY

Nigga, you live in the motherfucking projects. It's
an experiment. Projects experiment. Government
experiment. You serving time outside of the penitentiary, doing exactly what they want you to do:
pow pow, all day. That's the motherfucking master
plan, nigga. That's the motherfucking master plan.

MIKE

That's right.

CREW 1

No, Mike—

CREW 4

Let Mike make the call. Mike making the house
call.

MIKE

I'm making the call, man, you know? I want the
guns down, man. I want the guns down.

CREW 4

You heard what he said. Let's put the guns down.
Put the guns down.

MIKE

There was one last bullet was shot around here,
and that was the bullet in my head.

MUSIC MONTAGE #4. Mike takes off his bandages to reveal the scarred
and bloody place his eyes used to be.

The IMAGE DISSOLVES into a SERIES OF FLASHBACK IMAGES: the

shooting scene, jail, the cemetery, Lauren... ending with —

EXT. ANACOSTIA BRIDGE - EVENING

Ray crossing over the bridge into the other Washington, D.C. The last light of sun blazes orange on the horizon.

EXT. WASHINGTON, D.C.

Ray calls Lauren from a pay phone.

INT. PUBLIC BUS - NIGHT

Ray rides through the D.C. streets, stares out the window.

EXT. LAUREN'S HOUSE - LATER

Ray knocks on the door. Lauren appears.

> LAUREN
> I can't believe you made it.

> RAY
> I did.

> LAUREN
> Well, come on in.

INT. LAUREN'S HOUSE

It's a party/poetry reading. Lauren introduces Ray to her friends, all poets.

> LAUREN
> Ray, this is DJ; DJ, this is Ray. Friend of mine.

> DJ RENEGADE
> *(shakes Ray's hand)*
> DJ Renegade.

> LAUREN
> DJ's a phat poet, you got to hear his work.
> Actually, tonight you gonna hear some of his work
> because we're gonna have a little poetry reading.

CUT TO:

INT. LAUREN'S HOUSE - LATER

The reading is under way. DJ RENEGADE's holding court.

> DJ RENEGADE
>
> Brothers and sisters, love will leave you melancholy
> as a muted trumpet. Bluer than a cloudless sky,
> bluer than a Viking's eye...

CUT TO:

> DJ RENEGADE (cont'd)
> *(finishes the poem)*
> You see, love is a blue-bottled fly flitting between
> blue and green, wings raggedy as a pair of old
> jeans. Merci beaucoup. Love is Winnie the Pooh
> doing voodoo in corrective shoes.

They all laugh and applaud.

TIME CUT:

> DJ RENEGADE
> *(to Ray)*
> You write?

> RAY
> Um, a little bit, yeah.

> DJ RENEGADE
> You gonna kick a piece later?

> RAY
> Um, I don't know.

> LAUREN
> Yeah, he's gonna kick a piece later.

TIME CUT:

Ray and Lauren are alone, talking.

RAY

I got a million things going on in my head.

LAUREN

Oh, okay, so you're gonna freestyle.

RAY

No.

TIME CUT:

Lauren's trying out a new poem.

LAUREN

His intergalactic freestyle jazz licks
My ears
As I ride his tongue and groove to the sound of
chords no man has ever touched
His touch tempts me to taste flesh of my flesh
from which he is made

CUT TO:

LAUREN (cont'd)
(finishes the poem)
His invisible strokes are felt, as he stands on the
stage in front of me
A mike and a million miles away from me.

TIME CUT:

Ray sits next to Lauren and some of her friends.

RAY
(to Lauren)
Everything's kind of new now. Like, I wouldn't
want to read anything that I wrote before.

LIZA
(to Ray)
It's nice to have you on the outside.

Lauren turns on her, can't believe she said it.

>   RAY
>   (cool)
>   It's good to be on the outside.
>   (to Lauren)
>   It's all right, I'm not tripping.

                                                    TIME CUT:

Ray's standing before the small party.

>   RAY
>   (slow; beautiful)
>   You massage the universe's spine
>   the way you twirl through time and leave shadows
>   on the sun.
>   My love is the wind song
>   If it is up to me, I'll never die
>   If it is up to me, I'll die tomorrow a thousand
>   times in an hour and live seven minutes later
>   If it is up to me, the sun will never cease to shine
>   and the moon will never cease to glow and I'll
>   dance a million tomorrows in the sun rays of the
>   moon waves and bathe in the yesterdays of days to
>   come, ignoring all of my afterthoughts and pre-
>   conceived notions
>   If it is up to me, it is up to me
>   And thus is my love.
>   Untainted.
>   Eternal.

Lauren's rapt... devastated by the poem.

>   RAY
>   (finishing)
>   ...The wind is the moon's imagination... wander-
>   ing, it seeps through cracks, ripples the grass,
>   explores the unknown.
>   My love is my soul's imagination.
>   How do I love you?
>   Imagine.

DISSOLVE TO:

INT. LAUREN'S BEDROOM - LATER

Lauren and Ray sit on the couch, talking quietly.

> LAUREN
> I can't believe you actually came.

> RAY
> Glad I came. Very glad I came.

He fidgets uncomfortably.

> LAUREN
> I have thought of you. And...

> RAY
> And what else? What else is there? Today, now.

> LAUREN
> There's tomorrow. And the next day, and the next.

> RAY
> Not today. Not now.

> LAUREN
> Yeah, well.

> RAY
> Tomorrow, and the next day, and the next, for me,
> is not exactly... I'm sorry.

> LAUREN
> Ray—

> RAY
> If you want me to go—

LAUREN

Ray, I don't know what I want you to do, to be
quite honest with you. Today you're here.
Tomorrow and the next day and the next... you
still have to go to court. You still have to possibly
go away. And I still have to try to get back into
prison to do my job—

RAY
(leans in to kiss her)
Okay, please—

LAUREN
(pulls back)
No, I really can't—I can't go there right now, I just
can't.
(soft)
It's really difficult, Ray.

RAY

Who are you telling. You made an impression on
me. And, it's funny, I wasn't certain of when I'd be
able to see you again. But... And I'm not asking
for much more than that; that's all I want. Now.
This is all I'm asking for. Now.

MUSIC UP. He leans in again to kiss her. This time she lets him, and kisses
back. They undress each other, make languid love...

EXT. WASHINGTON, D.C. - EASTERN MARKET - NEXT MORNING

It's a colorful, lively outdoor market, made more alive by the Island drum
sounds of a rhythm band made up entirely of children banging on garbage
pails and pots and pans.

Lauren and Ray stop to watch and listen.

In the market, they come to a table of African and African-American literature, peruse the titles. Resting on the table is a framed blueprint of an
old slave ship, the *Slave Ship Brookes*. The CAMERA takes in the decks,
the gallows...

EXT. ALLEY BEHIND LAUREN'S HOUSE - LATER

Ray and Lauren round the corner on the way back from the market. Lauren has the slave ship picture under her arm.

> LAUREN
>
> So you coming to the slam tonight?

> RAY
>
> I don't know. I may.

> LAUREN
>
> You should.

> RAY
>
> I want to.

> LAUREN
>
> You should. You should. I can get you up on stage.

> RAY
>
> Yeah... I just—I'm not thinking about performing, I need to think. I just... I have to go to court on Monday.

> LAUREN
> *(it's a blow)*
> Wow. That soon. Damn, you just got out.

They've paused in the alley behind Lauren's building.

> LAUREN (cont'd)
>
> Have you thought about what you're going to do?

> RAY
>
> I have no clue. I need time to think it over, 'cause I can't see what I'm supposed to be doing now. None of this makes sense to me.

> LAUREN
> *(tries to stay cool, reason with him)*
> So you only have until Monday—

RAY
(no patience)
Yeah, I only have until Monday.

LAUREN
What did your lawyer say?

RAY
(Ray sits down on the stoop)
My lawyer told me to cop a plea, he told me that's
the best thing to do, he said if I fight it I'll probably just end up getting more time. It's just...

LAUREN
What's your charge.

RAY
Possession of illegal substance.

LAUREN
Are you guilty? Did you do it?

RAY
I had it on me.

LAUREN
(a long moment; quiet)
What's going to be is going to be. You stand up
and you face it.

RAY
(can't accept it)
It's a lot to face. It's a hell of a lot to face—for
some weed, you know.

LAUREN
Man, they caught you with the shit red-handed.
What are you gonna do, run?

RAY

No—I think there has to be another way out! I pray there has to be another way out. Copping a fucking plea?! That shit is not my way. I can't feel that shit, I can't see that shit—

LAUREN

Wait a minute, you acting like you did not do this shit—like copping a plea would be like lying to yourself. Well, you did the shit, Ray.

RAY

I did do the shit, but I don't feel guilty about it! I don't feel guilty! I'm sorry, but I don't feel guilty.

LAUREN

But you did it.

RAY

So the fuck what! I don't care. I did it! I did it! What the fuck did I do? And what are they doing to me? What the fuck is punishment for that shit? There has to be magical doors. I'm looking for the fucking magical doors. That's what I need. That's what I need. That's what's got to get me out of this shit. I mean... yesterday, I woke up in a fucking prison. I woke up on a fucking ship. I woke up there, you know? I woke up there! And then I went home. And I saw that for what it was. And then, I came here... and it was like a fucking new world to me. It was a new world. And I was like, Ah, this is fucking home, this is where I need to be, this is the shit that I've dreamt about. This is the shit that I can do, this is the new world that I want...
(desperate)
But I don't want to have to go through the fucking middle passage to get to the new world! That's not for me!

> LAUREN
> *(quiet)*

Look, Ray. All I'm saying is you made a mistake,
baby. We all make mistakes, I've made mistakes.
All you got to do is just walk up in that court
with your head up high, and accept responsibility
for what you've done. Go to jail, do your time,
make the most of your time, read, write, do whatever it is you gotta do—

> RAY

Man, what the fuck are you saying! What the fuck
are you saying! No, no, no, no, no, no, no... this
isn't class now. My only responsibility is to my
fucking dreams. That's my responsibility. Not to
no other shit like that.

> LAUREN

This is part of your dreams, Ray. You cannot have
your dreams if you don't—

> RAY
> *(explodes; leaps up)*

This is not a part of my dreams. This is not no
fucking metaphor! This is my life!

> LAUREN
> *(fights back; jumps up; furious)*

Motherfucker, who you think you jumping up
on?! You don't know this...
> *(stops; tries to calm down)*

Okay... okay... no.
> *(regards him; even)*

I know about your dreams. And I know about not
being able to get your dreams, and wanting them
and having them and all these roadblocks in your
way. I know something about that shit, Ray. I
haven't been in jail, I haven't done time, but I
know something about that, Ray.
> (MORE)

LAUREN (cont'd)

And all I'm saying is, this thing that you're going through right now is what is going to catapult you into the fucking dream. You can't see that right now because you haven't been there. I've been there—

RAY

You haven't fucking been there!

LAUREN

Don't you fucking tell me I haven't been there before! You don't know me! You don't know my fucking life story, motherfucker!

RAY

And you know mine.

LAUREN

Oh yeah, baby. You just spilled it all right here. You don't know what kind of prisons I've been a part of. You don't know what it's like to sell your ass on the street for a hit of crack. You don't know what that's like, motherfucker. I've been a slave! Fuck being a prisoner! Oh, don't come for me, motherfucker. Let me tell you something. You don't know me. Remember that. You don't know where I come from. But everything you telling me right now? I know it. I know it like the back of my motherfucking hand.

RAY

What the fuck do you mean I don't know.

LAUREN

You don't know!

RAY

You've been a fucking slave, what do you think
I've been? Where do you think I was in that fucking metaphor? Where do you think I was? When
you were the fucking slave, who was the fucking
overseer? Where do you think I was then? Who
was the one giving it to you, who was the one
selling that shit? That was me!

LAUREN

Oh! Oh! Awareness! Bing! Say that shit again.
Say it again, goddamnit. Say it again. Who was it?
Who was it? Who was it that put me in my
prison. Who was it that enslaved me. Who was it,
goddamnit?
        (holds up the slave ship picture; screaming)
Who the fuck was it?! Who was it!
        (throws the picture down; voice caught)
It was you. It was you. It was you.
        (a long moment)
It's not easy, baby. Escaping it. It hasn't been easy.
It hasn't been easy for none of us. You ain't the
first motherfucker to be up in this piece like this,
and you won't be the last. All I'm trying to do,
Ray, is help you, baby. Because I've been there,
that's all. That's all I'm trying to say. That's all that
was. That was just to show you that I've been
there. I know what it's like. I know what the fear
is like, I know what the pain is like, I know what
it's like... I know what it's like to be cornered. I
know what it's like.
        (slowly moving toward him; almost a whisper)
Just trust me, baby. Just trust me. All you gotta do
is go forward. Don't fall into their traps, don't fall
into their games. Please. Just go. 'Cause if you run
away from it, you just gonna get caught up later.
Trust me. Your freedom is there, it's waiting for
you. It's waiting for you. And oddly enough, baby,
it's waiting for you in the goddamn prison. It is.

> LAUREN (cont'd)
> *(reaches for him; holds him tight)*
> I know you can't see it. I know you can't see it,
> but it's there. It's there. It's there.

It's too much for Ray. He pulls back, picks up his bag, starts to walk away.

> LAUREN
> Ray. Ray! Ray!

But he's gone.

> LAUREN
> *(weeping; kicks the dirt)*
> Damn.

EXT. WASHINGTON, D.C. - ANACOSTIA RIVER - SUNSET

Ray stands on the bank, looking out over the river. The sun shimmers on the water... penetrates him, fracturing in the LENS.

DISSOLVE:

EXT. CLUB - WASHINGTON, D.C. - NIGHT

It's a scene. Crowds mill on the sidewalk outside.

> BOB HOLMAN (V.O. THE CUT)
> Come on, let's hear it from you guys.

INT. CLUB - POETRY SLAM

Veteran slam host BOB HOLMAN works the crowd from the stage, pumping them up, getting them going.

The AUDIENCE breaks into enthusiastic applause and shouting. It's a lively, happy mixed-bag crowd, psyched for the performances.

> BOB HOLMAN
> *(over the applause)*
> Welcome to the poetry club, where the words you
> say are the thoughts you live, and where nothing
> ever happens unless you say it first.
> (MORE)

BOB HOLMAN (cont'd)
Tonight, let's see who the first poet is who's going
to be coming up here for the slam tonight. Please
bring up... Liza Jesse Peterson!

The crowd welcomes her. Liza takes the stage.

LIZA

Ice Cream.

The crowd knows it, goes wild.

LIZA
(sensuously, sexily)

Ice cream.
Ice cream.
I used to be an ice cream fiend...
Mm mm mm mm mm mm mm....
You see, it all started when I had a large scoop of
Rain Forest Crunch with extra walnuts.
"Would you like a cup or a cone, miss? Cup or a
cone?"
Cup or a cone.
Cup or a cone and I was in a zone where I had to
make a wise choice between a cup or a cone. You
see, it's more fun with a cone, because I lick the
tip...

She licks her lips, the audience knows what she means and loves it.

LIZA

... and then I crunch and munch the cone.
And then I lick the tip again.
And then I crunch and munch the cone.
(rapid)
Until there's one sip at the bottom tip and I pop it
in my mouth and grin because I like that game.

CUT TO:

INT. METRO STATION - MUSIC UP

Ray waits on the subway platform as the train pulls in...

BACK TO:

INT. CLUB

DJ Renegade is on the stage, has the audience going...

BACK TO:

INT. METRO STATION

Ray boards the train.

BACK TO:

INT. CLUB

Another POET on stage, rapping into the mike...

BACK TO:

Ray rides the train, deep in thought.

BACK TO:

Bob Holman reads scores. The judges are giving 11's.

BACK TO:

Ray rides the train, writes in his journal...

The CUTS back and forth get faster and more frequent as Ray's train approaches its destination, Cleveland Park station...

Ray heads out of the station.

In the club, another POET holds court...

> TAYLOR MALI
> ...I'm writing a poem that will change the world,
> and it's "Like Lilly, like Taylor" at my office door.
> Lilly Wilson, a recovering "like" addict,
> the worst I've ever seen
> (MORE)

TAYLOR MALI (cont'd)
So, like, bad, that the entire eighth grade started
calling her "Like Lilly, like Wilson, like."
Until I made my classroom a like-free zone
And she couldn't speak for days...

MUSIC UP. In the alley outside the club, Ray pauses.

He moves through the crowds outside toward the door...

BOUNCER
Can I help you.

Getting ready to shoot Saul's performance in the climactic poetry slam scene.

RAY
Yeah, I'm supposed to be meeting someone here.

INT. CLUB

BOB HOLMAN
Every slam is a finality. Every slam is the end.

INT. CLUB HALLWAY

Ray walks down the dark hallway.

BACK ON HOLMAN:

> BOB HOLMAN (cont'd)
> And tonight there's no other way to end this slam
> but to bring up here one of the true heroes of
> poetry. Do you all remember when Lauren started
> out here?

APPLAUSE.

Ray enters the Slam.

> BOB HOLMAN (cont'd)
> Let's please bring Lauren up here to make it hap-
> pen for us right now.

The crowd eggs her on. Lauren gets up, heads for the stage... smiles when she sees Ray standing quietly near the door, taking it all in. They reach out to each other as she passes.

> BOB HOLMAN (cont'd)
> There's nothing else that can happen in the word
> but to make the word be the word itself.
> Something that you've heard before. Come on,
> Lauren!

She takes the stage.

> LAUREN
> This is a poem that I found when I was drowning
> one day. And it's for a friend of mine who's going
> through a hard time right now.

She finds Ray's eyes.

> LAUREN
> *(starts the poem)*
> i feel like my back is against a brick wall and I got
> a Mack truck two inches from my face. Every cell
> in my body is screaming, RUN! but I can't...

The audience is rapt as Lauren gathers strength.

LAUREN (cont'd)
...i'm kicking and stomping and running and jumping, wreaking all kinds of havoc, creating a bloody mess and i am going nowhere. Somewhere in my mind i think i am moving. Somewhere in reality i am running. Somewhere inside myself i am oh so still. Quiet. Dead. My soul is not rising. My spirit is not lifting. My life is not living. But i am running. Moving through the universe, a whirling dervish with no end, no purpose, no means, no life left to live. And yet, still, i want to go to that place where i can run, run free, my mind tells me. But those two words cannot occupy the same space in reality. run. free. My back is against a brick wall. i got a Mack truck two inches from my face. *Run free, baby, right now, it just looks hard, but it would be so easy. Just turn around and go. Clip all the wires, hookups and hangups and then you're home free. You can give birth to an excuse so easily, you'll believe it's always been there. Part of the natural order, made to order by your forever clever mind, constantly protecting you against things you no longer need to be protected from* ... and i believe. i believe like a Holy Roller singing sweating preaching go tell it on the mountain while speaking in twenty different tongues while diving in ten thousand feet of baptismal water without a life preserver. i believe like my bullet-ridden brother out there somewhere right now gurgling blood through his last breath spitting out a red ripe prayer so new so sweet so baby fresh so full of truth he thinks it can save his life...

The crowd gets more and more excited, swept away by her words.

LAUREN (cont'd)
...God does not exist in desperation and hope is lying dead somewhere in the sewer down the
(MORE)

                    LAUREN (cont'd)
street around the corner in the alley underneath
the feet of somebody itching scratching trembling
jonesing for their next hit and sucking somebody's
dick. i got two minutes - i got two motherfucking
minutes - before i run free or die, y'all. two minutes before i smash my face into the grill of a
Mack truck, before i get ten thousand bricks
shoved up my ass before i run   free   or die.

She leaves the stage as the crowd explodes. They want her back, won't stop
till she takes the stage again.

                    BOB HOLMAN
Let's have an encore!

                    LAUREN
          (back on stage; into the mike)
You know, it's about spreading the love. And I met
somebody recently who touched me, who moved
me.

Ray watches nervously from the back, not sure what Lauren will do.

                  LAUREN (cont'd)
And I hope he does the same thing for you. This is
his first time reading, and he's a big, big talent, and
he needs our love and our support, and I give you,
Ray.

The crowd is warm, encouraging. Ray hesitates... slowly approaches the stage.

                    RAY
          (on stage; starts slow; quiet)
if i could find the spot where truth echoes
i would stand there and whisper memories of my
children's future
i would let their future dwell in my past
so that i might live a brighter now

now is the essence of my domain
                  (MORE)

                        RAY (cont'd)
            but it contains all that was and will—

He stumbles over the words, stops, smiles shyly.

                            RAY
            I'll try it again.

The crowd is right there with him. They know he's breaking through
tonight. The applause is real, encouraging. He starts again.

                            RAY
            if i could find the spot where truth echoes
            i would stand there and whisper memories of my
            children's future
            i would let their future dwell in my past
            so that i might live a brighter now

            now is the essence of my domain
            but it contains all that was and will be
            and i am as i was and will be
            because i am and always will be
            that nigga

            i am that nigga

            i am that timeless nigga
            that swings on pendulums like vines
            through mines of booby-trapped minds
            that are enslaved by time
            i am the life that supersedes lifetimes
            i am

            it was me with serpentine hair
            that with a timeless stare
            turned mortal fear into stone time capsules
            they still exist as the walking dead
            as i do: the original suffer-head
            symbol of life
            and matriarchy's severed head
                            (MORE)

RAY (cont'd)

Medusa, i am

i am that nigga
i am that nigga
i am that nigga

i am a negro

negro from necro, meaning death
i overcame it
so they named me after it
and i be spittin' at death from behind
and putting "kick me" signs on its back

because

i am not the son of sha clack clack
i am before that
i am before

i am before before
before death is eternity
after death is eternity
there is no death there is only eternity
and i be riding on the wings of eternity
like: yah! yah! yah! sha clack clack

but my flight does not go undisturbed
because time makes dreams defer
and all of my time fears are turning my days into
day-mares
and i live day-mares reliving nightmares
that once haunted my past
sha clack clack
time is beatin' my ass

and i be havin' dreams of chocolate covered water
(MORE)

RAY (cont'd)

melons filled with fried chickens like piñatas. with
little pickaninny sons and daughters standing up
under them with big sticks and aluminum foil, hittin' them, trying to catch pieces of fallen fried
chicken wings. and aunt jemima and uncle ben are
standing in the corners with rifles pointed at the
heads of the little children. "don't shoot the children," i shout. "don't shoot the children." but it's
too late. they've already been infected by time. but
this shit is before my time...(i need more time! i
need more time!)...but it's too late. they start
shooting at the children and killing them:

one by one
two by two
three by three
four by four
five by five
six by six

but my spirit is growing seven by seven
faster than the speed of light
because light only penetrates the darkness
that's already there
and i am already there
i'm here at the end of the road
which is the beginning of the road bayond time
but where my niggas at?
oh shit
don't tell me my niggas are lost in time
my niggas are dying before their time
my niggas are serving unjust time
my niggas are dying because of time

The crowd doesn't know what's hit them. They go crazy, jump to their feet,
holler for him to come back. They want more.

INT. CLUB BATHROOM

Ray falls into the bathroom... escape. He's breathing hard. Lauren follows him in, shuts the door. In the background, the APPLAUSE rings out. Lauren and Ray regard each other a long moment... embrace, hold each other tight.

John Kirby

The crew sets up the final shot at the Washington Monument.

> LAUREN
> *(finally)*
> Look, I just... want to apologize for what happened earlier. I didn't mean for it to get out of hand...

> RAY
> *(tries to stop her)*
> No, you—

> LAUREN
> No, no, look.
> *(she's made a decision)*
> I just want you to know that no matter what happens on Monday, no matter what you decide to do... I'm gonna be here for you.

INT. CLUB

The crowd pounds the tables, chanting, "Ray! Ray! Ray!"

> BOB HOLMAN
> Go home and write your own goddamn poems!

INT. BATHROOM

> LAUREN
> *(happy for him)*
> You better get back out there. Can't you hear them? Just one more...

> RAY
> *(a trapped animal)*
> I need to get some air.

> LAUREN
> Then you'll come back?

> RAY
> Yeah.

> LAUREN
> Okay. Well, I'll hold the fort down till you get back.

> RAY
> *(starts to leave; looks at her)*
> Thank you.

She watches him leave, listens to the crowd chanting his name...

EXT. CLUB - MUSIC UP

Ray tumbles out of the crowded club, breathes in the night, heads for the street...

EXT. WASHINGTON, D.C.

He wanders through the streets. MUSIC MONTAGE #5.

John Kirby

Marc Levin composes the final shot.

IMAGES from the last few days pour over each other on the SCREEN...
jail scenes, kids from the neighborhood, his arrest, Lauren...

He breaks into a run...

The IMAGES keep coming... Mike's shooting, the cellblock, the poetry slam...

He runs and runs... walks past the Capitol... and straight toward the Washington Monument, floodlit in the dark night, shooting up out of the ground, a tall, impenetrable symbol of power.

CLOSE SHOT

Ray comes up against yet another cell door—locked in, locked out... puts his hands up on the bars, peers into the dark interior...

The CAMERA TILTS SLOWLY UP... AND UP, to reveal... the endless white expanse of the monument, shooting up into the night sky, FILLING THE SCREEN... the nation's great white phallus.

FADE TO BLACK

END CREDITS START TO ROLL...

Slam Goes
to Sundance

Slam Goes to Sundance

Donny Brice

Beau Sia, Alfre Woodard and Bonz Malone.

AND THE WINNER IZ

by Bonz Malone

And also what you have not requested I will give you, both riches and glory, so that there will not have happened to be any among the kings like you, all your days.
1 Kings 3:13

We'd been home from shooting in D.C. about four months, and the cast, including myself, had resumed our daily lives. The only thing on our minds was eating regularly. That's it! I got a call from Marc Levin, and all he said was, "Pack your stuff, we're going to Sundance!!" To those who don't know, Sundance is like the Cannes of America. If you don't know what Cannes is, you probably haven't heard of MTV either.

All we would have to do would be show up at showtime, shake a few hands, pass a few cards around and smile a lot. Big deal! We do that at ball games. Now it's time to play with the big boys—a role I've been waiting all my life to score. Saul, Sonja, Beau and I take a picture together in the airport, marking the start of a journey that could change all our lives forever.

Now I'm on my way to Park City to free the slaves out there with a little help from my friends. During the flight, I think about Judge Bell, who put me to sleep for four months. I bumped into him in the Macy's elevator a week before this trip and remembered the three and four hours laying up in a roach-infested bullpen of filth, and those biochemical sandwiches they threw at us at feeding time—all that came back to me as I looked into His Honor's eyes. I don't hold any grudge against the judge, though. If I did, we'd both be retired. Nah, I can smile now 'cause I've paid my fair share of debts across the bench—hard though it was to sit in my seat, screaming for a chance to win and never feeling that moment. Sort of like Patrick Ewing.

But then, just hours away from Sundance, it hits me: We're in the playoffs! One of the final fourteen out of 750 entries to ball in the Independent Film Championship of America. Starting today, the film that took us twelve days to shoot, with real characters throughout, will be shown to some of Hollywood's most influential players. I'm headed for a virtual winter wonderland where unknown actors can become Icons and a small-time filmmaker can sell a flick for millions before it goes public.

January 17 we arrived in Park City, one of the country's best spots for skiing. The minute we got to Main Street, we were mobbed by actors and directors. Established or not! The buzz was hot! People were talking about *Slam* like it was the greatest film ever shown at Sundance! I couldn't believe it.

Marc, Richard and Henri had the power of the people behind them, plus headliners out in front paving the way. Our multiracial gang, dubbed "The God Squad," had a sit-down to discuss our strategy. The mission was to bomb the festival with spoken-word explosions so as to give those Mormons and Moguls a blast of culture they'd never forget. We made a toast over Peking duck and pledged to "Come strong or don't come at all!" Then the executive producer passed out *Slam* baseball caps. After dinner we stepped out onto the sidewalk and showed the world we run it.

Without comps, we got into our first party—fifteen deep, just like in the ghetto—told 'em, "We're on a mission from God."

Immediately, the Big East took over the dance floor. We walked in listening to Willie Nelson and left to the Gap Band. Saul and Beau Sia started B-Boying in the middle of the room and the guests had a ball! Liza had the beauty and grace of a supermodel and watching her make her bones as an actress was spiritual ecstasy. Sonja got chased by every swinger on the hill. And me, I was the Intellectual Zen Gangster playin' the yard. For the remaining days, we lived each moment as if it were our last on earth, and it worked!

The freedom we had to live our lives to the fullest extent came without pretense of an award of any sort. The reason for our joy was that we had absolutely no money. Instead we had the richest itinerary: Hot Tubs, Jacuzzis, Skiing, Snowmobiles, Mansion Parties, the 20th Century Fox/Piper-Heidsieck party, the Miramax party, the Gap Jam. Interviews with *Premiere, Entertainment Weekly,* MTV News, *Detour, Rolling Stone, Vanity Fair, Entertainment Weekly* again, *Variety, L.A. Times* cover, *Washington Post,* cable TV in five languages. Offers by executives from all over the world—every day! It wasn't until one night back at the condo, we were all laughing and talking about how much fun this trip has been, when Saul said somberly, "Our lives are changing," and silence fell upon the room.

The sense of pride I felt representing the kind of film we made together and the type of jewels that were dropped therein was like defending the only thing that's still holy in a world that spends more on entertainment than food! Hope is what makes an underdog great and to come out of lockdown and make the kind of impact we made shows the watching world that there is a God and he has a squad and they ain't sleeping!

Sisters and brothers from every race and place want more than just bullets, explosions and car chases. They're not waiting for perfect writers. Not interested in perfect people or perfected characters. Perfect characters are found in a perfect society. "Hollyworld" wants to meet characters who've failed. I care about people who are scared, who ain't got shit, who are suckered by their vanity and gassed by their desires. We care about them because we see ourselves in them.

That's what the judges saw in us—in or out of jail—the unconditional courage to fight for focus! And they were proud of us, because we were young, black, in-between, and we loved each other. We displayed the kind of power, in both word and action, that inspired a message of hope and life to any listeners.

This was the closest we've ever been to Hollywood's elite inner circle. From Inmate Council to a contract with Trimark Pictures and dinner with an agent from William Morris—who but the Most High could have prepared me for this kind of inauguration?

Graduation to the third degree, on January 24, we are free. I knew I could fly, but I didn't try hard enough until now and with all the pain and suffering it takes to be an overnight success, never once have I cried 'til tonight. All those nights in jail pretending to use the toilet while cowriting this script, that was up for grabs. Only four representatives from each film were officially allowed to be in the audience for the ceremony, but all seventeen of us sat together—holding our hearts in our hands.

I prayed to Jehovah that this film would be blessed. Lisa West, who left East/West Records to join the revolution, passed around a program for us to sign. All I could think of was, "BZO WUZ HEAR! HOUSE GANG."

I was very scared, more than when meeting with the warden of Rikers or any of the gang leaders behind the brick walls of injustice. To sit in a darkened theater surrounded by people shedding tears of appreciation for our work is one of the highest honors that can be given to an individual. This is a very special event here.

The battle for bravery, a call for courage and two hours of decision were to pass before we would know who'd get the front page of the *L.A. Times*.

All the parties in the world couldn't hold a candle to the one that was being lit underneath my seat. Fear, to me, means: Fuck Everything And Run! It's been two years since I've had a drink of whiskey, or any mind-altering drug. In my abstinence, I've written my most personal and precious gifts to anyone who found themselves flawed like me. I had a Hellavision when I was asleep in jail and I've had it since I woke.

Today, the Country was not a joke, and Tomorrow the World is now. Up in the snowcapped alps of Utah, this was the mountain I saw in Job Korps, Eyes and Earz. I was the child who climbed that mountain and it was a great challenge indeed. I planted a tree for others to see years ago—when I was a boy addicted to pain and despair.

But here, tonight, I am a man with a heart as strong as the mountain upon which I stand. No other story I ever write will touch my soul the way this one does!

They bet against us! Didn't trust us! Wouldn't touch us! Thank Great God for Just Us, 'cause now they can't touch us! This film was distributed by God himself who hears the prayers of the imprisoned ones—in and out of jail—for He is mankind's ultimate Judge and He has found us worthy of praise!

At 8:25 p.m., we robbed the bank, and got the gold to lay the bricks for our yellow road. In search of glory, we danced in the sun—for the Grand Jury Prize, which *Slam* had won!

WHEN I GET BACK FROM SUNDANCE

by Beau Sia

When I get back from Sundance, I'll have pudding pops in Madagascar with Uma Thurman and Spock, and me and Tarantino are gonna buy the bones of Bruce Lee and put them in a movie called *The Bones of Bruce Lee Are Alive!*, and I'm gonna burn Doogie Howser's stupid computer diary, and I'm gonna have Punky Brewster in a nightgown reading me bedtime stories, and I'm gonna buy expensive crystal, because it's expensive.

When I get back from Sundance, I'll have a microchip in my head, so that I can say, "I have a microchip in my head!" and I'm gonna teach children how to fly, and the case of Melrose will be exiled to B movie hell, and Mel Tormé is gonna rap "Ice Ice Baby" to me while I shower, and I'm gonna kill Hanson before any of them reach puberty.

When I get back from Sundance, I'm gonna publish 382-page books with nothing but my name on the cover and people will buy them, and I'm gonna have benefit concerts where I sing everyone else's songs really badly, and I'm gonna eat barbecued Smurf every day, and I'm gonna reveal to the world that Jerry Springer is really Oprah Winfrey in disguise, and I'm gonna get an incurable cancer and cure it by applying a salve made out of the breast tissue of Gloria Estefan.

When I get back from Sundance, I'm gonna buy all of the baby kittens in the world, eagerly awaiting the second coming of Alf.

When I get back from Sundance, I'm gonna roam the galaxy in a Star Destroyer piloted by Bill Cosby and David Lee Roth in search of movie roles for Macauley Culkin.

When I get back from Sundance, I'm gonna have the actors from *The Breakfast Club* come over and watch the movie with me and they'll have to listen to me say repeatedly, "Wow, I really thought your careers would take off after that!"

When I get back from Sundance,
I'm gonna throw my weight around,
When I get back from Sundance,
I'm gonna use people,

When I get back from Sundance,
I'm gonna own Miramax.

And sure,
Sundance cannot buy you love,
but—
fuck it.
(Motioning to the cast and crew of *Slam*)
I got love right here.

THE SPIRIT OF ONE

Grand Jury Prize Presentation Speech

by Alfre Woodard

To the filmmakers—I was completely humbled by the experience of participating on this jury. As an artist, I understand it is futile to attempt to perceive as concrete heart and memory, pain and joy. So much of who you are and who you have known inhabits the stories you shared with us. As a mother, I know it is impossible to have a favorite child among all of your own, because you see the preciousness of identity of each unique soul, all of them quenching the thirst in so many parts of yourself. We dare to attempt to analyze and criticize films because we are touched or shaken or tickled by them—we are so personally affected, and we want to understand what has happened to us.

But it is like trying to hold light in our hands.

We jurors, official and unofficial, are just people. Trying to put into words and thought, you—who are creative and visionary, and elusive as the dreams you weave on film. But mainly we are exhilarated to have these films—to talk about and to think about and to argue about. You made your films without us. You made your pictures when nobody was looking. Out of a need to speak out into the space that separates us all, and let free an idea, a truth, a challenge... a whimsy. You did that not for prizes, but because you have an innate need to let the creative principle flow through you.

I believe there is one creator—one creative force. In that regard, we are inextricably bound together in our artistic endeavors.

I didn't come to this festival to judge films. I came here to be flooded with the fierceness of independent thought, and the perseverance to start with empty hands, some friends and a couple of bucks, and end up with these pictures, these offerings. I celebrate the films in dramatic competition, and I celebrate all of the filmmakers in this year's Festival.

You have marked a point of time for all of us. You have defined this moment by what you had to say. You are our griots, our storytellers. As your predecessors have done since we first stood up around the fire, you keep the lore of the tribe; our identity, our history. You lift up the mirror to the community—the whole one of man—for us to look at ourselves, and, hopefully, to grow. You weave your sacred story magic with humor, with rage, with pathos, with vital information. You are our perpetual healing.

As you continue to make it happen, know that no one can pay you what you're worth. Do argue the good deal—but know that it is a separate sport (and I hope one that you win, to eat). But you are a continuum of an ancient tradition. You are not working for prizes, you are not working for deals, you are not even working for our acknowledgment. You are making history. You are telling the stories. You are giving us the view from that very particular place where you stand and live. You are blessing the earth, and us on it. You are documenting the fact that we have been here. And I thank you for this work, and for all the work to come, on behalf of all the people on all the corners of the world who you will touch for as long as that piece of film can roll.

In the spirit of one, in its own time, the film that is to be named the Grand Jury Prize winner of the 1998 Sundance Film Festival, is *Slam*.

CREDITS

Directed by	MARC LEVIN
Written by	SONJA SOHN
	MARC LEVIN
	BONZ MALONE
	SAUL WILLIAMS
	RICHARD STRATTON
Story by	MARC LEVIN
	RICHARD STRATTON
Produced by	HENRI M. KESSLER
	MARC LEVIN
	RICHARD STRATTON
Executive Producers	DAVID PEIPERS
	HENRI M. KESSLER
Director of Photography	MARK BENJAMIN
Music by	DJ SPOOKY
Edited by	EMIR LEWIS

CAST

Ray Joshua	SAUL WILLIAMS
Lauren Bell	SONJA SOHN
Hopha	BONZ MALONE
Big Mike	LAWRENCE WILSON
Jimmy Huang	BEAU SIA
China	ANDRE TAYLOR
Bay (Jail Rapper)	MOMOLU STEWART
Doo Wop Cops	RON JONES
	REAMER SHEDRICK
Chief C.O.	ALLAN E. LUCAS
Officer Dom	DOMINIC CHIANESE JR.
Jail Class Poet "Why"	JEROME GOLDMAN
Party Poet "Diminuendo in Blue"	DJ RENEGADE
Slam Poet "Ice Cream"	LIZA JESSE PETERSON
Slam Poet "Like"	TAYLOR MALI
Slam M.C.	BOB HOLMAN
Public Defender	RHOZIER T. BROWN
Prosecutor	RICHARD STRATTON
Judge	MAYOR MARION BARRY JR.

CREW

Associate Producer	DAPHNE PINKERSON
Creative Consultant	BONZ MALONE
Technical Consultant	RHOZIER T. BROWN
Production Coordinator	ELENI TSOKANOS
Business Affairs	LISA WEST
Sound	DAVID HOCS
Gaffer/Grip	JOHN P. SIMS
Assistant Camera	TONY HARDMON
2nd AC/Title Concept	JOHN KIRBY
2nd Camera/Club Shoot	ALAN S. DEUTSCH
Assistant Camera/Club Shoot	CHRIS PAUL
Videographer	DAPHNE PINKERSON
Additional Editing	BRIAN COTNOIR
Editorial Consultants	TIM SQUYRES
	ALISON ELLWOOD
Assistant Editor	DIANE BUTLER
Script Editor	PAM WIDENER
Security	MARCUS GAINES
Makeup	ZEAL HARRIS
FX Makeup	JEREMY SAULNIER
Still Photography	WALTER WOODWARD JR.
	JOHN KIRBY
	FIONN REILLY
Craft Services	CIRCA CATERING
Production Assistants	FREDERICK BRUST
	DOMINIC CHIANESE JR.
	OLUMIDE EARTH
	ROBERT LEAVER
	CARLOS E. McBRIDE
	ERIC RIVAS QUIROGA
	ISABELLA VON ROTH
	JENNIFER M. WARNER
Production Accountant	AMY SAZAMA
Web Designer	JENNIFER R. MEAGHER
Post Production Assistants	OLUMIDE EARTH
	DESIRE ORTIZ
	RACHEL P. GOLDSTEIN
Laboratory Services	DU ART FILM & VIDEO
Color Timer	KENT McGREW
Avid Conform	MOVING PICTURES
	ALAN MILLER

Title Design	DU ART DIGITAL
	MARKUS JANNER
	HOLLY KEMPNER
Negative Cutter	IMMACULATE MATCHING
	ELLIOT GAMSON
Re-Recording Mixers	DIGITAL CINEMA
	RICK DIOR
	DAVID JAUNAI
	SYNC SOUND
Sound Design	RAY PALAGY
	PHILIPPE DESLOOVERE
Dialogue Editors	NEIL CEDAR
	TONY SLOCUM
Legal	SLOSS LAW

D.C. DEPARTMENT OF CORRECTIONS

Director	MARGARET MOORE
D.C. Jail Warden	PATRICIA JACKSON
Coordinator	LT. SAMUEL RICHARDSON
Media Relations	WALTER WOODWARD

DODGE CITY CAST

Weed Buyer	WEUSI BARAKA
Dodge City Crew	EDDIE BLACK
	HARRY CAMPBELL
	ROBERT PHILSON

JAIL CAST

Jail C.O.	DANIEL M. FAVORS
Jail C.O.	JOHNNY FOYE
Command Center C.O	JESSE HICKS
Hallway C.O.	CAROLYN MORRIS
Bullpen Inmates	LEONARD A. THOMPSON JR.
	TODD BAKER
Poetry Class	JOSEPH WILSON
Thug Life Crew	TALIB WILSON
Van Inmates	KEVIN KENNEDY
	DONNELL ROBINSON

SPECIAL THANKS

Nancy Abraham, Bill Adler, Rick Blume, Alvin Bowens, Paul Brennan,
Ellin Burke, Paul Devlin, Howard University, Fez Under Time Café, NYC,
Henry O. Eshelman, Magdalynne Gates, Denise Greene, Beth Hyman,
Phyllis Johnson, Brian Kelly, Hartford Park Apartments, Arlene Kessler,
Steven Kessler, Theodore Kessler, Ned "Ebn" Leiben, Al Levin, Daniel Levin,
Hannah Levin, Sara Levin, Jamie Lusberg, Kathy Martinis, Lissa Mattson,
Robin Mayemura, Geoffrey Miller, Bill Moyers, Mayor's Office of Theater and
Film, Emilio Murillo Film & Broadcasting, Sheila Nevins, Joy Newhouse,
Michael de Haven Newsom, Annie Nocenti, David and Ann Peipers,
Peipers & Company, Inc., John Sloss, Benjamin Productions, Blowback
Productions, Alan Solow, Eric St. Michaels, Ron and Claudia West,
Denise Vende Cruze, Kim Wozencraft, Max and Dash, Irwin Young